Woman-to-Woman
Sexual Violence

Other titles in

THE NORTHEASTERN SERIES ON GENDER, CRIME, AND LAW
edited by Claire Renzetti, St. Joseph's University

▼

WOMAN-TO-WOMAN SEXUAL VIOLENCE

Does She Call It Rape?

LORI B. GIRSHICK

Northeastern University Press

BOSTON

Northeastern University Press
Copyright 2002 by Lori B. Girshick

Library of Congress Cataloging-in-Publication Data

Girshick, Lori B.
Woman-to-woman sexual violence : does she call it rape? / Lori B. Girshick.
p. cm – (Northeastern series on gender, crime, and law)
Includes bibliographical references and index.
ISBN: 978-1-55553-527-8
1. Abused lesbians. 2. Sexual abuse victims. 3. Violence in women. I. Title. II. Series.
HO75.5 G56 2002
362.82'92–dc21   2001051183

Designed by Gary Gore

Composed in Electra by Coghill Composition in Richmond, Virginia. Printed and
bound by Edwards Brothers, Inc., in Ann Arbor, Michigan. The paper is EB Natural, an
acid-free sheet.

Manufactured in the United States of America
06 05 04   5 4 3 2

For those who are still silenced

Contents

Acknowledgments

There are times when an idea takes root so firmly that nothing can stop you. The idea for this project felt like an obsession to me, and waiting for several years for the right time to proceed proved to be a challenge. Like most things in life, challenging projects cannot be accomplished alone. Working on an issue that is surrounded by so much silence is not easy, and I have many people to thank for their input, their encouragement, and, of course, their stories.

The process of creating a major research and writing project is my greatest love—regardless of the overwhelming responsibilities along the way. I want to thank Anne Alexander for reading the early drafts of questionnaire, flyer, and letters and for listening to me think out loud while I planned my next steps. Thank you to Beth Leventhal of The Network/La Red: Ending Abuse in Lesbian, Bisexual Women's, and Transgender Communities (formerly The Network for Battered Lesbians and Bisexual Women), and Diane Dolan-Soto of the New York Anti-Violence Project for commenting on drafts and encouraging the project from the beginning. I appreciate the early encouragement and feedback on the entire manuscript at numerous points from Claire Renzetti, who is one of a kind in her presence and support. I am grateful for helpful comments and insights from Melissa Burchard on the language chapter, Katie Fisher on the legal chapter, and Carol Plummer for feedback on theoretical ideas. Thanks also to Crissy Stewart for legal research. My anonymous reviewers helped strengthen the book through their perceptive comments.

I spoke to scores of staff people at rape crisis and domestic violence agencies across the country, who helped spread the word about the study and affirmed the need for this work. Thank you for telling me this work was so important and needed to be done and for offering to help me in any way possible. To all of you who posted my flyers, sent out an Internet notice, spoke to friends, and printed a paragraph in your newsletter, you helped make this book possible.

My full gratitude goes to the librarians at Warren Wilson College, especially Mary Brown, who filled countless interlibrary loan requests for me and helped me track down research sources. Without their help and generosity of spirit I would have been bogged down in research quagmire. Several colleagues helped stuff envelopes for the initial nationwide mailing or listened to me prattle on about the details that preoccupied me. I am appreciative for my sabbatical leave that allowed me to write full-time—a delicious way to spend a sabbatical, I might add—made possible by the Andrew W. Mellon Foundation Trust, the Appalachian College Association, and Warren Wilson College. Thank you Dr. Virginia McKinley, academic dean of Warren Wilson, for supporting my work.

Friends around the country and here at home allowed me to let off stream when I needed an outlet for what I was absorbing. They encouraged me in every way. To mention only a few of the many, thank you Anne Alexander, Cathleen Desjardins, Bob Overby, and Cynthia Shaeffer.

To Sarah Rowley and Bill Frohlich of Northeastern University Press, thanks is not enough. You believed in the project and in me, and I am appreciative of your support, your time and energy in listening to my concerns, and for understanding the process I was going through. Sarah, to you especially, thank you for those long conversations and e-mails that helped me push on with a project many might not give the time to understand. It isn't easy to say, "The rapist was a woman" and be taken seriously, but you knew better.

It is satisfying that as I write these words, the domestic violence agency in my city is starting a support group for battered lesbians. I pushed for this group for many years, and now it is happening. I hope this stands as an example for those of you who don't yet have that support group; I encourage you to keep working on it. I hope the rape crisis agency will next be providing targeted services for women survivors of woman-perpetrated rape.

To the brave women who came forward—those whose words you are about to read, and those who sent me e-mails with stories, comments, and questions—you are my sheroes. I am grateful that you contacted me, spoke to me, and in some cases, allowed numerous follow-up calls. Thanks for keeping in touch with me, and especially for caring enough to help others. I hope you are proud of what we have accomplished together. One of you told me to "stay open and courageous," and I now say that to all of you.

Woman-to-Woman
Sexual Violence

Introduction

In 1984 it was a bit of a shock to me when I dated a woman who told me she had been battered by her former partner of several years. Of course I'd heard of battering. But by a *lesbian?* I never discounted her story, and years later when I worked at a domestic violence shelter agency, I was mystified by the lack of services for and discussion about battered lesbians. However, I was even more upset when our agency hired a part-time staff person to facilitate a battered lesbian support group and do outreach to the lesbian community but drew hardly any clients. By then I had heard more stories; I knew that such abuse existed in my own community. Where were the survivors of this abuse?

Today, early in the third millennium, the situation has barely improved, but some changes have taken place. Articles have appeared in the queer press,[1] some agency staff are talking about lesbian abuse, and some specific lesbian services are now available. Some. But the idea that women might be violent is not palatable; we don't know quite how to place it, and as feminists, we are worried about possible consequences to our patriarchal analysis. The thought of a woman *rapist* is even more removed from our sensibility. A woman sexually harming another woman? Penetrating her with an object or her fingers? Tying her up and anally raping her? Holding her down? Verbally harassing her? *Her against her?* This is tough stuff. Just ask the women it happens to.

Aileen confirms that abuse by another woman is not taken seriously. She felt she would not be believed:

> Anyone I talk to whether they are lesbian, bi, whether they're a woman, whether they're a man, whether they're gay, it doesn't matter what their sexual orientation is, it's just the assumption that women cannot first of all be violent or even [be] more so than men to other women, but also that [the] violence cannot hurt as much.

3

I have worked in the domestic violence field since 1990 in various capacities: community educator, volunteer coordinator, support group facilitator, shelter staff member, volunteer advocate on a crisis line, and educator in volunteer trainings. I also teach about it in my college classes. I have worked on a county domestic violence council and on other community committees. I have counseled women of every age, from teenagers to retirees, and spoken to women in all kinds of circumstances, including women in prison. I have written about teen dating violence and lesbian battering. Over the years I have followed the resistance in our society to holding batterers accountable, and I have wondered if we have come very far in the last decade. And then I come to the topic of lesbian battering. The silence is deafening. Knowing what I know, I do not want to be haunted by Audre Lorde's words: "Your silence will not protect you";[2] and so, I speak out.

Daphne McClellan points out that lesbian battering is a new problem "as far as public consciousness is concerned" and that it requires advocacy.[3] There is resistance to both the survivors and the perpetrators, and they

> need to be defended in the general community and the criminal justice system against those who would rather not acknowledge their existence or who find their existence repulsive. They need to be defended against those that are aware of their existence but see such abuse as mutual fighting or scuffling, or even worse, as amusing.[4]

I agree with this assessment and seek to be such a defender.

In this research I focus on sexual violence specifically rather than lesbian battering per se. The work on sexual violence, especially regarding lesbians and bisexual women, rests on the foundation of research on same-sex domestic violence. Much of the sexual violence in the stories that follow takes place within a battering relationship. As such, much of what I write applies to both. The permission to speak about same-sex sexual violence has emerged from the public discussion of lesbian and gay male battering.

The legitimacy to seek help for woman-to-woman sexual violence is reflected in what Allison has to say:

> Another thing that I think is important when you try to target women or just get women to see that they can go in for help with their woman-to-woman stuff, I think it's also important to have them feel like their experience is valid even though [maybe] it wasn't raucous, forced, violent rape. 'Cause another thing I remember feeling like—this isn't now but it was then—"Oh, well what happened wasn't that

bad because it was a woman and it wasn't forced, and I didn't get pregnant, VD, or whatever." So, I didn't get any support.

In the past decade as I worked with battered lesbians, I heard stories of sexual abuse yet I rarely found anything written about it. The extent of woman-to-woman sexual violence outside of partner relationships also remains unknown. As a feminist, I believe that sexual violence is one of the main mechanisms of patriarchy. I wondered how this fit with women perpetrators and women survivors and felt a need to bring this type of abuse into view. Sexual violence has both a physical component and a psychological component and can be hidden within those categories. Power and control are the major motivations for sexual violence and battering, again blurring distinctions. I decided to focus on this most difficult topic because the hidden nature of it helped reinforce the shame of survivors, often preventing them from getting help and support. And on the most personal level, I wanted to work on sexual violence because I had been sexually abused as a girl and raped by a man as an adult, and this violence has had a very big impact on my life.

Liz speaks of the repercussions of sexual violence within her abusive relationship:

At first, and for a long time, I tried to ignore it and blocked it out. I had emotional problems resulting from it, but I had no idea of the source. My first awareness (looking back) of the emotional impact of the violence was shortly after I left [my partner]. I moved in with another woman, and one night we were getting ready to have sex when she asked me to "rape" her. I thought she meant playacting, but she told me she meant "for real," and that she could not "get off" any other way. I jumped out of her bed and went for a walk. I felt sickened and disgusted. The next day I found another place to live and moved out. Through therapy and talking about it, I realized that my intermittent fear of my partner(s), the unexplained bouts of crying and the need to be able to get away from them (i.e., leave during an argument), resulted from the rape. I had fear of intimacy, fear of sexual abandon and pleasure, and a strong need to be in control during sex (or more accurately not to be vulnerable), and eventually suffered depression because I didn't seem very interested in sex with any partner I stayed with for any length of time. I believed something was inherently wrong with me, that I was defective in some way (low self-esteem). By no means was the sexual abuse the cause of *all* of my emotional problems with intimacy, but it did seem to be the direct cause of my fear and reluctance to be in a vulnerable position during sex.

A slight majority of women who requested my survey did not return it. To tell someone your sexual violence story is not easy. To talk about lesbian and bisexual abuse is to air dirty laundry about the lesbian and bi communities. The seventy women who came forward fully supported the goals of the study and enthusiastically helped me. Ninety percent agreed to follow-up conversation, primarily by phone. They not only wrote about it but also talked about it with me. This research was not only a process that I experienced but also something that affected the participants. Responding to the survey "set the ball in motion," "gave me words," "helped me clarify," and "helped me so much to put together." For some, it was "the first time I've actually been able to tell somebody about that aspect of what happened to me."

Marcia shares her process of recovery:

Looking back I just can't believe that woman was me—it seems so unreal. But it was. I was meeting with [my therapist] sometimes twice a week and sometimes that didn't even feel often enough. The other major emotion that added to the anger was feeling isolated. I remember searching the Web for anything that included me, anything about woman-woman assault and there was practically nothing. I searched all over for anything, anyone who was like me—anyone who had a similar experience. I wanted to read someone's story and be able to see myself in it. I have found some books but they're more educational than healing. I doubted myself a lot—still do sometimes, that maybe I was making a bigger deal out of what happened than I should be. I kept hoping to find an article or a story somewhere about a woman who had been assaulted by a female acquaintance. But nothing. I knew there had to be someone out there like me—but where was she? I felt really alone. I just noticed that I'm writing in the past tense and I'm really excited about that. For so long it felt like I had to relive it all every time I thought about it. My stomach would tighten until I felt ill and my heart would race. But it's slowly gotten different these last few weeks. I feel more in control and like I actually have some say and power about how I'll handle it. And my sex drive is finally waking up. . . . I still think it's going to be a long time before we're that intimate again, but when we talk about it now, it feels like more of an adventure than of an albatross.

When my obsession with this subject began, there was very little written on lesbian battering and even less on woman-to-woman sexual violence. But in the past five to ten years, these issues have drawn more attention as activists and researchers began speaking out, asking questions, and writing. The focus has primarily been on lesbian battering, but there is some work on same-sex sexual violence. These works are generally feature articles in the queer press or research papers published in academic journals documenting abuse, suggestive of models, and criticizing the lack of services. So while there are resources, they are not readily available to the general public. Feature news articles in the queer press reach a limited audience and rarely go beyond establishing that the problem exists. Journal articles are generally aimed at other academics rather than service providers or violence survivors. The technical language and the circulation of professional journals limit the accessibility of the research.

What is different about my work? What am I adding or confirming? In the pages to come, I use the experiences and understandings of seventy women to document a hidden reality. I look at what happened and what they called what happened to them, how they responded, and whether they received any help to cope with the emotional impact of their abuse. Their stories reveal how the queer communities reacted and what role societal homophobia, biphobia, and transphobia has in all of this. I look at what the survivors themselves say would be the best agency services. The stories are in-depth and provide us with a fuller understanding of woman-to-woman sexual violence than exists anywhere else. These are the women who can tell us what happened and what we need to do.

Throughout this work I use the word "we" to refer to the lesbian and broader queer communities. As a lesbian it does not feel right to say "they" when talking about my own reference group of women who are woman-identified. In other cases when I say "we," I will specify who that is, as in the cases of feminists, women in general, service providers, or the larger society. One of the dilemmas in speaking of "we" is that rarely is there one united community. So "we" will of necessity refer to a generalized group. In fact, there are limitations to the sample of women who speak through this book. The sample is primarily white, middle-, and lower-class lesbians, with little variation by race and only a small number of bisexual women. Further research that specifically includes more nonwhite women and bisexual women is clearly needed. The complete lack of research on interpersonal violence among transgender people and transsexuals also points to a serious gap.

I admit that I am exposing a side of life many would prefer to keep secret. I do not believe these stories show that women are more violent than men are or that lesbians are some sick subset of all women. The fact that some men batter or rape does not mean all men batter and rape. The fact that some lesbians and bisexual women batter and rape does not mean all lesbians and bisexual women batter and rape. What this study demonstrates is that within our relationships we also have problems; we come from the same distorted aspect of society that produces some people who want to have power and control over others. Susan Brison, in processing her rape (by a man) and whether or not to go public, concluded, "I'm much more afraid of what *will* continue to happen if I don't [speak out]."[5] Sexual violence, like other types of abuse, thrives on secrecy. Many of the study participants have realized this and feel there is too much at risk to *not* speak out. It could never be truer than in the case of sexual violence that we need to listen to what we may not want to hear. We must acknowledge this reality if we want to change it. If we shut these survivors out, we sacrifice them. I can't do that, and I hope you can't either.

1

Speaking the Unspeakable

I wish I would have been more aware what woman-to-woman sexual violence was—what it looked like so that I might have acknowledged for myself what had happened to me, that I had been violated. I felt violated but didn't have words to put to the experience or the knowledge to put words to it. (Judy)

I always suspected that men could hurt you, but never, ever fathomed that a woman would take that away from another woman. It left me absolutely unable to trust another woman's sexual advances and to be able to trust my body for betraying me with pleasure response. (Lauren)

I buried it initially so I wasn't looking for anything in particular. I had packed it up and moved on. When I unpacked it though, I searched for anything in the literature that included me—but there's nothing really out there. The only very little there is about woman/woman sexual assault is either mother/daughter or within the context of a battering relationship. There's literature about heterosexual date rape/assault but nothing for lesbians. I wish there could have been just one book about a lesbian who experiences the date/acquaintance assault I had so I could have known I wasn't alone. (Marcia)

It has scarred me emotionally. I have had to overcome feelings of helplessness and unworthiness. I continue to battle with self-esteem and being a victim—which makes me feel less than I am. (Ariel)

Judy, Lauren, Marcia, and Ariel (all names are pseudonyms unless otherwise noted) are four women who responded to my appeal to participate in a study of woman-to-woman sexual violence. They are four lesbians who represent thousands of others suffering—in silence and isolation—from sexual abuse by another woman. They are this book's *raison d'être*, my work's driving force. To these women I say: Suffer in silence no more.

To speak of woman-to-woman sexual violence breaks a barrier of silence, to admit what society denies, and to debunk a myth of lesbian utopia.

What, sadly, many women say they might expect from a man (everyone knows that rapists are *men*) is unexpected from another woman. As women we are not prepared, we feel totally without safety, and the depth of our betrayal is greater. While rape and battering are different experiences, they share the societal belief that women are not violent—women do not rape and women do not batter. This denial of female perpetrators means they are free to move on to the next victim.

Definition of a Social Problem

Many kinds of relationships are open to all of us, from casual coworkers and acquaintances to close friends and intimate partners, and generally we are involved in many kinds of relationships at any given time. Several factors influence the point at which relationship dynamics begin to take on a public quality, or become a social problem. Behaviors are not inherently good or bad; rather social norms establish what is acceptable or unacceptable. If, in a relationship, you are beaten because your partner "loves" you, we know there is a problem. When boundaries are crossed, others—perhaps law enforcement officials, hospital workers, work supervisors, or therapists—are forced into what was before a private relationship.

Same-sex interpersonal violence has not always been defined as a social problem; in fact, activists and organizers are struggling to construct this now. Same-sex relationships are not given the same legitimacy as heterosexual relationships, so it has been nearly impossible to recognize same-sex abuse within relationships. Our culture defines the appropriate acting out of love or commitment, and these feelings and their accompanying behaviors and ceremonies are not easily ascribed to same-sex relationships. The mass of studies on relationship issues—love, attraction, intimacy, courtship, dissolution, stability, and so forth—generally exclude the experiences of lesbians and bisexual women. Researchers, journalists, therapists, and other professionals look to fit lesbian and bisexual women into the heterosexual woman's mold.[1] Identifying a social problem and its solution may, therefore, be off the mark. Issues of socialization, societal pressure, sexism, and more, need to be understood within the even broader context of homophobia and biphobia. This is lacking if lesbian and bisexual experiences are invisible.

Joseph Gusfield refers to the "ownership" of the definition of a problem as the ability to create and influence the society's definition.[2] As such, the battered women's movement owned society's understanding of what battering was and who the victims of battering were because movement activists were the ones speaking out and writing about the issues. To gain societal acceptance that women were, in fact, battered in their homes meant the early organizers of the battered women's movement had to portray "acceptable" female victims.[3] An acceptable victim was the woman with whom everyone could sympathize, who in the eyes of mainstream culture could not be blamed for the violence against her. In the 1970s that woman was heterosexual, white, and middle-class. This has meant downplaying or avoiding the battered lesbian or bisexual woman. Since it would discredit this image to point out that she might be nonwhite, or poor, or not heterosexual, these and other statuses remained invisible, marginalized. There was no analysis of who these women were, and this early imprint of the "battered woman," the one who could stand for all, has left us with no race analysis, no lesbian or bisexual analysis, no class analysis. To be a woman and to be battered was enough to establish the credibility of the definition of the new social problem, but the legacy has been the exclusion of many key dimensions of who these women really are. Though "any" woman *can* be a battered woman, the image that comes to mind is rarely the lesbian or bisexual woman. The lesbian and bisexual communities have had a hand in this outcome, as they have colluded to avoid making the problem known. Community members told survivors to not talk about their abuse to protect the community from even greater stigma—at the price, of course, of abused lesbians and bisexual women.

Because lesbians and bisexual women are battered, the established definition needs to be altered. The push to view *lesbians and bi women* as battered women means forging a new analysis requiring new literature, programs such as battered lesbian support groups, staff and volunteer trainings that include discussion of battered lesbians and bisexual women, and so forth. It means accepting women's same-sex relationships as legitimate. This has proven to be a tall order, and the resistance continues.

The same holds true when considering woman-to-woman sexual violence. Antirape work has been similarly inseparable from the feminist analysis.[4] Consciousness-raising groups and speak-outs at antirape workshops and conferences worked to spread the feminist challenge of traditional assumptions about rape. The conceptualization was premised on "woman as man's property" and that women submit to men. Women-oriented women have no place in this formulation, similar to the cultural contradictions found in the concept of "marital rape."[5] While reports of same-sex rape are found occasionally in the gay press, no movement (antirape or domestic violence) has claimed it. Feminists, for the most part, have ignored it up to now.

The Prevalence of Same-Sex Abuse

Whereas estimating the prevalence of domestic violence and rape for heterosexual women is difficult, it is even harder to do so among lesbians and bisexual women. Hindrances all abused women share include underreporting to authorities based on distrust of the legal system, personal feelings of shame and embarrassment, not wanting to name someone they know (as is most likely) as a batterer or rapist, and not labeling their experience as battering or rape. Another problem is found in the difficulty in comparing studies and their findings because they use differing definitions of what constitutes battering or sexual violence (or both). A main factor here is whether the abuse is defined broadly or narrowly. For lesbians and bisexual women, add to this the lack of random samples (making it difficult to generalize findings to the broader population) and denial that woman-to-woman battering and sexual violence even exists. The need to hide gay identities impacts the identification of the population by researchers. All prevalence studies of antigay violence share this problem, and most studies are done in gay/lesbian/bi-identified settings.[6] Researchers do not always ask the right questions to tell us if perpetrators of sexual violence against lesbians and bisexual women are females, if responses include stranger assault as opposed to relationship abuse, and if incest is included along with adult victimization. Sexual violence itself is defined differently in the studies, so sexual assault is sometimes mixed with, for example, unwanted kissing. These differences make it impossible to truly compare study findings.

But researchers do attempt to learn about these phenomena. Studies on sexual violence of lesbians conducted during the 1980s and 1990s range from a low of 5 percent to a high of 57 percent. In a study by Pamela Brand and Aline Kidd of 130 lesbian college students and lesbians in a discussion group, 5 percent had experienced attempted rape by a date, and 7 percent had been date raped by male or female perpetrators.[7] Seventeen percent of lesbians in a nonrandom survey by JoAnn Loulan said they'd been sexually abused in a lesbian relationship.[8] Lacey Sloan and Tonya Edmond found that 23 percent of lesbians had experienced sexual assault and another 35 percent had experienced attempted sexual assault by male or female perpetrators.[9]

Waterman, Dawson, and Bologna, in a study of sexual coercion among lesbian and gay male college students, found that 31 percent of the lesbians had been sexually abused by other lesbians.[10] In examining lifetime sexual victimization of college students, David Duncan reported that 31 percent of lesbians in his sample had been forced to have sex against their will by male or female perpetrators.[11]

In Claire Renzetti's study of 100 battered lesbians, 48 percent were forced to have sex by their partners.[12] Lisa Waldner-Haugrud and Linda Gratch found 133 instances of unwanted sexual behavior by their female partners among the 118 lesbians in their study. Fifty percent of them encountered unwanted penetration.[13] And Lie, Schilit, Bush, Montagne, and Reyes discovered that 57 percent of their lesbian respondents had experienced some type of sexual victimization by a female partner (of that, 19 percent forced or hurtful sex).[14]

Prevalence of lesbian domestic violence is estimated to approximate that in heterosexual relationships, between one-fourth and one-half of all relationships. The American Bar Association estimates the prevalence of domestic violence among gay and lesbian couples as between 25 and 33 percent. It claims that each year, between 50,000 and 100,000 lesbians are battered.[15] Brand and Kidd found one-fourth of their sample of lesbian couples had been physically abused.[16] Vallerie Coleman reported that 46 percent of the 90 lesbian couples she studied experienced interpersonal violence.[17] And Gwat-Yong Lie and Sabrina Gentlewarrier found that a female partner or lover abused 52 percent of the 1,099 lesbians who participated in their study at the Michigan Womyn's Festival, and that 30 percent admitted abusing a female partner or lover.[18]

The National Coalition of Anti-Violence Programs (NCAVP) is a coalition of Lesbian/Gay/Transgender/Bisexual (LGTB) victim advocacy and documentation programs that formed in 1995. In 1999, eleven reporting organizations documented 3,120 cases of domestic violence. Of that number, 1,458 (47 percent) were females.[19] While this does not represent a scientific study, the work these agencies are doing is the first of its kind — documenting both domestic violence cases and hate crimes and providing services for primarily gay, lesbian, and bisexual victims of domestic violence.

Theoretical Questions

Do survivors of woman-to-woman sexual violence and battering need different interventions than heterosexual women? If they do, and if the point of theory is to form the basis upon which service providers can base intervention,[20] does the theory need to be different? Given that lesbian partner violence is approximating the same frequency, with the same abuse types, and for the same purpose of control as heterosexual abuse, do the theoretical models used to explain heterosexual male abuse of females hold for lesbian abuse? Can different theoretical gender explanations—biological, gender role, and systemic male dominance—simply apply to lesbians and bisexual women?

Present feminist perspectives do a poor job of explaining woman-to-woman battering and sexual violence.[21] Essentialism—treating all women the same—has obvious weaknesses. "The same" has meant white, middle-class heterosexual women as the standard, since that is who authored the early theories. This theoretical exclusion of lesbians and bisexual women, women of color, immigrant women, and Native American women does not work.[22] What remains is an understanding without any analysis of the different situational locations of race, class, and sexual identity and how those locations affect both survivors and perpetrators. Particularly in the case of female abusers, they are put in an awkward position. As Ellen Bell writes, "In becoming an abuser, of her child or lover, a woman is not rendered sexless or an honorary man."[23]

Randy Thornhill and Craig Palmer assert that rape is behavior by men that is biologically determined and tied to the need for successful reproduction.[24] Consequently, men attempt to copulate with as many women of reproductive age as possible, which if the women resist, become acts of rape. Their argument rests on the premise that every aspect of life is biologically motivated. In their view, the evolution of male and female sexuality explains the causes of rape. The evolutionary factors of natural selection have resulted in males viewing any female (though especially those of childbearing age) as a suitable mate, while females act as if only certain males are good mates. This is because males have a minimal parental effort in offspring—primarily mating—while females have a high investment in parental offspring: carrying the fetus to term and taking care of it.

The biological determinist view posits that rape is based on male sexuality and that rape is a sexual act involving sexual arousal. It is *not* an act of power and control. Males are biologically selected to control the sexual behavior of females because of paternity identification, not for some "metaphysical" notion of cultural gender roles or male privilege. In fact, Thornhill and Palmer have clear disdain for feminist theory that examines power and control dynamics in society. Society, to them, is a "non-corporeal reified entity," and hence an abstraction without merit.[25]

My problems with the ideas of evolutionary psychologists are several. First, the theory is heterosexist and ignores same-sex rape.[26] When I asked Professor Thornhill how he would explain women raping other women, he suggested that "these women may be highly androgenized."[27] I am not sure how even highly androgenized women act on the role to impregnate. An argument based on natural selection does not account for why woman-to-woman sexual abuse appears to be so similar to heterosexual sexual abuse, as the stories in this book demonstrate. Then, they discount the possibility of motivations for rape other than impregnation. Thornhill and Palmer state that if rape were about control, then men would control in other, nonsexual ways. Clearly men do. I can only assume these authors are unfamiliar with domestic violence, sexual harassment, the distribution of political and economic power, and control over the media. Ironically, in the Darwinian argument, there is a complete inability to see "science" itself as a construct—which is how they view social science—and a discounting of choices of how to respond to sexual drive. Rather than rape unwilling females, why not masturbate or pay for sexual services? Power and control provide a reason for rape choice—whether male or female perpetrator.

Sex-role conditioning views violence as a learned behavior. Males are battering and raping women, the argument goes, because they have been socially conditioned to be aggressive, to sexualize women, and to win at all costs. They learn that violence gets results. Women have been socially conditioned to be passive, dependent, nurturing, and obedient. They learn that violence is used against them. In the gender perspective, feminism has defined victims as primarily female and perpetrators as typically male. By default, Waldner-Haugrud maintains, same-sex abuse does not have both the required participants.[28] Some argue that lesbians and bi women learn these roles so that lesbians and bisexual women who internalize socially feminine ways are more likely to be victimized, while lesbians and bisexual women who internalize socially masculine ways tend to be abusive. This is clearly a heterosexist model, which does not account for other variables such as the role of homophobia and biphobia in keeping lesbians and bisexual women closeted and unable to leave abusers. It also promotes the heterosexist idea that lesbians and bisexual women mimic heterosexual relationships with one partner more dominant (and "male") than the other.[29] But lesbians and bisexual women do not always conform to these expectations. Neither do heterosexual females in the estimated 5 to 10 percent of abuse cases where females batter males.[30] The gender role socialization explanation of power-over becomes much less clear-cut when the exceptions to the rule are not simply a minority of cases.

The basic explanatory concepts for both domestic violence and rape are power and domination, but they are applied in an analysis of how heterosexual men oppress heterosexual women under patriarchy. Male power is seen as operating in a system that legitimizes male control primarily through gender role socialization and mechanisms such as denied access to civil rights (liberal feminism) or control over women's bodies through the threat of violence and actual violence (radical feminism). In this analysis, women's experience has been universalized—all women regardless of differences are under the power and control of men. However, this system of male dominance is built on aspects that have little relevance to the lives of nonheterosexuals—the institution of marriage, women as the property of men, women's economic dependence on men, and the home as a private sphere.[31] So while there are certainly some structural aspects of sexism that apply to lesbians and bisexual women as females (women are paid less than men, for example), many of the structural relationship issues do not apply to them, weakening the applicability of the male dominance analysis of domestic violence. This analysis was easier to uncritically accept before women spoke up and acknowledged same-sex abuse.

David Island and Patrick Letellier dismiss the feminist analysis and view abusers as sadists with a personality disorder that is diagnosable and treatable. They do not believe abuse is a gender issue at all but a psychological one. The theory should focus on the behavior of abusers.[32] However, this focus does not tell us why males are overwhelmingly batterers in heterosexual relationships or why males are predominantly the rapists of women. This approach also does not call for societal changes, and isolates abusive behavior from the social context to center on the behavior of individual actors.

Greg Merrill and Joan McClennen advocate using a social-psychological model, though in slightly different ways.[33] Based on the writing of Beth Zemsky,[34] Merrill attempts to integrate feminist theory with the psychological theory of Island and Letellier in a three-part social-psychological model. He sees gender as one of several factors in interpersonal violence.[35] According to Zemsky, abuse is the result of learning to abuse, having the opportunity to abuse, and choosing to abuse. By acknowledging both the social and psychological aspects of battering, sex role socialization helps explain why more men abuse women than vice versa, but also that women can internalize the hierarchical modeling found in our culture. Learning to abuse is one element that combines with social status location and with individual psychology.[36] The three factors of learning, opportunity, and choice exist within the context of heterosexism. Individual psychological variables influence the three factors.[37] McClennen calls for one theory for lesbians and one for gay males. She bases her theoretical approach on Merrill's but factors in the oppression lesbians face as women because of sexism and the different gender socialization they experience compared with men for what she calls a patriarchal social-psychological theory.[38]

But violence is not primarily about gender; it is about power and control, gender socialization, and family and relationship dynamics. Barbara Hart reminds us that "lesbians, like their non-lesbian counterparts, are socialized in a culture where the family unit is designed to control and order the private relationships between members of the family. . . . Lesbians batter their lovers because violence is often an effective method to gain power and control over intimates."[39] George Appleby and Jeane Anastas similarly suggest looking at socialization in cultural institutions, specifically the family. Regardless of sexual identity, males and females are born and raised within family units.[40] The family structure is a hierarchy of unequal power, where lessons about power and control over resources are absorbed. Family members often learn the negative consequences of resistance to power and use of violence.

Ellen Faulkner suggests, "Lesbians need to look at power and how lesbians use it. Butch and femme sexuality is about power, as is sadomasochism, class, race, and ability."[41] Understanding that power relations run through all aspects of who we are as individuals and not just targeting some dimensions is important in challenging the misuse of power. Melanie Kaye/Kantrowitz asserts that as lesbians we don't want to deny our power, but states, "[T]he power to act at all includes the power to act wrong. A lesbian who beats her lover is a woman abusing the power available to her." She asks, can we use our power well? "How do we learn that we can use power responsibly? Having never had power, how do we develop control?" And, she wonders if men and women are batterers, what do violence and control have to do with patriarchy?[42]

Mary Eaton seeks a separate theory to explain lesbian battering that can coexist with a theory of heterosexual abuse. She suggests that lesbian battering is part of the larger context of heterosexist and homophobic antilesbian policies and practices. The need to remain closeted; silence around lesbian abuse by legislatures, courts, the lesbian community, and service providers; and the denial of services (including sometimes even the protection of safe shelter)—all of these reinforce lesbian invisibility. Says Eaton, "If erasure is understood to exist on a continuum, from closetry at one pole to physical annihilation at the other, the phenomenon of intralesbian violence can be seen to span its entire spectrum."[43] These factors are unique to a theory of woman-to-woman abuse.

Early feminism began as a movement to achieve women's equality to men. But sexism is not the only societal inequality. bell hooks looks at the politics of domination where interconnections exist between various systems of domination. She calls the overriding system the white supremacist, capitalist, patriarchal class structure. In her view the need is to transform society, not reform aspects of it so that women can be equal to men of their social class. There is, she states, a cultural basis to group oppression. Moving beyond the view that men are the enemy, hooks says, "we are compelled to examine systems of domination and our role in their maintenance and perpetuation."[44] With the development of a political consciousness, feminists will recognize the need "to eradicate the underlying cultural basis and causes of sexism and other forms of group oppression."[45] Women and men are socialized to accept the maintenance of power by force. Both women and men condone violence in our culture, and both women and men act violently. The theoretical premise is not patriarchy alone or capitalism alone, or any one form of oppression alone, but the organizing principle of power-over—"the idea that hierarchical structures should be the basis of human interaction."[46]

Whether to use gender as the key explanatory variable, analyzing cultural, psychological, or structural factors alone or together, questioning the use of power by disenfranchised group members within their relationships, or examining the impact of homophobia and biphobia presents challenges to our theoretical understanding of woman-to-woman violence. Is our main concern to have *one* theory to explain all abusive interpersonal violence? Is our key concern to understand why *perpetrators* (male or female) act in violent ways? Are we trying to make sense of why *women* (lesbian, bisexual, or heterosexual) are violent? Our theoretical premises matter—what proposals for social change shall we theorists put forward? I will return to these questions in the concluding chapter, where I will expand upon the premises that hooks proposed.

Design of the Study and the Research Process

Similar to the use of action research by Rebecca Dobash and Russell Dobash,[47] my original goals for this work included documenting stories of sexual violence, validating individual lesbians and bisexual women who experience a type of abuse that is often denied, pushing for acknowledgment in the lesbian and bisexual communities that this violence occurs, and advocating that social service agencies need to provide services for these women who are chronically underserved. These goals involve grassroots groups, community resources, media, policy makers, and lawmakers.

I encountered some of the same methodological constraints as others who work with marginalized groups. Because this is not a prevalence study, I did not need a random sample. In my case, response to the outreach I did all over the country (described later in this chapter) depended on a participant's voluntary request for the survey. All of the participants have experienced sexual violence in some form.

In my survey, I defined sexual violence to mean "any unwanted sexual activity. Contact sexual activities include: touching parts of the body, kissing, vaginal penetration by objects, vaginal penetration by fingers, oral sex, anal sex, rubbing, and being forced to do things to yourself. Noncontact sexual activities include forced viewing of pornography or other sexually explicit material and being forced to watch sexual activity of others." In my work I use Hart's definition of lesbian domestic violence: "Lesbian battering is that pattern of violent and coercive behaviors whereby a lesbian seeks to control the thoughts, beliefs or conduct of her intimate partner or to punish the intimate for resisting the perpetrator's control over her."[48] Abuse types include physical violence, emotional and psychological control, verbal abuse, financial control, sexual violence, property destruction, companion animal abuse, and threats.

As a feminist, my design of the survey and my interaction with the study participants do not follow traditional social science "objective" criteria. Listening to stories and emotional reactions does not lend itself to numerical measurement. Many aspects of social life do not "work" with objective measurement, and in my opinion this then does not mean there is a problem with the research. Rich information and understanding result from qualitative research methods employing narratives and the personal meanings attached to them.

I have certain biases that influenced this study. For example, I believe that homophobia and biphobia are closely connected to this social problem of woman-to-woman sexual violence. Implicit in the topic, I believe that some women are violent (in fact capable of rape), contrary to traditional gender role notions. I feel that the lesbian and bisexual communities have certain myths that need debunking, that feminist theory needs reexamination when it comes to interpersonal violence, and that social services are inadequate for the needs of the abused lesbian and bisexual woman. As a feminist, I am invested in this work. As Elizabeth Stanko discusses, there is a personal stake in studying sexual violence.[49] As a lesbian, I worry about woman-to-woman sexual violence for myself and for my lesbian and bi sisters.

Stanko says, "Emotion and pain are never far from teaching and research on sexual violence."[50] Reading, conversing about, and transcribing stories of sexual violence are painful. There were times I felt overwhelmed with feelings of enormous discomfort and vulnerability, as well as times when I wondered how participants could have pulled their lives together, how they could have survived their situations. At one point in the research, when I was single, I felt that I would never find someone to date because she might turn out to be an abusive partner. Often, when I present this research at conferences and I share some of the stories, I feel guilt for traumatizing the audience. I see teary eyes and am met with silence. While this reaction is appropriate, it is also difficult to manage.

Yet, because I feel it is so important to confront these issues, it is crucial that I do manage my feelings of discomfort, fear, or guilt. On the most personal level, when I have nightmares or when I feel overwhelmed by the painful experiences I hear, it is important to talk to someone about how I feel. Other outlets I use include writing poetry and crying. On the more political level, I work on these issues as an educator, as a support group facilitator, and as a writer. Volunteering at an antiviolence agency is an important physical response to working out my emotional pains.

The "experts" on this topic are the women who experience sexual violence by other women and the advocates and staff working in this field. When I first designed my flyer, cover letter, and questionnaire, I asked several women in the field around the country to review the outreach pieces. Our collective experience in working with (or being) abused lesbians and bisexual women was vast. I approached the project as a facilitator who is working with seventy direct participants and a multitude of other indirect participants who I am in touch with by phone or e-mail—all who have had input into the study. Ninety-four percent of the women who filled out the survey agreed to a follow-up. Eighty-eight percent of them did this follow-up in a phone conversation. I was heartened that so many women wanted to continue talking about such painful and personal experiences.

The process of this research is as important as the product. The scores of people I spoke with in my initial outreach contact, the e-mail correspondence that developed, the agency staff who called me with support, researchers asking me for information, and most of all, contact and conversations with participants created a process that lasted about a year and a half and that was rich and important in and of itself. Participants were more than willing to help in any way they could and have ownership in what they realized is groundbreaking work. Participants often saw this as part of their own personal healing process. For example, Nora said, "It was extremely therapeutic, very difficult, but extremely therapeutic. And it really helped me through some things and helped me realize some areas where I'm really stuck." Marcia filled out the survey over several therapy sessions with her counselor. And countless women thanked me for the opportunity to name what happened to them, to work on their issues, and to talk about their experiences.

The choice of topic had several consequences. I am dealing with sexual violence *and* women as perpetrators *and* lesbians and bisexual women. Sexual matters are difficult to discuss, women are not viewed as sexual perpetrators, and those of us who are not heterosexual are a stigmatized population. I found it difficult to discuss my research with others. Somewhat like Christine Mattley, who writes about responses to her research on phone sex workers,[51] I felt my topic was seen as questionable (and perhaps, *I* was questionable). Similar to Renzetti, who studies lesbian battering, I felt many people did not take the topic seriously or didn't believe it was an issue of much weight.[52] While some of this may have been pure surprise (that women might sexually violate or that lesbians and bisexual women were abused), some of it may have been amusement. I feared a voyeuristic response due to the focus on two women together sexually—in spite of the abusive nature of what I was exploring. I felt uncomfortable talking about the study to people outside of it, yet that is also part of the social change process and certainly part of the motivation for the project itself. When asked what I was writing about, I sometimes said it was a book on rape, which was true enough but certainly sidestepped crucial aspects. Mattley suggests that when working with marginalized groups or issues, researchers need to be prepared to answer tough questions and not be caught off guard.[53] I did not want my work trivialized and felt very protective about the women who are survivors, and I now realize how I discussed my work with others was the part of the process at which I was weakest.

I began drafting the materials for the study in January 1999. At the end of April 1999, I sent out over three thousand flyers with cover letters nationwide to domestic violence and rape crisis agencies. I sent hundreds of flyers to be posted in feminist bookstores and at gay, lesbian, bisexual, and transgender community centers. I sent three different press releases (May and November 1999, and March 2000) to about one hundred nationwide gay media sources. I targeted bisexual organizations, African-American, Latina, and Asian organizations, and contacted transgender groups. I sent mailings to therapists working with primarily lesbian, bisexual, and gay clients in the Bay Area. I sent notices to women's organizations and human rights groups. There were postings on electronic bulletin boards. I called and spoke to staff that had programs for battered lesbians and bisexual women. I constantly asked for referrals.

I had 15 requests from agencies for surveys and 167 inquiries from individuals about the study. Of the individuals, 67 received the survey and did not send it back. The majority of these women received at least one reminder from me, and often a second survey. Some of the women contacted me and told me they did not plan to respond because the topic was too emotional, their battering didn't include sexual violence, they were too busy, and so forth. Seventeen expressed interest but never sent me their addresses to send them the survey. Thirteen returned surveys I could not use because the respondents were not sexually violated by another woman. The remaining seventy women returned the survey and are the participants of the study.

Of the participants, more women (29 percent) heard about the study from the queer press than any other source. Nineteen percent heard about it via the Internet or an e-mail message, and another 19 percent heard about it from a friend or colleague. Eleven percent of the women learned about the study from a domestic violence or rape crisis agency. Publications other than the queer press (such as health publications, the NOW Times, Ms. Magazine, or organization newsletters) accounted for 9 percent of the women's source of information. Seven percent of the women learned of it from a gay community center or bookstore bulletin board. Four percent of the women heard about the study directly from me, and another 3 percent from their therapists.

The women came from twenty-six states, and one participant was from Canada. Regionally, they came from the Midwest (37.1 percent), Southeast (21.4 percent), New England (14.3 percent), Pacific West (14.3 percent), Middle Atlantic (7.1 percent), and Southwest (4.3 percent). More respondents came from North Carolina (nine) than any other state (followed by eight from Massachusetts). Interestingly, the majority of participants did not come from the cities believed to have the largest lesbian, bisexual, and gay male communities, such as San Francisco, New York, or Los Angeles, but from smaller towns and cities.

I corresponded with over one hundred people through e-mail or on the phone in addition to those who requested surveys. These contacts ranged from people offering assistance, asking for referrals or research information, telling me their stories, or offering me moral support in my efforts. This part of the process was quite exciting because it showed the interest and concern nationally on the topic and helped end my own isolation as a researcher and activist pursuing this work.

While I felt I made considerable outreach efforts, my sample shows a marked lack of diversity. I have come to the conclusion that to achieve greater racial diversity (that is, nonwhites) and participation from the transgender community, I needed to have had co-researchers from these communities with connections directly in these communities. Mailings of flyers and letters did not prove sufficient in these cases. As shown later, there was class diversity when looking at income, but not when looking at educational level. Basically, the result is a white and well-educated group, similar to other studies of self-selected participants, as noted by Brenda Riemer and Jeanne Thomas.[54] The women are not necessarily all "out" lesbians or bi women, since they came forward individually with assured confidentiality, so there is some diversity on that dimension.

Demographics of the Study Participants

Who are these seventy women who responded to my appeal for stories and interviews about their sexual violence experiences? They are women who hope telling their stories will help others who might experience something similar, women who want to end their silence and found a forum for doing so, women who view their participation as part of their healing process. For some of the women, this was the first time they told anyone of this sexual violence. Nora points to the major reason: "Even though the physical violence was much more violent, I think the sexual violence had a lot more impact on me psychologically, emotionally. . . . It's one big secret. So many people knew later on that I had been in an abusive relationship. I told nobody about the sexual violence because there's so much shame about it." The combination of sexual secrets with denial of women as perpetrators silences most abused lesbians and bisexual women who are survivors of this type of violence.

The vast majority of the study participants are lesbians (81 percent).

Sixteen percent are bisexual women, one woman (1 percent) is heterosexual, and one woman identified as transgendered (though she identified as a lesbian at the time of her abuse). Most of the women (53 percent) are single, while 41 percent are partnered. Two women (3 percent) are in a relationship of less than one year, and another 3 percent are in a relationship with a male. The women are overwhelmingly white, not Latina (86 percent). Six percent identified as white and Native American, 3 percent as white Latina, and one woman each identified in these four categories: South Asian, Middle Eastern, Latina, and mixed white and black.

In total, ninety-one situations of sexual violence were described. Some of these are one-time-only events; some of them may have been twice with the same person; or there may be an ongoing sexually abusive situation involved. Forty-three events are one-time situations, and forty-eight events are twice or ongoing situations.

Respondents ranged in age from 18 to 64, with the average age 36.7 years old. More of the women are in their thirties—41 percent—than any other age category. The next largest category is 40 to 49 years old (24 percent), followed by 20 to 29 years old (20 percent). Nine percent are 50 to 59 years old, and only 3 percent each are found in the age categories of 18 to 19 years old and 60 to 64 years old. These ages represent their age at the time of the study. If one looks at the time of their sexual violence, a different pattern emerges.

In examining age at sexual violence for the ongoing situations, I counted the age it started. So, for example, Ariel's sexual violence within a battering relationship occurred when she was 23 to 30 years old. I count this as age 23 for this purpose. A majority, 60 percent, of the sexual violence occurred when respondents were between 15 and 25 years old (56 percent between 18 and 25 years old). Forty-six percent of the women were in their twenties when the sexual violence occurred or started. Seventeen percent of the violence happened between the ages 18 to 19 and also ages 30 to 39. Ten percent of the women experienced their sexual abuse when they were between ages 40 and 49, and four women, or four percent, were minors when they were sexually violated by other women.

The sexual violence was concentrated at younger ages (under twenty-five). So, while almost half of the women were recounting events that happened within the past ten years (48 percent), more of the women were discussing events that occurred more than ten or even thirty years ago. Forty percent of the women told of violence from the 1980s, 11 percent of abuses were from the 1970s, and one woman's sexual violence occurred in the late

1960s. Several significant points should be made about this: sexual violence incidents carry enormous stigma for decades, and survivors find them difficult to talk about; memories of events are usually very clear; and the emotional impact is severe and long lasting. Furthermore, when these abuses occurred and whether the survivors could speak publicly about them is related to what was happening in the lesbian and gay rights and women's rights movements at the time. Speaking out in the 1970s and 1980s guaranteed a response of silencing, while today abuse survivors have the support of ten years of early research and writings to validate their experiences. That doesn't mean it is necessarily easy for the survivors, but the fact that this violence occurs is finally being acknowledged. In talking about this work, I was met with constant surprise and confusion, but I have been able to work on it nonetheless. I have been able to assert what I know rather than be silenced by those who don't know or don't want to hear of it.

This is a well-educated group of participants. Most of the women in the study are either college graduates (40 percent) or have advanced degrees after college (29 percent). Thirty percent have some college, and only one participant (1 percent) has less than high school. Three women have additional educational certificates. Over one-fourth (26 percent) of the women work in business/managerial jobs. Sixteen percent have jobs in professional fields, and another 16 percent work in social services. Women who are retired, disabled, or unemployed make up 13 percent of the sample. Ten percent are students (graduate or undergraduate), and 9 percent are writers. Four percent are craftspeople, and 7 percent hold other jobs not fitting in the prior categories. Despite their high educational levels, these women do not have high incomes. One-third (33 percent) of the women make less than $15,000. Six women (9 percent) make between $15,000 and $19,999. One-fifth (21 percent) make between $20,000 and $29,000. Nineteen percent earn between $30,000 and $39,000. Eleven percent earn between $40,000 and $49,000, and only five women (7 percent) earn over $50,000.

The type of sexual violence these women experienced is difficult to categorize because the labels they used at first to name what occurred usually differs from what they label it later. And, more important, because the laws vary as to whether sexual violation by a female perpetrator is punishable and these acts are vastly underreported, there is no generally recognized vocabulary to discuss sexual violence by females against other females. I discuss these issues in the following chapters. However, the survivors ultimately considered the majority of the ninety-one situations rapes or sexual assaults.

Fifty-six percent of the time, the perpetrator was a partner, lover, or girlfriend. Twenty-five percent of the situations involved acquaintances or friends and three percent involved dates. Women reported sexual abuse by professionals (therapist, teacher, doctor, mentor, or supervisor) in 7 percent of the situations. Coworkers were perpetrators in 4 percent of the cases. Two perpetrators (2 percent) were strangers, and there was one case each of an ex-lover, an adopted sister, and a sex partner as perpetrator. For most of the women (79 percent), the perpetrator was no longer in their lives. Eleven percent said the abuser was somewhat still in their lives, and for 11 percent, the perpetrator was involved in their lives, usually as a friend.

Of the seventy participants, more than half (53 percent) had been in one or more battering relationships, and thirty-three women (47 percent) had not. Of the ninety-one sexual violence situations I discuss, 45 percent took place within a battering relationship; 55 percent did not. Thirty-four (37 percent) of the events involved alcohol or drug use by the perpetrator, survivor, or both, while 57 (63 percent) did not. In only seventeen cases (19 percent) was legal help sought, usually in seeking a restraining order or calling the police.

This sample represents a group of women with a heavy abuse history in addition to their adult sexual violence by other women. Seventy-one percent experienced incest as children or adolescents or statutory rape, and 51 percent have been raped by a male as adults. Forty percent have a history of both incest and rape by a male. With previous abuse histories, it is likely that these women were more able to recognize the abuse they suffered later in life as well as the importance of speaking out about it.

I discuss the issues of revictimization later in chapter 6, but I believe it is important to state here at the outset that I do not interpret revictimization to imply an individual woman's pathology. That is, these women are not primarily mentally ill, borderline personalities, or masochists. Instead, I believe symptoms of posttraumatic stress and temporary coping behaviors (as opposed to personality characteristics) that arise in response to abuse are the key factors that place women at risk for further abuse. The other unfortunate factor is that many women and men in society are abusers, and they are going to victimize or attempt to victimize others—the women in this study or, perhaps, you the reader—regardless of abuse histories.

The Respondents as Real People

Sexually abused and battered women come from every walk of life and meet their abusers in very "ordinary" ways—at work, in school, through friends of theirs. Like other people, they deal with family problems growing up, need ways to support themselves, move for jobs or school or new opportunities, and seek loving and trusting relationships. Following are a few snapshots of four study respondents, offering a glimpse at their lives.

Evon: Evon is a white lesbian. When she answered the ad for the study she was twenty-six years old, working as an administrative assistant. When I asked her to reflect on her experiences a year after the survey and interview, she had this to say:

> I grew up in a strong, loving family with the knowledge that I could do anything I set my mind to. My mother especially brought me up on independence, creativity, and the courage to always move forward. I have obtained much success in reaching my goals, but along the way I have also experienced sexual assault and domestic violence. As a seventeen-year-old woman, I was raped by my first boyfriend who told me it was love and that I was nothing. This relationship lasted two years and included sexual violence and domestic violence. I then moved on, went to college, came out as a lesbian, and began to enjoy a full-on pro–woman powered life. I lived courageously with strong women friends secure in my wisdom of experience. What I didn't expect, again, was rape, this time by a man I called my friend, who did it in spite of my independence and lesbianism. Soon after this experience I met "her" and fell in love. She was a survivor also of rape and abuse and this is how we connected. Within a month she was my abuser full-on 24/7. I was in shock and disbelief. It took me a year before I could escape. I lived in fear and [in] the fear of reaching out to a stranger who wouldn't believe me, or even worse, [would] disrespect me because I am a lesbian. It never occurred to me that I could experience this level of abuse at the hands of another woman. Now I am working in the domestic violence movement. I am no longer unaware that SA [sexual abuse] and DV [domestic violence] do occur in a woman-to-woman society and can happen to anyone. My vision for the future is to end SA and DV through outreach and education so that all are aware and empowered to create true social change.

Giselle: When I first spoke to Giselle, a biracial (European-Hispanic) lesbian, she was thirty-nine and a social worker. She says of herself:

> I am a forty-year-old lesbian, musician, artist, Gemini, which is just another excuse for having a hard time making decisions! My "abuse" was subtle and insidious and continues to puzzle me and seep into my life and relationships in a myriad of sneaky ways. As I enter the second half of my life, I have a longing to put the past behind me with less blame and less judgment. It was no one's fault, it was everyone's fault, it was my fault. It doesn't really matter anymore. What matters to me is having energy for my four-year-old daughter and her mother. What matters to me now is

being awake and fully alive for my life. What matters to me is to not miss any more moments being resentful, angry, or confused. What matters to me now is NOW.

Rita: Rita was forty at the time she responded to the survey. She is a white, bisexual woman in a long-term committed relationship. She is disabled. She writes:

I grew up in a rural town that is only two miles square in New Jersey. I was teacher's pet. I thought I was the only gay teen there in 1972 when I entered a private all-women's Catholic high school. I had "fag" written on my locker, but I didn't know what it meant. I endured a childhood with a father who was both physically and verbally abusive. I became interested in art and writing. They both were outlets for me. I wrote poems all through high school and college and kept a journal. I graduated Georgian Court College in 1980 with a B.A. in art. I was also accepted into *Who's Who in American Colleges and Universities* and Sigma Tau Delta.

Currently, I am a survivor of an industrial accident and I am disabled from back surgery. I have taken up ceramics again and throw pottery on a wheel in my basement. I also volunteer for Habitat for Humanity. I work with children at my church teaching them art and religion. I love children and encourage every child I meet to a fault. The abuse in my past has given me the tools to cope with serious illness and the frustration of our current medical care system.

I have learned to say: "Take your hand out of my face and don't abuse me" to my father and still say it. In 1982, I was almost married to a handsome Italian man from South Philly, but he was an alcoholic and I chose to avoid any more dysfunction in my life. Instead, in 1990, I married a woman in a Unitarian Church. We have been together for eleven years happily. We celebrated our tenth anniversary by renewing our wedding vows in Vermont with a civil union this past fall. I feel truly blessed to have someone so devoted to me and to have a healthy loving relationship. I like to think that we all can grow and change, but you have to have the courage to do it. Believe it can happen to you!

Lila: At the time of the survey, Lila was a public policy program manager. She is a white lesbian, thirty-seven years old, and a former prostitute. She writes:

I was sexually abused for twelve years in my childhood and for thirteen years in the sex industry. One of the ways I healed was through speaking and acting for myself and other women like me. I published research and essays about stripping and prostitution and developed programs, public policy, and educational materials to benefit the women and hold the men accountable. I wanted other women to feel about themselves the way I finally felt about myself, so I created a residential therapy program for prostituted women.

Now I am in law school and am interested in family law because I see my role as attorney as a healer, not a soldier. I will continue to help women realize their feminine power, be independent of violent and exploitive people, and be leaders in their families and communities.

As a stripper, the violence perpetrated against me was very public. As an activist, I was very public about abuse. Now I want privacy and intimacy. We don't always have to be on the front line to make a difference for other women. We can work at different levels at different times depending on all the other things going on in our lives. Surviving violence, maintaining health and integrity, and speaking the truth are ways to make a difference. It challenges those people who brutalized us and makes us role models for women and girls struggling to survive violence. And so, I will quietly practice law, salsa dance, and make love.

What's to Follow

In the next chapter, I present a discussion of the broader context of our lives as lesbians and bisexual women—homophobia, the irrational fear and hatred of homosexuals; biphobia, the fear and hatred of bisexuals; and transphobia, the fear and hatred of transgender people. No social change is possible unless these phobias are factored into the analysis of our societal and internalized oppression. Many of the problems in the queer communities are due to the stress of coping with homophobia, biphobia, and transphobia and the resulting distortion it creates in our lives. These phobias also play a major role in our problem with admitting woman-to-woman sexual violence.

I explore the myth of lesbian utopia in chapter 3. The need for community, development of a distinct lesbian culture, denial of violence, merger in woman-focused relationships, silence, fear of not being believed, and the consequences of denial are issues I examine here. Chapter 4 focuses on the personal stories of women who have experienced sexual violence by other women. I cover stories of sexual harassment, date rape and acquaintance rape, domestic violence, and abuses of authority, along with a discussion of how the women responded to what happened to them.

The issue of language and labels is the focal point of chapter 5. I look at how survivors define what happened to them, how the labels shift, and why they shift. I follow with a discussion of terminology of sexual violence. In chapter 6 I deal with the emotional impact of sexual violence on the women in the study. I discuss incest and rape by men as well as the issue of revictimization. The women talk about coping with this previous abuse and violence from a woman.

Chapter 7 examines heterosexism in the legal system and how laws are not lesbian- and bisexual-friendly. Both the laws and the application of the laws are problematic. I look at state laws, as well as the opinions and experiences of the women in the study with the legal system. Chapter 8 takes the same approach regarding services for survivors. I examine why women abuse and the issues related to healing from abuse regarding what services survivors want and need as compared with what actually exists. I end with concluding comments in chapter 9, including a theoretical framework for social change.

2

The Societal Context of Homophobia, Biphobia, and Transphobia

The hot line worker didn't know how to react because it was a woman who attacked me. She could not even tell me if I was entitled to a protection order. She didn't seem to understand and she didn't seem concerned. It took so much for me to dial that phone number, and it just made me feel worse. (Christy)

I was very concerned about outing the professor and our relationship and this factored hugely in my not reaching out. (Erin)

[I wasn't worried about a homophobic reaction] because I was talking with other gay individuals who knew me better than they knew her. But it took four years before I spoke of it with a straight person (my counselor). (Marcia)

Yes, [I was] afraid I would be told I deserved it because of my lifestyle or that it (the violence) would be minimized. Being shut out of some people's lives due to my lifestyle made it even harder to know who would support me. (Maureen)

How is it that these women felt they could not reach out for help after their sexual violence? And why were the women who weren't worried about a homophobic or biphobic reaction to their victimization not worried because primarily they were telling someone else who was gay? To answer these questions we must explore the societal context of heterosexism, monosexism, homophobia, biphobia, and transphobia and how this impacts the lives of lesbians and bisexual women.

The women in the study didn't simply experience sexual violence; they did so in an environment that discriminates against them and hates them for who they are. To function in such a society means to live without the necessary supports heterosexuals take for granted. As we will see, lesbians and bisexual women felt there were few services they could turn to after their experiences of sexual violence. They doubted whether they would be welcome at crisis service agencies and even wondered if they could call crisis hot lines. They wished for support services provided by and designed for lesbians or bisexual women where they felt they would be accepted and understood. Agency support groups that usually provide safety and trust for group members are not necessarily safe for the lesbian or bisexual woman joining a group of heterosexual women violated by men. The unknown factor is if these women will be homophobic or biphobic—a variable the lesbian or bisexual woman survivor usually does not want to test. To have to defend your sexual desire is an inappropriate burden; to be negated during crisis is too painful.

To realize the pervasiveness of antilesbian and antibisexual sentiment in society and how this affects survivors of woman-to-woman sexual violence, it is necessary to explore the concepts and the research that empirically tests those concepts. In the following sections I introduce these concepts. I explore the nature of oppression and heterosexism and its impacts on those who are discriminated against. This discussion helps all of us in understanding the predicaments of these women, as well as points to underlying societal attitudes and assumptions that need to change.

Definitions

Homophobia is the irrational fear and hatred of gays and lesbians. It is, as Mary Louise Adams points out, a condition of individuals,[1] whereas *heterosexism*, the belief that heterosexuality is normal, natural, and right, and that any other sexual orientation is abnormal, is institutionalized in our larger sociopolitical system. It is the system itself that mandates "compulsory heterosexuality" through laws, gender roles and expectations, cultural practices, mass media, and religious and other social institutions.[2] *Biphobia* refers to the discomfort and fear individuals feel around bisexual people, while *monosexism* relates to the structural and cultural privileging of sexuality directed toward only one gender (heterosexuality or homosexuality). *Transphobia* is the fear and rejection of those who attempt to construct their own social identity regardless of external genitalia. Because of homophobia, biphobia, transphobia, monosexism, and heterosexism, the lives of lesbians and bisexual women are circumscribed through stigma, shame, and threats of violence and actual violence. These interlocking oppressions around gender definition and acceptability form the background for our identity formation.

The term *homophobia* has its roots in Wainwright Churchill's use of the word "homoerotophobia" in 1967 when discussing the cultural fear of sexual contact between same-sex partners. In 1971, Kenneth Smith used the term "homophobia" in describing the personality profile of people with a negative reaction to homosexuals. It was George Weinberg in his 1972 publication *Society and the Healthy Homosexual* who shifted the term to a focus on societal attitudes.[3] While some see the use of the word *phobia* as an overstatement of what a clinically phobic reaction entails, Weinberg's stress was on the irrational, fear-driven aspect of the view.[4]

While *homophobia* is a common term used in the media during coverage of hate crimes, in discussing civil rights legislation, and in academic writings and activist literature, the term *biphobia* is not. This is emblematic of the invisibility of bisexuality as a valid sexual identity and of bisexuals as a minority in need of civil rights. Consequently, myths about bisexuality abound. These myths and stereotypes include that bisexuals are confused, that bisexuality is a transition stage to homosexuality, that bisexuals are promiscuous and untrustworthy in a relationship, that they are obsessed with sex, that they are nonmonogamous, and that they spread STDs and HIV. Because of their supposed high levels of sexual activity, they are expected to be good lovers.[5]

Perhaps the issue most "unnatural" and unsettling about bisexuality is that it runs contrary to monosexism, the idea that sexuality is dichotomous. It is not acceptable to be attracted to both women and men. The fear of biphobia rests on the inability to place bisexual people in a box and set them apart. Consequently, the biphobic individual may think: *If they are not different from me, then maybe there is the possibility I could be like them*—which creates personal anxiety.[6] The direct challenge to the dual gender system is unfathomable to the biphobic person. Bisexuals are seen as people who are sexual in an "uncontrolled and uncontrollable way."[7]

Bisexuals are stigmatized not only by heterosexuals but also by lesbians and gay men. From the vantage point of the lesbian and gay communities, bisexuals blur the boundaries between insider and outsider. Given their access to heterosexual privilege, some queer community members wonder how committed bisexuals are to lesbian and gay causes.[8] This issue of who is in and who is out as community members resembles the prejudice of African Americans and their views on skin color privilege—will the lighter skinned black choose to "pass" for white when it is convenient? From a lesbian feminist position, bi women are "collaborating with the enemy" and may be seen as more harmful to feminism than heterosexual women.[9]

Identifying who you are and what community you belong to is particularly complicated for the transgender individual. For trans folks, the challenge to conceptualization that there is a biological dichotomy of two sexes that correlates with two distinct gender identities is no abstraction. Rather, they experience a lack of fit between biological assignment at birth and how they feel. The most blatant form of transphobia is found in the fact that in the last decade, one person per month has died because of transgender-based hatred and prejudice. Transgender people are mistreated by police and medical providers, verbally abused on the street, and subjected to partner abuse and sexual violence.[10] Certainly, transgender people are the least understood and least accepted of the sexual minorities.

The oppression of minorities is a consequence of power relations—the power to control access to resources, the ability to construct dominant ideologies, and the authority to determine the structure of the hierarchical system we inhabit. The binary sexual system is a major aspect of our social system and is subject to power relations and all that it entails. Marilyn Frye writes:

> The experience of oppressed people is that the living of one's life is confined and shaped by forces and barriers which are not accidental or occasional and hence avoidable, but are systematically related to each other in such a way as to catch one between and among them and restrict or penalize motion in any direction.[11]

She refers to a birdcage, where looking between the wires gives one the impression of choice and movement, but viewing the entire structure shows the obvious barriers to freedom. The consequence of powerlessness is a negative impact on one's mental health and a diminished sense of mastery.[12]

The Interlocking Nature of Oppression

The weapons that those in power use against those with less power are experienced simultaneously on multiple dimensions—sexual identity, sex, race, class, ability, and age—as each individual occupies a social status on these different dimensions. For example, the Combahee River Collective states, "We believe that sexual politics under patriarchy is as pervasive in black women's lives as are the politics of class and race. We also find it difficult to separate race from class from sex oppression because in our lives they are most often experienced simultaneously."[13] Further, they state that organizing against the power of dominant groups was especially difficult, since (in their case) as black lesbian feminists they were not just fighting one oppression but a "whole range of oppressions."[14] Lorde reinforces that there is no hierarchy of oppressions. She writes, "I cannot afford the luxury of fighting one form of oppression only. I cannot afford to believe that freedom from intolerance is the right of only one particular group. And I cannot afford to choose between the fronts upon which I must battle these forces of discrimination."[15]

Struggling against one form of oppression is "inextricably linked to all struggles to resist domination," explains hooks.[16] It is never a matter of one form of oppression taking precedence over another, but seeing via critical consciousness the nature of our hierarchical system and understanding the links.[17] The interlocking nature of oppression is important because fighting against one type of oppression in isolation can leave societal members oppressed in other "equally dehumanizing ways."[18] Still, hooks and Valli Kanuha point to the difference between race, which often cannot be hidden, and sexual identity, which is not externally seen. Other complications, such as the historical legacy of slavery or attempts at genocide, need to be taken into account. So, while oppressions should not be ranked, neither are they synonymous. Furthermore, since they are experienced simultaneously, some individuals are more disadvantaged than others are. Kanuha points to the low status of the nonwhite lesbian, for example.[19]

Those who are members of privileged groups have invisible and unearned advantages, as Peggy McIntosh discusses.[20] The dominance of white, heterosexual males is the result of interlocking hierarchies of privilege, which women, lesbians, gay men, bisexuals, and nonwhites challenge on a daily basis. Heterosexism rests on patriarchal male privilege. Many lesbian feminists see sexism and heterosexism as "hopelessly intertwined, and the oppression of women and lesbians as the prototype for all other oppressions, since the oppression of women and of lesbians crosses boundaries of race, class, and age."[21] This interrelationship is crucial because it points to the cultural, institutional, and personal entrenchment of homophobia and heterosexism. Gender as a socially constructed typology establishes what "normal" femininity and "normal" masculinity are. Homosexuality and bisexuality violate these gender norms, which are taught in the key societal institutions of family, religion, schools, and mass media.

To violate these expected norms stigmatizes the social and personal identities of lesbians and bisexual women; they have a "spoiled" identity. Those associated with lesbians and bi women, such as family members,

may experience a "courtesy stigma," making coming out a more complicated issue, since it involves others beyond the self.[22] Since stigma results
in the individual feeling abnormal, social worth may be low, and the lesbian
or bisexual woman may feel imperfect in terms of societal standards.[23] Parents and other family members often turn to support services such as therapists or groups such as Parents and Friends of Lesbians and Gays (P-FLAG).

The Cultural Level of Heterosexism

Cultural norms, such as monosexuality, traditional gender roles, and
the definition of family, are major elements of heterosexism. Because of the
widespread knowledge of these norms, lesbian baiting as an element of
sexism is a powerful tool of homophobia. Women who are outspoken about
their rights or speak out about violence against them, who dress in "man-
nish" ways, who work in traditionally male occupations, or who resist male
sexual advances are at risk of being called "lesbians." Feminists are often
assumed to be lesbians, as are college students taking women's studies
classes. Lesbian baiting is an attempt to control women by labeling them as
lesbians for their unacceptable behavior (i.e., resistance to male domination). Whether they are lesbians or not is beside the point. The goal is to
stigmatize them and silence them.[24] Fear of being labeled a lesbian keeps
many women from forming strong bonds of solidarity and support because
the label "lesbian" sexualizes their relationships in a way that may not be
accurate.[25]

Public opinion polls about homosexuality continue to show that while
the public does not favor outright discrimination, a majority still believes
homosexuality is wrong. A 1994 poll revealed a negative view of homosexuality by most respondents, though 75 percent opposed discrimination.[26]
During the 1990s, research by the National Opinion Research Center
showed that 50 to 66 percent of people believed homosexual relations were
immoral.[27]

The powerful influence of media contributes to shaping these views.
News reports cover gay bashings; television talk shows exploit gay, bisexual,
and transgender "freaks"; and pornography trivializes lesbians by portraying
two women together as a prelude to "real" sex with a man. Joshua Gamson
explores how talk show producers use lesbians, gay men, bisexuals, and
transgender people to distinguish between normal and abnormal sexual beings. This fits in well with talk show fascination with the taboo, the sexual,
the controversial, and the newly politicized. While lesbians and gay men

are often affirmed in these shows ("Be proud of who you are!") that is not always the case, and bisexuals and transgender individuals are particularly vilified. Negative portrayals include the deceit of lesbians and gay men who come out after being married (hence, they deceived their spouses and ruined their lives), transsexuals who are defined as gender liars (the girlfriend who turned out to be a man), transsexuals who ruin their children's lives (because of family conflict and strain), the falseness of bisexuality (you can't be both, you have to choose), and the promiscuity of bisexuals (they can only be satisfied with simultaneous male and female partners). These shows play to the anxieties and hostilities that public visibility of queers provokes. The fact that sometimes the guests on these shows are actors or that the conflicts that emerge are rehearsed is irrelevant to the prejudice and discriminatory attitudes that are reinforced. It is the rare talk show that allows any queer to contest this oppression, though that can occur.[28]

Leigh, a heterosexual woman in the study, was surprised by people's reaction to what happened to her. She was held against her will for three days by her best friend and that woman's boyfriend, and was forced to perform sexual acts on them both. She said,

> It didn't occur to me that I'd get a homophobic reaction. Because I was trying to tell people "this is what happened to me." And I got both from men and women who I told, when I told them I was forced to have oral sex with a woman, "Oh, ick, oh, yuck, oh, my God!" And I said, "What is your problem with this? Men do this and you don't have a problem when men do this. So, it's like, it's not some disgusting thing." And I continued telling people until pretty much everybody I told who was heterosexual had that same reaction or else they would look at me like why didn't I have a problem with this. Like, the problem for me was the fact that I was forced to do this, but they didn't get that. So, that's why I stopped [telling].

While cultural heterosexism is rooted in our ideas about "normalcy," this does not mean that the ideas go unchallenged. The American Psychiatric Association (APA) defined homosexuality as pathological until 1974 when it was removed as a mental disorder from the *Diagnostic and Statistical Manual of Mental Disorders*, second edition (*DSM-II*). Until that time much energy went into curing what was defined as abnormal. However, in the past few decades, the APA has been very clear that homosexuality should not be stigmatized.[29]

Another highly contentious cultural arena is that of religious values, whether a form of Christianity, Judaism, Islam, or Hinduism. Most traditional religions preach that homosexuality is a sacrilege, that it is evil, and that it is perverted. The antihomosexual views of the dominant religion in America, Christianity, are shared by the most visible minority religion, Judaism. The same passages pointed to in the Bible to prove homosexuality as an aberration are contested in interpretation by more accepting religious leaders.[30] However, given the power of conservative televangelists, decrees from the Vatican, and the coming together of the religious right around this single issue of antihomosexuality, the cultural power of religious homophobia is potent. Kara grew up where the Corn Belt intersected the Bible Belt. She says, "You had these fears that all queers were going to hell. People just really got off on beating up gay people."

hooks, writing about homophobia in black communities, points to the strong influence of church teachings that encourage homophobia. Combined with the other cultural ideas that coupling should be for the purpose of having children (lesbians are not naturally seen as mothers) and that interracial relationships are frowned upon (more lesbian relationships than heterosexual ones appear to be interracial), homophobia is widespread.[31] Harlon Dalton adds that "homosexuality [in the black community] carries more baggage than in the larger society" because "openly gay men and lesbians evoke hostility in part because they have come to symbolize the strong female and the weak male that slavery and Jim Crow produced."[32] Brenda Blasingame writes about the struggle for many African-American lesbians and bisexuals who fear they would lose the support of their community in their struggle against racism if they were true to their sexual identity and came out.[33] Factors of gay liberation versus black liberation also confuse existing microlevel support of lesbians, bisexuals, and gay men with broader liberation struggles. hooks advocates an emphasis on the commonality of struggles rather than the divisions between them.[34]

The Institutional Level of Heterosexism

The institutional level of heterosexism, built upon cultural norms, spans an enormous gamut of our lives. Lack of civil rights protection, lack of legal avenues such as marriage, discrimination in housing and employment, media control, religious hierarchies, public policy decisions—the list of institutionalized heterosexism is a very long one. Given the invisible nature of heterosexism to heterosexuals, it usually comes as a surprise to them to realize the extent of its institutionalization. In fact, it often looks like lesbians, gays, and bisexuals have won our rights because of activism and political visibility. However, Urvashi Vaid writes:

The irony of gay and lesbian mainstreaming is that more than fifty years of active effort to challenge homophobia and heterosexism have yielded us not freedom but "virtual equality," which simulates genuine civic equality but cannot transcend the simulation. In this state, gay and lesbian people possess some of the trappings of full equality but are denied all of its benefits.[35]

For example, there is a range of civic rights denied us. While we may co-habitate, lesbians or two bisexual women do not have the rights and privileges of marriage. In response to the Supreme Court of Hawaii agreeing to hear a lawsuit in 1992 that denial of access by gays and lesbians to marriage was illegal under the state constitution, states across the country jumped into action to make sure gay marriage would not be legal in their jurisdiction.[36] In 1996, the federal Defense of Marriage Act was passed, stating that the legally recognized marriage was only between a man and a woman. The consequences of these actions denies women in intimate partnership access to health and life insurance, tax code benefits, social security and pensions, joint credit policies, inheritance laws, bereavement and medical leave plans, and so on. Marriage allows spousal visits to hospital intensive care units, as well as automatic legal and medical powers of attorney. And equally important, lesbians and bisexual women are denied the social legitimacy of our relationships.[37] Deirdre comments on one consequence of this lack of legitimacy:

> Society needs to recognize us as human beings. I mean, if I'm a human being capable of being in a loving relationship with another human being, and that relationship is a valid relationship, then if that person turns around and abuses me or rapes me, then I am a victim of abuse or rape. But if A and B isn't accepted then C and D aren't going to be accepted.

Some cities have extended family benefits to same-sex partners. For example, New York City gay city employees have funeral leave benefits, and San Francisco allows unmarried couples to register their relationships.[38] The most recent challenge to homophobic marriage laws is the Vermont Supreme Court decision in 1999 wherein gay and lesbian couples can register civil unions granting all of the benefits of heterosexual marriage (without being called "marriage"). While a promising step forward, the struggle continues as we must wait and see whether this can be extended to other states and whether it will be allowed to stand in Vermont.[39]

Another area where cultural heterosexism is strong is the notion that

lesbians and bisexual women are not fit to be parents. This has been institutionalized into laws around child custody and adoption. Many cases have
been documented where lesbians lost custody of their children to their ex-
husbands solely because of their sexual identity. Sometimes the visitation
rules include no overnights if the lesbian mother has a female roommate.[40]
Most states do not allow adoption to same-sex couples. If one member of
the couple adopts as a single mother, the other may never be able to adopt
as the second parent.

Probably the case that most captured the nation's attention was in 1995,
when Sharon Bottoms lost custody of her son, Tyler, to her own mother.
The Virginia Supreme Court ruled that Sharon was not a fit mother because of the gender role "confusion" in her home. Tyler called Sharon's
female partner, who provided the primary financial family support, "da da."
Sharon's gender "errors" included that she lived with a woman and that she
was too assertive. She was, therefore, a "bad" mother.[41]

Sodomy laws represent another realm where law has stepped in to enforce cultural notions of gender correctness. The right of states to outlaw
private consensual acts was upheld by the U. S. Supreme Court in 1986 in
Bowers v. Hardwick. While the Georgia antisodomy law does not specify
sexual orientation or gender of the people involved in the sexual acts, the
law is primarily used against men who are engaging in oral or anal sex
with men. Sixteen states still outlaw these sexual acts, demonstrating the
importance of forcing people to adhere to "appropriate" gender norms.[42]

Nor are lesbians welcomed in the military. They are discharged from
the military at a rate seven to ten times that of men, often simply on the
suspicion that they are lesbians. One major difference between gay males
and lesbians who are discharged is that women are more often caught up
in a mass purge, referred to as "witch-hunts." To save themselves from dis-
charge, women are forced to name others who might be lesbians or are
lesbians, resulting in the mass purging of women. Military women most
often targeted for investigation are those who work nontraditional jobs and
those who spurn the attention of heterosexual men. In this latter case, lesbian baiting intersects with sexual harassment.[43]

Other aspects of institutional heterosexism include the controversy sur-
rounding hate crimes legislation, congressional budget cuts to the National
Endowment for the Arts, exclusion of people with AIDS in the Americans
with Disabilities Act, voter actions such as Colorado's Amendment 2 (no
longer in effect as of December 1993), and more generally, the mainstream
media's reinforcement of stereotypical images of lesbians and gay men, sen-

sationalization of news stories, or omission of lesbian and gay characters, thus reinforcing our invisibility.[44]

The Individual Level of Heterosexism

On the personal level of heterosexism, lesbians and bisexual women are affected in a multitude of ways. A major problem is coming out to family, to others in our daily life, and to others more broadly in society.[45] Rochelle Klinger, for example, in speaking about lesbian couples, reports:

> A major problem for the lesbian couple is the uncertain outcome of coming out to the family. If family members have sufficient psychological resources, they may go through a process of grief and readjustment and may eventually be a good support for the couple. If they lack the resources or are influenced by things such as fundamentalist religious beliefs, disclosure may cause rejection. In a couple, rejection by one or both families can reawaken internalized homophobia and feelings of lack of legitimacy.[46]

The juggling act that lesbians manage is "impressive," according to Laura Markowitz. They have to "balance stress in so many systems at once—their own families of origin, their relationship, the gay/lesbian community, their ethnic or religious communities, and mainstream society."[47] Unlike race, except in the circumstance of passing as white, homosexuality is not usually visible. Passing as heterosexual becomes an option for those individuals who either assess the danger of a situation or have internalized the homophobia of the society. As Margolies, Becker, and Jackson-Brewer point out, the hidden lesbian may have a harder time balancing the public self with the private self. She may experience isolation from her peers, while fearing discovery from straight society.[48]

Bisexual women have similar coming out issues to lesbians. Influenced by the negative images of same-sex couples and of bisexuals, they may experience shame, ambivalence, and discomfort.[49] Many bisexual women first identify as heterosexual, then as lesbian, and may go back and forth before they admit their bisexuality.[50] In this process, women may experience isolation, invisibility, and oppression. But to not come out invites the dilemma of passing as heterosexual. The bisexual woman who passes for heterosexual might feel disingenuous and invisible, and might also have more trouble finding other bisexual people. As Robyn Ochs tells us, the "privilege" of passing leads to a heavier burden of having to actively announce your bisexuality if you don't want incorrect assumptions to be made.[51]

Loulan reinforces that living in a homophobic, misogynist world has an impact on lesbians' sense of self and self-worth. In her study of 1,566 lesbians, she asked about hand-holding. Eighty percent of respondents said they held their partner's hand. Yet only 27 percent said they held hands in public. As Loulan states, "This is a shocking reality for most lesbians: holding hands in public is off limits."[52] One study participant, Brooke, mentioned this issue. "[Impacts of homophobia] came mostly from [my partner]. She wouldn't hold hands in [public]. She didn't see it as a 'lesbian relationship.'"

Alice Moses found that the major determinant of identity management (or being out as a lesbian) for lesbians in her study was the extent to which they were around straight women. It is when a lesbian is around nonlesbians that she worries about being identified. "The more a woman worries about being identified, the more difficult she finds a number of situations, the more behaviors she is liable to engage in in order not to be identified as a lesbian woman, and the fewer risk-taking behaviors she will engage in in some situations."[53] Examples of how this plays out in public life include whether to have a picture of your partner on your desk at work, talk about what you did over the weekend, share stories about parenting your children, or bring your partner to work-related activities such as the holiday party. Claudia remarked in her interview that she believes in mainstreaming, "but I also believe there is this knot in your stomach that only relaxes when you know you're safe."

Consequently, homophobia and heterosexism have an impact on the mental health and well-being of lesbians. Authors of the National Lesbian Health Care Survey found that lack of social support, negative public attitudes, barriers to community institution participation, and degree of "outness" all have implications for mental health. Their study revealed a "distressingly high prevalence of life events and behaviors related to mental health problems," such as histories of abuse; tobacco, alcohol, and drug use; thoughts of suicide and suicide attempts; counseling for depression; and problems with money, relationships, and work.[54] Some studies show that gay people are twice as likely as the general population to seek therapy because of stresses of coming out and internalized homophobia.[55] Gays and lesbians have high rates of mental disorders and are at great risk of suicide. While individual biological factors can't be ruled out, living in a homophobic society adds incredible stress.[56]

Internalized Homophobia and Internalized Biphobia

The consequences of homophobia, biphobia, and heterosexism that mental health concerns display cannot be separated from the impact of internalized homophobia and internalized biphobia—the internalizing of the dominant views of society that homosexuality and bisexuality are wrong. This is especially a problem for lesbian, gay, and bisexual youth that experience social isolation during adolescence, when fitting in is a major component of self-worth. Gay teens have higher rates of suicide, alcohol and drug abuse, and HIV infection than other teens. Many teens withdraw from their families for fear of being "discovered" as gay and becoming "throwaway" youth. Lesbian, gay, and bisexual youth also suffer from a lack of positive role models to help them resist societal homophobic messages.[57] Studies on heterosexual teen dating violence among high school students show that a range of 9 to 39 percent of respondents are affected.[58] Irene Basile, working with lesbian and gay teens in Philadelphia, adds that lesbian and gay youth also face high rates of teen dating violence. She believes this is in part a result of the pressures of homophobia and sexism.[59] Lack of positive role models, disapproval and rejection from parents and friends, lack of information about being a lesbian, and isolation are other factors identified as problematic for lesbian teens in abusive relationships.[60]

Internalized homophobia can result in the distressing questioning of sexual orientation and identity by women who reject or are uncertain about their attraction to other women. Or they may wonder if they are "lesbian enough." Indeed, this is a major reason for entering therapy. As Joan Sophie states, "Internalized homophobia makes consideration of lesbian identity for oneself extremely threatening to the individual's self-esteem."[61] To embrace one's lesbianism is not only a personal decision but also a political statement to the society. A parallel can be seen to racism. hooks writes about "loving blackness as political resistance."[62] Internalized racism functions in a manner that encourages black individuals to hate their skin color, hair texture, facial features, and general nonwhite aspects. To embrace blackness or to proclaim "Black Is Beautiful" and affirm these denigrated aspects of self is a powerful attempt to overthrow internalized oppression.[63]

Internalized biphobia is an obvious consequence of societal messages that one's sexual identity is invalid. Bisexual role models are few, and bisexuals are rarely represented in the mainstream or queer media. While the number of organized bisexual groups is growing, especially in major cities, the sense of a bisexual community is in its early stages. Bisexuals who are in stable relationships may be confronted with nagging questions about holding on to a bi identity. If you are committed, why not claim to be heterosexual if partnered with a man or a lesbian if partnered with a woman? These questions reflect societal pressure to bend to a monosexist standard. Bisexuals who work within the lesbian community may feel like second-class citizens because of the lack of recognition in lesbian events and organizations. Given all these circumstances, it is difficult to form a positive, well-integrated bisexual identity.[64]

Dawn Szymanski and Y. Barry Chung state that internalized homophobia scales measure five dimensions of lesbian existence: connection with the lesbian community (isolation versus social support); public identity as a lesbian (passing and fear of discovery versus disclosure); personal feelings about being a lesbian (self-hatred versus self-acceptance); moral and religious attitudes toward lesbianism (condemnation versus tolerance); and attitudes toward other lesbians (horizontal oppression/hostility versus group appreciation).[65] So, for example, one scale designed to measure internalized homophobia among lesbians includes items such as the following: "I have tried to stop being attracted to women in general"; "I feel alienated from myself because of being lesbian/bisexual"; "I have tried to become more sexually attracted to men"; and "If someone offered me the chance to be completely heterosexual, I would accept the chance."[66] Bisexual internalized oppression taps into similar dynamics: "If we 'get a chance to get married,' we will take it"; "We are hiding behind heterosexual privilege"; "We are 'on the fence,' incapable of commitment"; and "We are untrustworthy, unreliable, and fickle."[67] Scales that measure internalized oppression are useful to therapists because they can indicate the extent of psychological distress caused by oppression, they can help measure the reduction of internalized homophobia with lesbians in therapy, and they can indicate areas of psychological distress unique to lesbians.[68]

Several study participants mentioned feeling that their abuse was a result of their lesbianism. Erin says,

> Definitely I think it's one piece of something that ends up "I don't deserve it" or "I deserve to be abused." "It's a choice," "I'm a deviant anyway," "I got myself into this by choosing this perverse lifestyle," "I shouldn't have been going to sex clubs if I didn't want sex," all that stuff. "I'm getting punished because I have these desires."

Sonia echoes, "I think a lot of women think [being a lesbian's] what their problem is and not that it's an abuse situation." And Ariel ponders,

What does it mean to be a healthy lesbian? Get rid of the inner homophobia. Be able to deal, or learn how to deal with society and not look at it as overbearing or overwhelming but more of an opportunity to educate. That's the only way I can look at it. To me, and this might sound really strange, but to me God put us all on this earth for a reason, and He made each and every one of us for a reason, and I'm a lesbian for whatever reason, and to me I don't believe I'm right or wrong because of it, but this is who I am. But I think that that has a lot to do with it, the self-acceptance, the misogyny and hatred of women, the hatred of society, and the condemnation that you live through however long you've got has a lot to do with the domestic violence, has a lot to do with the drinking problems, the drug problems.

Dealing with internalized oppression means first recognizing that these feelings have become part of our beliefs, and then acknowledging that they work to deny who we are and affect how we deal with the issues in our lives.[69] The Bisexual Resource Center further suggests finding safe places to talk about our feelings and our pain, build relationships and allies around homophobia, and get involved in liberation work.[70] Gail Pheterson sees overcoming internalized oppression work as simultaneously operating with overcoming internalized domination. Those who have internalized feelings of superiority, normalcy, and self-righteousness work in "a mutually reinforcing web of insecurities and rigidities." Oppressed people cannot end oppression by themselves.[71]

Service Providers, Homophobia, and Biphobia

Homophobia, biphobia, and heterosexism have major implications for service providers. Many social workers in the course of their work are not considering the full range of issues for their client because the client does not feel she can come out.[72] Therapists may be limiting their usefulness to their clients because they are giving messages that they don't want to deal with sexuality issues,[73] as they are insufficiently trained about human sexuality.[74] Many therapists are not screening for same-sex relationship battering.[75] Health care providers may make assumptions of heterosexuality and stigmatize patients or may ask inappropriate questions about, for example, birth control. Many lesbians avoid seeking health care because of uncomfortable encounters with providers.[76] One study respondent, Giselle, who works in social services, talked about the homophobia of her peers. They had been discussing child abuse and

the comment was made, something like, "and some people even become lesbians."
Like that. And I thought, wow. And . . . I wanted to stand up on my chair and say,
"You know, it's a pretty good choice." You know, 'cause that's what everyone
thinks, horrible things happen to you so you become a lesbian. I think of my girlfriend, and I think, that's a good reason to be a lesbian.

As survivors of interpersonal violence, lesbians and bisexual women
have been silenced because of homophobia and biphobia. We are afraid of
adding to society's hatred of us by pointing to any negative behavior. We
don't want to subject ourselves to the homophobia or biphobia of the police
or court system. Our internalized homophobia and biphobia lead us to
question if our abusers are acting "like men" or if our survivors are being
stereotypical "heterosexual victims."[77] If we feel ashamed of being lesbian,
we might feel that "battering comes with the territory."[78] We can't risk being
outed or outing our abusers. On the other hand, abusers might threaten to
out us as a form of control over us if we attempt to seek help or leave the
relationship.[79]

Neither are shelter agencies necessarily safe. Not being lesbian- or bi-
friendly is demonstrated in a number of ways.[80] Volunteers who work on
the crisis line and with clients in the office or at the shelter are exposed to
diversity issues in most training programs. However, there is no guarantee
that this sensitizes them to the needs of lesbians and bisexual women. Staff
are also supposedly nonheterosexist, yet might be aware of, and feel threatened by, the stereotype that the agency is full of "man-hating dykes." Any
lesbian staff could be dealing with internalized homophobia as bisexual
staff could be dealing with internalized biphobia. And there is no way to
insist that clients not be homophobic or biphobic. A shelter resident might
be insensitive to the needs of another resident who is a lesbian. Any number
of these women—volunteers, clients, or staff—might believe that lesbians
are sick, deserve what they get, or are a danger to children in the shelter.[81]
Susan Schechter points out that living or working in an all-woman environment raises questions about what it means to be a woman. Both shelter
residents and staff might seek to protect themselves from lesbian baiting by
making "derogatory comments about lesbians, thus assuring themselves and
others they are not 'deviant.' "[82]

The presence of a lesbian or bisexual female client flies in the face of
the feminist analysis that batterers are male, an analysis that many staff have
built years of work upon. Funders also have accepted this rationale of domestic violence, and especially if they are also homophobic or biphobic,

may deny funding to agencies that seek to include programs for lesbians and bisexual women. Lesbian and bisexual clients challenge their understanding of abuse and may threaten their motivation for why they should continue to fund this agency.

Homophobia's Impact on the Women in the Study

When asked about their concern about a homophobic or biphobic reaction to what happened to them, only a bit over one-quarter of the women expressed concern. However, over one-third weren't concerned because they did not respond immediately to what happened to them. The other women who said they weren't worried about a homophobic reaction said this was so because they were talking to other lesbians or people who they already knew weren't homophobic. So, when they did respond and it wasn't to another lesbian, bisexual, or ally, they had definite concerns about homophobia.

Another way to look at fears of homophobia and biphobia is by looking at what services the women wished had been available. Half of the women needed a more responsive societal environment (lesbian-specific services, lesbian-friendly services, or validation of violence by women) or felt they wouldn't have used any services regardless. Almost one-fourth of these women wished there had been lesbian-specific services (hot line, support group, therapist, or literature) or explicit lesbian-friendly programs. Nora recounts, "After I left, I went to a domestic violence agency out of town. I wanted to join a support group, but was told that the other group members might feel uncomfortable with the lesbian relationship. I wish the domestic violence agency was more aware/responsive." And Christy had an agency problem as well. "I wish there would have been a *gay and lesbian* violence hot line. The DV hot line I called said they trained all their volunteers in same-sex DV, but obviously the one I got didn't get it." Adele simply wished for "queer sensitive rape crisis services."

Maureen felt lucky. "I was referred to an agency that could deal directly with me and the abuse—and I was *extremely* glad that there was a lesbian counselor available." Cecile's situation worked out, but help was delayed. "Eventually I found a support group for battered lesbians, after the relationship was over. I wish there had been more education and outreach so I could have identified my situation and gotten support sooner. I wish the local battered women's shelter (where I was volunteering) had mentioned the issue, ever." This latter point—lack of awareness of same-sex abuse at domestic violence agencies—was repeated often. For example, Meredith said, "I wish the Women's Center in [my town] recognized violence between women, and recognized that women can be as responsible, as consciously responsible and accountable, for their actions as men can."

Almost the same number of women said they wouldn't have used any services. Their reasons varied; one feared the abuser ("I was too scared to do anything about her. She threatened to kill me and I believed her." [Marti]). Melanie dissociated: "Had I not blocked out what occurred, I am certain, feeling confident a sexual assault crisis service would have been supportive, I would have called." And Carole said, "I wasn't ready to hear the truth."

Eleven percent wished they had known that woman-to-woman sexual violence existed. Liz speaks to this point: "I wish I had known that rape/ sexual abuse between women was possible and that it happened. Perhaps if I had known it could and did exist, I may have defined it differently and gotten help." And Andie voices a basic concern: "If society as a whole were more open about woman-to-woman violence I would have felt less alone."

To address the issue of woman-to-woman sexual violence requires having to address homophobia, biphobia, and heterosexism simultaneously. As the context of our lives, the impact is enormous. Whether dealing with acknowledging that woman-to-woman abuse exists, looking at laws and services we can turn to for protection and help, or simply being able to proclaim that we are lesbian or bisexual women and our partners are not men, we are met with substantial hurdles. Breaking silence about woman-to-woman violence means tearing down the walls of prejudice, hatred, and fear in all realms.

3

The Myth of Lesbian
Utopia Unraveled

I have to say the aspect of the incident that feels the most painful is the amount of disbelief that existed among other lesbians, from those who knew me casually to those who didn't know me or her, and the audacity of people who said that because I had had sex with her previously that then the incident couldn't have happened/or really been an assault. (Gita)

Lesbian Utopia and the Need for Community

The mythology of women's nonviolence and lesbian egalitarianism has proven to be a formidable block to admitting and dealing with same-sex sexual violence and domestic violence perpetrated by women.[1] It is not only that others in the community believe in the utopian vision; survivors of this abuse internalize the myths and want to believe that they are safe from other women. For example, Marcia stated, "Women are supposed to travel in packs. You're supposed to protect each other. And it's just never mentioned that a woman could attack you the same way that a man could." And Aileen reminisced that

> when I was first coming out people were constructing safe space as women space where [it turned out] there were more perpetrators in the room than there were in any other kind of group I went to. So, it's about the way that safe space had been constructed by the fact that women do feel comfortable with other women 'cause we've been socialized differently for the most part than men. And there's a shared something there. You need to trust somebody. . . . It completely cracks apart the belief in lesbian utopia.

49

Clinging to a belief in lesbian utopia is all the more understandable when examining the issue of lesbian invisibility. Whether absent from dictionary definitions as Frye points out,[2] or because of the lack of legitimacy of female-oriented couples, or as a consequence of compulsory heterosexuality as Adrienne Rich discusses,[3] the result has been that the conceptualizing of lesbian and bisexual women's lives is a struggle and must be constructed and fought for. Lesbians and bisexual women are absent from history (largely written by men), contemporary lesbian and bisexual role models are few (as a result of homophobia and biphobia), and coming out or being visible is always at the risk of physical or psychological harm (or both). Male dominance demands lesbian invisibility, since the threat of total independence from men is implied. If heterosexuality were not compulsory, women might not choose it, given the inequality built into the system of patriarchy.[4] Lesbians are not who they are *as* lesbians; they are considered man-haters, women going through a phase, women who cannot get a man, or men trapped in women's bodies.[5] Numerous forms of male power over women are found in heterosexism, prostitution, pornography, rape, domestic violence, sex role stereotyping, and media images. Rich has constructed a "lesbian continuum" in which we can understand a range of women-identified experiences over time and cultures to assert lesbian existence as natural. She claims that the "deviant" labeling of lesbianism is at the heart of lesbian oppression. When looked at in this way, lesbianism is an "act of resistance."[6]

Similar to dynamics with other stigmatized groups, lesbian and bisexual communities, loosely defined, provide support from a hostile society. Connection to community becomes all the more imperative when this negativity and the lack of acceptability create a need for the self to be part of a larger group to help sustain that sense of belonging.[7] The development of a distinct women-focused culture of coffeehouses, bars, feminist bookstores, publishing companies, recording companies, music festivals, women's health clinics, gay pride parades and events, coming out stories, rainbow flags, and other organizations, national events, and rituals "serve as social, political, and psychological buffers to the hostility of the dominant culture."[8]

Lesbian and bisexual communities provide for many a sense of camaraderie, a sense of support and understanding, a shared vision, and sense of self as a lesbian or bi woman.[9] Some lesbian and bisexual communities are geographic, some within institutions, some social, and others ideological. Additional factors in community culture may include variation by race, social class, social or political focus, and urban or rural location. While individual lesbians and bisexual women may be very involved in their communities, other women may be loosely affiliated.

Development of a Distinct Woman-Identified Culture

Perhaps the biggest influence in the development of twentieth-century American lesbian culture was the shift beginning in the late 1950s and early 1960s away from the view that lesbianism was pathological. Instead, the new view was toward greater acceptance that it was a personal identity reflected in a certain lifestyle and within the range of normal sexuality. Sociologists, psychiatrists, and social psychologists led the way in promoting that this was not a sexual disease but a problem of the views of the broader society.[10]

In the decades before second wave feminism (the 1930s through the 1950s), the center of woman-identified culture was found in the bars, the most public place lesbians could gather at that time. Certainly many of these women were bisexual, but their existence was not acknowledged or supported. They were assumed to be lesbians, leading to their invisibility. While there were problems of alcoholism, fights, and police raids, bars also became a place to assert identity, socialize, and meet other women, including potential lovers.[11] It was within the bar culture that butch/femme roles became entrenched as the stereotypical manner of lesbian presentation (aside from the "kiki" women who were not welcomed, since they would not adhere to these roles). Many interpret these roles as role-playing mimicry of heterosexual couples. Nichols, Pagano, and Rossoff view the roles as giving an illusion of power we did not have as an oppressed group, while others regard them as "survival strategies" for lesbian existence or as "complex erotic statements."[12]

While butch/femme styles evolved over the decades, the primary assertion was made through appearance. Butches basically wore men's clothing, and femmes wore women's clothing. Behavior was another stylistic marker. Butches behaved more aggressively, opening doors, lighting cigarettes, and making the "first move" sexually. Butches were supposed to pair with femmes to protect them from the outside society and from other butches. Fighting, drinking, and "tough guy" demeanor were part of the butch comportment. It is easier to understand this "street dyke" personality when placed in the 1950s context of rigid sex roles, McCarthyite political repression, and the early emergence of the gay community. Butches defended the right to lesbian existence and were highly visible targets in public because of their dress and behavior. In this sense, butch/femme was a political statement at the same time as it was the assertion of self.[13]

The "stone butch" developed as the ultimate butch emotional and sexual behavior. This lesbian was untouchable, and her goal was to satisfy her femme sexually but never be touched herself. She would usually be in bed with her clothes on. In an oral history of lesbians in Buffalo, New York, between 1940 and 1960, researchers Madeline Davis and Elizabeth Kennedy found that stone butch was held as ideal butch behavior but also varied. Some untouchables claimed they were never touched, while others revealed that stone butches never existed, claiming you could never keep a lover for long if you refused to be touched.[14] Still, butches and especially stone butches held higher status than femmes, creating something of a hierarchy within lesbian culture. This was shown best in the ridicule of the butch who became a femme.[15]

Sheila Jeffreys suggests that less is known about the femme compared with the butch because femmes occupied a low social status. The majority of narrative studies of butch/femme from the 1950s focus on the voices of butches because few femmes came forward to be interviewed. Instead, researchers depended on what butches said about femmes; femme voices are absent. The low social status of the femme seems comparable with the low status of women as compared with men. This inferior role was found in femme jokes and put-downs, and an undercurrent of doubt that they were "real" lesbians. At the same time, butches devoted enormous energy to courting femmes, and in fact, femmes provided some security for butches, as they were more acceptable in public and had greater success in stable employment, hence helping to support their butch partners.[16]

Like the rest of society, social class divided the lesbian communities. The bar culture and butch/femme involved mostly working-class lesbians. Middle-class lesbians met in academic environments or at women-sponsored events such as dances, and were more likely to go to gay male bars when they did go to bars. Class splits also were reflected in ideological splits that developed in the 1970s with feminism. Working-class lesbians remained focused on the bars as the main place to socialize and often worked alongside men; middle-class lesbians had wider options than the bars, and many pursued a separatist ideology in early feminism.[17]

By the 1970s, butch/femme shifted once again, this time as a discredited pattern. Women's Liberation and feminism condemned the masculine-identified butch and the feminine femme as sexist. These roles were not consistent with the alternative counterculture many feminists strove to create. Women's music, open discussion of lesbian sexuality, the political agenda of feminism, lesbian separatism, women's institutions, and feminist views of nonhierarchy, leaderless movements, androgynous dressing, and other "politically correct" values enhanced the vision of the Lesbian Nation. Bisexuals who risked coming forward were treated as "sex traitors" and were excluded from lesbian utopia. As Becki Ross narrates, reaction (or overreaction) to heterosexual male sexual violence against women, as well as the promiscuity of gay males, resulted in many lesbians creating an identity that had little to do with sex. Loving women was pleasure-based, but not necessarily orgasm-based. Nineteen-seventies lesbian feminists saw most heterosexual acts as exploitative and objectifying.[18] The notion of the "political lesbian," the woman who made a choice to be a lesbian as opposed to the woman whose sexual attraction was to women, was put forth as a further way for women to bond sexually with other women and reject men.[19] The oppression of women was central to the analysis, and simply because women might make pornography for women or women strip for women, that didn't make it any less exploitative. Feminist political organizing led to rape crisis centers, battered women's shelters, women's health clinics, and an analysis that advanced a new consciousness of lesbian oppression and activism.[20]

Butch/femme continued in working-class bars and pockets outside of the mainstream feminist movement, and Davis and Kennedy remind us that the feminist movement has its roots in the struggles that butch/femme took on.[21] Many lesbians felt that freedom from these roles was desirable, but they also recounted personal experiences of "role change, role evolution, and role flexibility."[22] While many lesbians and bisexual women today protest against these roles, they also are quite familiar with them. Furthermore, butch/femme reemerged in the 1980s as a way to break from the rigidity of lesbian feminism[23] and to say, "It is all right to have different sexual tastes, not just in what or whom one is attracted to, but in what one does in bed: It is all right to prefer an active or passive role."[24] Rarely, however, does the contemporary butch feel she is a man. She feels she is acting in a way that is who she *is*.

What many lesbians viewed as an ideal community, others saw as rigid, exclusionary, and too dependent on a denial of difference.[25] In the 1970s and 1980s, the hotly contested arenas where theory and practice clashed, known as the "sex wars," around pornography, sadomasochism, bisexuality, sex with men, butch/femme roles, and nonmonogamy created schisms in the lesbian feminist utopia. Cultural feminists claimed that women-centered sex is best when it was absent of control, domination, and violence. Lesbian ethics were nonviolent ethics. But sexual radicals wanted freedom from sexual repression and women to express their full sexuality.[26] The more these "bad girls" felt attacked, the louder they became. By the mid- to late 1980s, unheard voices were raised from "working class lesbians, butches and femmes, socialist lesbians, s/m dykes, lesbian sex trade workers, lesbians living with HIV, disabled lesbians, Black, Latino, Native and Asian lesbians" shifting the "substance and direction of current sex debates and strategies."[27]

Survey participants reflected a mixture of references regarding butch/ femme roles. Blair gives us some insight from her experiences in the 1970s:

> Twenty-plus years ago some sexual assault was a bit of the norm. There were "butch" and "fem" women. You were one or the other. This is when I first came out, in 1976. I look back and see that there was a lot of frustration in the women's world with continual roadblocks for equality. In the "dyke" world (which is where I was trying to fit into) there was an even greater frustration as the opportunity for equal employment for jobs in the nontraditional world began to open up. The frustration was dealing with the men and verbal assaults, straight women and their verbal assaults (taking the jobs away from "the men"). Having few other women with experience in dealing with this to lean against for support and no women in upper management to counsel with, left many frustrated as hell. This frustration went home with a person.

Two women mentioned that their abusers were butch and seemed very male-identified. Carole, for example, said, "This was the first time in my relationships with women that I was involved with somebody that was truly butch. In fact, there were more things about her that were more like a man, like a woman with too much testosterone, or just in the thinking . . . in everything, dress, behavior, attitudes." And Deirdre's partner, who was a stone butch and never wanted to be perceived as weak, said to her, "The reason I never told you you were pretty was because you wanted me to tell you so bad and if I told you I would have been weak." Deirdre felt that "some of her male traits, or what you would characterize as male traits, were much more male than any men I ever met." On the other hand, Wanda, who dated a femme, had been tied to a tree and raped anally with a dildo. She said, "Being a butch woman, it was especially degrading."

Admitting Violence

Discussion of same-sex domestic violence is fifteen to twenty years ahead of discussion of same-sex sexual violence. It is important to remember that not all domestic violence contains sexual abuse and that sexual violence can take place outside of battering relationships. We have much to learn from the domestic violence discussion and the overlapping similarities, but there are also distinct issues. In terms of admitting the abuse, domestic violence and sexual violence share many similarities.

Acknowledgment of butch/femme creates something of a challenge when looking at violence in same-sex relationships. The myth that within a violent relationship it is the butch who is the aggressor (or that only in relationships with identifiable roles is there violence at all) obscures the fact that abuse is about power and control and not about roles. A gender analysis that puts forth the idea that male-identified—or butch—lesbians are more likely to be violent will not stand when applied to actual cases (as exemplified by Wanda's case, described earlier).[28] As Connie Burk discusses, domestic violence is not only men battering women:

> When heterosexist assumptions of butch and femme interact with this faulty logic, it results in an inevitable assessment that butches are batterers and femmes are victims. This is perhaps one of the most common ways that butch dykes are misassessed as abusive—by an advocate's heterosexist conflation of masculinity with abusiveness. This can result in police arresting or domestic violence programs identifying a butch dyke as the primary aggressor, simply because to their heterosexist eyes the butch "looked like the man."[29]

But it is the myth that women aren't violent because of their socialization and that two women together have egalitarian, loving, and passionate relationships that is the more insidious belief leading to the denial of violence between women in same-sex relationships. Lauren echoed what many study participants said when she claimed, "To me, women above all should nurture women, whether that's in a lesbian relationship or in a friendship or whatever. And it just appalls me that women can take that power from another woman." The feminist analysis views violence as inherently male—look at war, look at domestic violence, rape, incest, pornography—and to admit woman-to-woman violence would discredit this analysis. Pam Elliott points out that male-to-female domestic violence has been used as a tool to fight sexism, which effectively then excludes lesbians and bisexual women.[30] And Ellen, a study participant who also has published on this issue, writes, "Lesbians felt that our relationships were utopian since they did not involve men. We did not want to imagine that women could do harm to another woman in a relationship."[31]

Consequently, Bell says, "We don't expect it from each other. . . . It is men who are violent, not women, not lesbians and especially not lesbian-feminists."[32] A study by Sloan and Edmond that measured the perception of sexual assault danger for lesbians and gay men in their community showed that the majority did feel there was a problem. However, lesbians saw the biggest sexual threat as coming from heterosexual male strangers.[33] As an example of the consequences of such thinking, Christy, whose obsessive partner physically and sexually abused her, had trouble recognizing what was happening to her: "If it had been a man I think it would have been easier to realize that it was unacceptable no matter what. I think also coming from a feminist perspective, I didn't want to see that a woman would do that, so I was denying it." And two women who had previously been abused by men before they came out said, "I had subjected myself to contact with another abuser and could not believe that a woman would do that to another woman" (Hannah), and, "I naively never thought that a woman would do that to another woman. . . . [I was thinking,] I'm finally with the right gender, everything will be wonderful now" (Deirdre).

Reasons for Denial

The general evolution of lesbian and bi culture and community, from the bar culture to butch/femme roles to lesbian feminism to gay liberation to today's more assimilationist agenda, has given us a certain legacy. This legacy is *not* completely unified, since many in the queer community, such as lesbian and bisexual women of color, butches, femmes, differently abled women, transgender women, and lesbians and bisexual women who primarily identify with the leather community, do not identify with lesbian utopia. We are in actuality many communities. However, part of our generalized identity is that women are not violent and that banding together in solidarity against the homo-, bi-, and transphobic culture is necessary. For many lesbians and bisexual women, admitting woman-to-woman violence is just too painful. Identifying with the female victim of violence means that it is just too difficult to acknowledge that another woman was the victimizer. "We wanted lesbians to be the good ones, the innocent ones," Kaye/Kantrowitz reminds us.[34] The fact is, lesbians can be violent. Interpersonal violence does exist in our communities, and our denial is killing us.

Many lesbians and bisexual women feel that admitting the reality of violence will hurt us in the larger society—another major reason for denial. Ellen "was told that this was something that needed to be kept quiet since we already had enough going against us."[35] And Aura, representing the experience of many women, claims, "What I had to deal with much more [than homophobia] were lesbians trying to silence me because *they* felt that acknowledging the existence of violent women would increase homophobia and misunderstanding." Some fear that revealing this violence would provide more homophobic and biphobic ammunition to generate even more negative views of lesbians and bisexual women.

A third reason for denial that violence occurs in same-sex interpersonal relationships is that it is overwhelming to admit this could happen in our personal relationships when we simultaneously face external threats of harm.[36] A fourth reason for this denial is that many heterosexuals active in the battered women's movement worry about their funding and their public image if they start to serve lesbian and bisexual women survivors. Finally, feminists, gay and straight, are concerned about what would happen to the analysis they had constructed, which is built around male power and privilege, if woman-to-woman violence is addressed.[37] Aura bore the brunt of this aspect when she told her story of abuse as a teen by a much older woman in the local feminist newspaper. She was attacked in print, told that she "was drawing attention away from the serious problem of male/patriarchal violence and attacking feminism in the process."

Given the important role the lesbian, bisexual, and gay communities play in the individual identities of most lesbians and bisexual women, the individual's commitment to community is generally demonstrated by conformity.[38] This tension is played out in many realms but particularly in the area of abuse. The lesbian, bisexual, and gay communities have generally denied abuse, silenced victims, and protected abusers. This loyalty to the community has made it difficult to expose the negative aspects of abusive same-sex relationships. In fact, lesbians or bisexual women may blame survivors for their abuse rather than hold an abuser accountable, since this would require community acknowledgment of the abuse.[39]

Lesbian Couples

Couples in general must balance the need for intimacy in their relationships with the desire for independence and autonomy. For same-sex partners, this aspect is heightened because their coupling is the most secure way that lesbian and bisexual individuals are tied to the community.[40] The breakup of a couple becomes a threat to other couples, given the insular nature of the community that protects itself from external homophobia or biphobia, and the relatively small number of partners from which to choose. Everyone in the subsystem tends to know everyone else; common banter within friendship circles is the frequency with which so many of the women have at one time or another been partnered with each other.

Another aspect of being part of a couple in a same-sex relationship is that the couple tends to have the same friends, or at least considerable overlap, whereas a heterosexual couple may have more distinct friendship circles (the man with some separate male friends and the woman with some separate female friends). As a consequence, breakups threaten friendship bonds, and choices are made to side with one partner or the other. In a violent relationship this might create the dilemma Christy faced: "I figured if I told my friends then they would not socialize with us and they would do something that would make her more angry and she'd take it out on me or something. And I even had friends who would ask and I still wouldn't [tell], I would hide it."

What is known as the "problem with fusion" in lesbian relationships has been widely written about.[41] The problem has several facets. One, as women socialized to put the needs of others first, two women are vulnerable to developing an unhealthy interdependence on each other. Two, women who are feminists may stress equality in their relationships, which puts pressure on the couple to maintain the balance of equality. Three, living in a homophobic and biphobic society that does not validate their relationships may cause them to turn to each other for especially high levels of support and draw tight boundaries around their relationship. These factors might combine to create an isolating, "merged" or "fused" relationship. While it *may* become difficult to simultaneously foster emotional dependence and personal autonomy, Klinger points out that a certain degree of fusion is healthy for lesbians dealing with homophobia and invisibility.[42] While we need to examine this issue, fusion should not automatically be identified with pathology. However, when one woman attempts to assert greater independence, problems might arise. If the other partner feels threatened by this, the isolation of the relationship may have created an environment in which power and control are expressed unchecked as the threatened partner tries to prevent this independence. For those relationships in which abuse does occur, the dynamics of jealousy and possessiveness are perhaps freer to operate in such a setting. As such, it is important to recognize the dynamics unique to same-sex couples that may be related to abuse.

Silence

The silence around lesbian and bisexual battering and sexual violence has been deafening. Hart, in her preface to Kerry Lobel's *Naming the Violence,* published in 1986, eloquently recounted how woman-to-woman abuse was occurring and no one was willing to speak out or condemn it. In the late 1970s and early 1980s, Hart was organizing and speaking out in the initial years of the National Coalition Against Domestic Violence (NCADV). In those early attempts, homophobia and the need for separate lesbian services were constant themes; they remain so today with the added awareness to include bisexual women. In 1983, the Lesbian Task Force of the NCADV issued statements regarding lesbian battering that acknowledged it as a problem as serious as heterosexual battering. They declared that it cut across all demographic lines; that the lesbian community must address it and hold batterers accountable; that battered women's service providers must confront their homophobia and serve lesbian clients; and that the lesbian community must develop an analysis that adequately listens to and assists lesbian victims.[43] Still, almost thirty years after publicly admitting same-sex abuse, we continue to struggle with deeply entrenched denial and the lack of services.

When discussing the physical and sexual abuse that occurred in the late 1980s by her partner of a year and a half, Cecile's comments reflect the reality of community inaction:

I mean, I think the lesbian community I was hanging out with was people who defined themselves as feminists, and I was also working in a [battered women's] shelter at the time, so that was part of my community. And yeah, people just didn't want to hear it. I mean, the incident where she started screaming at me and pounding her fist into her hand, everyone walked away. It was kind of typical of how people, they just didn't know what to do. They didn't want to deal with it.

Cecile faced the same problem of denial when she tried to discuss her rape by her partner:

People had never heard of it and they, they couldn't believe that it really happened, and that's not what rape is, you know, how can a woman rape? Like those kinds of things. And I got a lot of responses about how the dynamics of our relationship just weren't very healthy but there were two of us and how was I playing out my old issues, and maybe we needed to work on communication.

Telling

Telling others about the sexual violence perpetrated against them was a big issue for most women respondents. Those who held no concerns about being believed generally told new lovers, family members, or people they felt knew them well or they trusted. Some women didn't have this concern because they just didn't talk about it. For those who were concerned about being believed, the primary reasons related to our mythology. For example, "Why would a stranger believe female/female abuse?" (Rita); "Because of not taking it seriously—it was by another woman" (Aileen); "It is virtually [impossible] to prove female to female violation" (Oona); "Didn't think someone would believe that a woman could/would attack another woman" (Maureen); "Because she said a woman can't rape another woman" (Roxanne); "Women don't do these things to each other" (Patti); and "[It] would not hold up as 'real' " (Evon). Other reasons leading to concern about being believed included having a promiscuous history, feeling it was her own fault, being drunk, cooperating to get it over with, and the abuser being held in high regard within the community.

The Consequences of Denial

The consequences of believing that women do not physically, emotionally, or sexually harm other women are many. Survivors of violence are isolated; they are blamed and sacrificed. Denial of violence means that abusers can freely move on to the next victim. Women are placed at risk because others bury the problems. The lack of services is perpetuated because the need is not acknowledged.

The terrible isolation and abandonment many lesbians and bisexual women face when their abuse is denied is shown in this comment of Aura's: "Most lesbians I knew were very willing to sacrifice survivors such as myself for their own sense of comfort." Cecile told me, "I think what happens so much of the time is that the survivors are the ones who lose their community because people don't want to deal with it, and they need to get away from their abuser or people take the side of the abuser for all kinds of weird reasons." Becoming an outcast from your community is far from uncommon, as this woman communicated to me in correspondence: "The hardest part of this was the lack of support that I received from people who knew me and the local lesbian community. I became a 'pariah.' I had overreacted. . . . I had aired our 'dirty laundry.' But no one had lived those twenty months with me, and few chose to understand."

Gita related that in her case, her rapist drew sympathy from her friends and the larger community by claiming herself to be the victim. Gita said, "I think this is something that is particular to the lesbian community and particularly insidious because so many women know the language of victimhood and so many people have been in therapy that women often can't see other women as anything but victims." Gita's abuser carried out a campaign of harassment involving Gita's friends and workplace that turned sentiment against her and effectively silenced her. Discrediting the victim is a not uncommon technique that lesbian and bisexual female abusers use, and it is effective perhaps because so many are willing to cast aside any thoughts of possible violence on the part of women. If the community does not want to hear about this abuse, it encourages survivors to suffer in silence. As McClennen writes, "In essence, when same-gender individuals experience partner abuse, they virtually have no community."[44]

The lack of effective means to confront abusers means that they are left free to move on to their next victim. Several women in the study mentioned that they heard of their abusers' next partners and subsequent violence. Some of them met these new partners and recognized the similar denial patterns that they themselves had gone through. Patti, attending a support group for battered lesbians in Seattle, said, "Someone said when we were in this group, gosh I wonder if . . . we've dated the same people because we have the same personalities."

Because violent lesbians and bisexual women are not confronted, they do not have to deal with their problem of violence, and they generally are not charged with rape or assault, do not serve time in jail, pay any restitution, attend batterer treatment programs, or go through any of the mechanisms that heterosexual male rapists or abusers might face. They are not labeled "rapists" or "batterers." The lesbian, bisexual, and gay male communities have rarely advocated for these mechanisms, and the mainstream legal system has not promoted them. Cecile mentioned, "I would rather see the abuser ostracized than the survivor, but I don't know if that's the whole solution either." In fact, staff at the Asian Women's Shelter in San Francisco have pointed out that admitting the problem of lesbian and bisexual violence and holding abusers accountable *is* helping the community. Breaking this cycle of violence is a community issue—this is where the abusers and the survivors live from day to day, who they interact with, and where accountability is played out.[45]

Looking at this issue in context—struggles for lesbian existence, lesbian feminist ideology, and other issues influencing our communities' mythology—we can see how the problem has reached such proportions. But it is catching up with us. It is becoming harder to run away from the problems we face, which as Rich wrote, "has included role playing, self-hatred, breakdown, alcoholism, suicide, and intrawoman violence; we romanticize at our peril what it means to love and act against the grain. . . ."[46] As Marianne pointed out, "We come from the same families everybody else does with the same problems, so it happens to be a problem in the lesbian community. Why wouldn't it be?"

The mythology of lesbian utopia no longer serves us. Erin claimed that "I really did have this fantasy myth that women can't hurt each other. . . . Now I have to deal with this." Missy also was facing the stark reality after being in two sexually abusive situations. "I think we've got to be more honest with what's actually going on versus these little myths that we've constructed for ourselves. It's damaging. . . . It was really horrifying, 'Oh, my God, what am I going to do?' These are people, too, they're not these mythical creatures." Female nonviolence is "far from the truth," echoes Ariel. It is time to create a new vision of giving voice, not silencing, of preventing harm, not perpetuating it.

4

"I Couldn't Believe a Woman Did This to Me"

My ex-wife and I do not speak any longer. She's very upset with me for leaving and identifying her behaviors as abusive. I sleep with mace at my headboard, and I'm hoping to move soon so she'll no longer have my address. It all takes time. (Ariel)

She still threatens me through my friends when she sees them in the local lesbian bar. She told one of my friends she has a gun and is "looking for me." I have seen her in crowds at Pride events. I ignore her completely. I will never speak to her again. I carry a cell phone and I will call the police if she ever approaches me or tries to follow me. (Christy)

She harassed me by phone for a year or so, and then moved on to someone else. Haven't seen her in years. (Cecile)

I ran into her at the grocery store one and a half years later and talked briefly. I was terrified. In March '94, she invited her [estranged] partner for dinner and killed this woman and herself. I'm glad she's dead. (Nora)

The sexual violence that the seventy women in this study experienced spans a continuum of the types of violence that a range of female abusers perpetrate. A continuum of violence has been written about regarding heterosexual women; this is the first time such a range has been verified for lesbians and bisexual women with female perpetrators. This confirms that lesbians and bi women are at risk for sexual violence in their relationships, on their dates, at work, among their friends and acquaintances, and from strangers. It also confirms that this violence is significant. Because up to this point as a society we have not admitted this violence, we lack an adequate response to it.

My use of the word "continuum" is similar to that of Liz Kelly's.[1] Items on a continuum have a basic underlying character, and the elements pass into one another. The continuum does not imply a linear line of events, nor does it insinuate a statement of relative seriousness. Rather, all the forms of sexual violence are serious, they can be named, and the continuum allows us to link behaviors and to analyze them in the context of the society. Carole Sheffield offers one example of an analysis of the continuum of sexual violence that heterosexual women experience. She uses the term "sexual terrorism" to describe the way men in the patriarchal system frighten and control, and hence dominate, women. Writes Sheffield, "The essence of terrorism is that one never knows when is the wrong time and where is the wrong place."[2] This terrorism includes, among other forms, the fear women feel when they walk alone at night, exposure to pornography, workplace sexual harassment, and domestic violence. Once society acknowledges female perpetrators, we realize that sexual terrorism applies to lesbians and bisexual women as well.

In this chapter I examine the types of sexual violence by different female perpetrators to document this hidden violence and to uncover some of the issues involved. My hope is that now society will begin to seriously grapple with the existence of this violence.

Sexual Violence within Battering Relationships

More than half of the women in the study (thirty-seven out of seventy) discuss one or more abusive relationships. Of ninety-one situations of sexual violence, forty-two (46 percent) were in the context of battering. I begin by examining sexual violence within battering relationships.

Marital rape accounts for approximately 25 percent of all types of rape.[3] A number of studies estimate that 10 percent to 25 percent of married heterosexual women experience unwanted sex at least once during their marriages.[4] Studies examining sexual assault of battered heterosexual women find an incidence ranging from a low of 40 percent to a high of 70 percent.[5] Rape within an intimate relationship is different from stranger rape in that the assaults tend to be repeated more than once or are ongoing during the relationship, and that sexual abuse within domestic violence tends to occur within the more severe battering relationships.[6]

No study of marital rape has included women in same-sex relationships who cohabitate. However, I believe that there are parallels between the experiences of battered lesbians and bisexual women who are subjected to sexual violence by their intimate partners and the findings of the studies on marital rape just cited based on heterosexual women. Marital rape studies have not focused on the legal status of heterosexual couples but on the characteristics of a long-term cohabitating relationship.[7] The sexual abuse of same-sex cohabitating couples can be called marital rape.

If I substituted the pronoun *he* for the *she* in the stories that follow, I am certain every reader would feel the story was about marital sexual abuse. Similar to studies that have found that men who rape their wives are especially violent and that they often demand sex after battering,[8] these stories reveal the same findings. Raquel Bergen cites four main reasons why men rape their wives: entitlement to sex, sexual jealousy, as punishment, and as a control mechanism.[9] Control is the overriding reason for the rapes—to force the victim to do what the rapist wants her to do. This holds not only for husbands; abusive women in same-sex relationships share this motivation. And Basile's research on how wives acquiesce or "give in" to unwanted sex with their husbands also holds parallels with situations in which many of these lesbians and bisexual women have found themselves in their partner relationships.[10]

Battered lesbians and bisexual women have the same struggles with low self-esteem, terror, confusion, and isolation as battered heterosexual women. As raped partners, these women share the same sense of betrayal, disbelief, disgust, and fear as other raped wives. Within battering, sexual violence is one of the major tools used to control and dominate. Nora, a white, forty-five-year-old lesbian and currently unemployed, told me, "I realized there is no separation for me between the domestic violence, the physical battering, the emotional violence, and the sexual violence. It was all part of the same picture." Evon's story reveals this blurring between sexual and physical violence. A twenty-six-year-old white lesbian working as an administrative assistant, Evon's abuse occurred two years ago. She wrote:

> During the relationship I did not "see" the sexual abuse occurring. I was up to my ears in the domestic violence happening—but blocked so much out—a lot of the sexual assaults blended into my mind as DV or went missing altogether. I did know and realize not wanting to do certain things, fearing not wanting to do certain things, fearing if I did not do them what the outcome would be. I remember hating what was being done to me sexually—and how I would feel when *having* to perform certain acts or have them performed on me. I remember being hurt physically on many occasions while engaging in sex.

Evon lived with her partner for one year. She describes the sexual assaults, which occurred when her partner was drunk and sometimes also high on pot.

These assaults happened about three to five times a week. She would tie me up and force her fingers inside of me, and sometimes she would leave me there. She would forcibly attack me, physically hurting me and at the same time forcing herself inside of me. Sometimes she would use objects. There were times when I would be forced to perform acts on her; she would demand oral sex, "or else" situations . . . she would demand that I fuck her, "or else" situations. Many times after a physical assault from her, she would end it with sexual violations against me to show she was always in control. There would be times she would be so forceful I would bleed, and it was always painful. On occasion these acts happened in public places, but mostly it happened in our apartment.

Eventually because of the extreme violence, Evon did call the police and had her partner escorted out of the apartment. They knew their relationship was out of control and mutually decided they needed to split up. Evon gave her partner money to go home to her family, and the relationship ended.

Marianne, a thirty-eight-year-old, white, lesbian Ph.D., was in an explosive relationship in her early twenties for four years. Thinking back on those years, her words echo what many battered women say:

I knew I didn't like how she was treating me, but I also thought I deserved or caused her to do those things to me. I also believe, now, that she intended me to think so. I tried to pretend none of it happened or that it wasn't real or painful. I think if you asked me at the time I probably would have covered for her or said it was "not too bad" or consensual.

Here is her story:

[My partner] was quite a bit older than me (about eight years). She seemed very world-wise, had an authority about her that amazed and intimidated me. I was sort of awestruck by her when I got involved with her. I soon discovered that she liked controlling what I did, who I had as friends, what we thought about and did. She seemed at the beginning to be "safe," she had a job, apartment, parents she visited often, friends, etc. Things started to fall apart after about four months. She'd get mad and throw things around the apartment, she'd take things of mine and throw them (or throw them out), she tossed the TV out a window and smashed it, etc. After awhile she'd hit me or push my face, hard, if I did something she disliked or didn't do what she asked or demanded. She constantly threatened to leave, told me I was worthless or dumb, told me my friends (I didn't have many) were idiotic, told me I was unattractive or ugly, and so on. I was extremely anxious that she would leave. I also hated how things were going, and thought it was all my fault. After about a year she'd progressed to full-blown rampages, beating on me with things (a chair, thrown books, pans from the kitchen). I tried fighting back but she was strong and completely wild. Sometimes she would beat on me until I was crying and subdued (and hurting), then she'd tear my clothes off and force me down, then force her fingers or other objects inside of me, kiss me roughly, suck on my skin to make marks that sometimes bled, hit me on the breasts, etc. She'd ask me to "do" her and I'd try to do what she wanted, but it was hard, she wanted me to almost hurt her or actually hurt her. I felt awful about this but she'd destroy stuff if I didn't, and at the time I owned very little. One time she literally raped me with a plastic dildo. This went on for several years. I finally left her when my current lover (who is not abusive *at all*) gave me safe haven.

Jannette, a white bisexual, now thirty-five and a therapist, had two different abusive relationships with similar dynamics. In each one her partner was sadistic, taking advantage of her low self-esteem and trauma from unresolved incest over many years. Jannette knew she didn't want to engage in these sexual acts but said, "I didn't know that I had the right, within these relationships, to refuse to do certain things or have certain things done to me and not be punished for it and to still maintain the relationship. I had no concept of mutuality in relationship, of open communication and negotiation. . . ." In her first year of college she was taken "under the wings" of her sorority graduate assistant and her pledge mom, who started to include her in all their activities.

They basically included me in their lives at a time when I was very lost and lonely. The first time that we engaged in any type of sexual activity, I was the one who initiated it. While [the graduate assistant and I] were sitting on her couch at this extremely tense moment she was looking at me very expectantly and, I thought, almost beckoning for me to kiss her. So, I did. She said she wondered when I would finally do that. She said that she did not want to push me because she wasn't certain what my expectations were. After that point, we began sleeping together and engaging in various sexual activities. The frequency and type of activity gradually intensified. At one point, I was performing oral sex on her and I had a severe flashback regarding my mother. I stopped what I was doing and I began to gag and to cry. She became enraged by my reaction and she beat me. After that point, she was violent, aggressive, and insistent regarding our sexual relations. Much of the time, we both had been drinking. If I refused to have sex in any way, she would hit me or beat me. Several times I attempted to avoid the situation by staying away. She tracked me down at my sorority house and would twist my arm behind my back and force me to go with her to her apartment. If I was not compliant to her demands in bed, she would beat me or, sometimes she would tie me to her bed and stick objects in my vagina and my rectum. One time, when I was tied to her bed in that way, her roommate returned home with several friends. She got dressed and dragged me naked into the TV room and ordered me to masturbate in front of the people there.

Jealousy appears to be a major spark for sexual violence, where the "taking" of a woman proves a sense of ownership. No one else can have her. The situations of Kara, Christy, and Maureen demonstrate this motivation. For example, Kara, a thirty-six-year-old white lesbian, was involved with a woman for two to three years when she was in her early twenties. She recounts:

[My partner] came in from work (we worked at the same place but I was on surgical leave at the time), in an upset/angry frame of mind. She had discovered, while at work, that BEFORE I had even met her, I had gone out with a couple of the guys (not dating, but friends) from work. She hit me upside the head, restrained me (handcuffs, other binds), then proceeded to rape me (penetration with a dildo) and sodomize me.

Kara left her partner after this and fled to a shelter. However, her partner found the shelter and sat outside it, putting other women in danger. Because of her fear of this woman, Kara returned and, as she said, for the next two years "waited for her to kill me."

Maureen, age forty-two, a white bisexual social worker, was in an abusive relationship ten years ago. Her partner

became extremely jealous of a friendship that I had with a male that went back many years. On several occasions her jealousy was out of control and she took it out on me sexually, by holding me down on the bed, grabbing my breasts, and trying to force something into my vagina, insisting that "this is what you want from him" or words to that effect. I tried to resist and was quite upset; I was left in tears. . . . While I was with this same partner, I was sexually assaulted by a male that we both knew. My partner became furious that I had "had sex with a man" and said that I was a willing participant. She then slept with him to "even the score." She also sexually abused me by asking "did he do this" and "did you like it when he did this" as she pulled my head back (by my hair), kissed me, sucked and bit my breasts, groped my body in several areas, and stuck her fingers inside me, moving them back and forth quite roughly. She actually tried to get her fist into my vagina, but I yelled in pain and she stopped.

Maureen's partner used her bisexuality against her, as an excuse to rape her in her rage that men had had sexual relations with her. Although one man had sexually assaulted Maureen, her partner refused to see the situation as an assault and reacted with jealousy as if it were consensual and a threat to their relationship. Biphobia within the lesbian community is as problematic as it is within the straight community. The lesbian and the straight woman may feel distrust, hatred, or fear of bisexual women, who then become targets for abuse.

Christy, a white lesbian, now twenty-seven and an attorney, suffered when she partnered with a woman during graduate school who was obsessed with her. Fierce arguments and fights accompanied their intense sexual relationship. Sex after fights became a pattern. Her partner's possessiveness showed itself in constant phone calls throughout the day and a refusal to accept Christy's decision to break off the relationship.

One weekend, I went to her house . . . I planned to break it off. We began discussing ending the relationship. She became enraged. We were standing near the bathroom. She pushed me inside the bathroom and held me down and wouldn't let me leave. She was holding me down and I tried to get away. She told me I couldn't leave her; she would kill herself if I left. I struggled and began crying hysterically. She held me down until I stopped struggling and was just weak and sobbing. She then began kissing me and had sex with me. She held me down the whole time. I knew I couldn't get away and I couldn't make her stop.

When I quit taking her phone calls, after that, she drove two hours to [the city I moved to] and showed up at my apartment. She was crying. I wouldn't let her in. The doorman said it was an emergency so I talked to her on the phone. She said her uncle raped her and she had no place to go. I let her in. We talked. I felt horrible. I let her stay. She found out I talked to an ex-girlfriend. She became angry and pushed me onto the bed. She sat on my stomach and held my arms down. She said she wouldn't let go until I called my ex and told her I never wanted to speak to her again, even as a friend. She held me down for over an hour as I apologized. She grabbed the phone and dialed the number. She continued to sit on me as I talked. I did what she said, hung up, and sobbed. She then hugged me, kissed me, and had sex with me as I cried. I later found out she lied about her uncle because it was the only way she knew how to get me to see her.

[Another time] she held me down at knifepoint for three hours when I tried to make her leave my apartment. When I got free and ran to the phone to call 911, she ripped it off the wall and smashed it. [In another incident] she was chasing me when I tried to get away from her. I tried to close a door to a room to keep her out. I was pulling it shut; she was reaching through to grab me. She grabbed my leg and pulled it through the door and I fell down. She then slammed it in the door as hard as she could. I thought my kneecap was broken and went to the hospital.

Using sex with others as a sexual manipulation also figured into some stories. In Maureen's story, told earlier, her partner had sex with Maureen's male rapist to "even the score." Rhonda was in her twenties when, after five years together, her partner started to have an affair. Rhonda, white and bisexual, age thirty-two and currently unemployed, agreed to a threesome as a way to end the affair. "At first, my significant other expected me to watch, only. It hurt. Things were all messed up. We tried two times with this other woman and when it came to me being involved, my girlfriend got upset to see someone else with me. To me it was sex only with the other girl and a way to stop the affair."

In another situation, Samantha's partner brought a minor into bed with them. "She brought that girl into bed with us. I did not want to have sex with the girl so I didn't, but I had to witness [my girlfriend's] seduction of that girl. I felt trapped and I did have scary sex with that woman while that girl was in that bed with us." In reflecting back over ten years to that time, Samantha, a white lesbian, now thirty-three and an artist, admits, "I didn't realize at the time how out of control we were. I was scared of being beat by this womon [sic], afraid of pissing her off and getting my butt kicked but I didn't question what was happening in bed. I did not question it because I was still obeying the message implanted by my grandfather to just 'take it.' "

Samantha brings out one of the implications of the incest connection to later adult sexual activity—that is, the inability to respond to, and stop, further abuse. For some women, such as Jannette, cited earlier, incest flashbacks or issues enrage the abuser. Cecile's partner of one and a half years used both her incest background and a rape by a male against her.

> We'd been together only a few months. We were on a camping trip with a large group of friends. She was angry at me for spending too much time with a friend from out of town who was with us on the trip (mind you, I was doing exactly what we'd agreed upon before the trip). We went for a walk on the beach at night. She started pressing me for details on a previous sexual assault. I said I didn't want to talk about it, but she kept making up details herself until I finally said what really happened. She then declared that I had turned her on so much with this story that she had to have me right there on the beach. I said I really didn't want to and she kept pushing. I kept saying no, and she kept insisting that I wanted it. She pushed me down on the sand and raped me with her hand. I felt that I could physically fight her off, but I was afraid of hurting her. I was even more afraid of what she would do to me later if I used force to resist. . . . When she was done I was crying and she comforted me (well, tried, it wasn't comforting). She then got outraged on my

behalf that my sexual experiences with my father and sister have made it impossible for me to enjoy lovemaking under the stars.

In another example with this same partner, Cecile, a white lesbian, now thirty-three, said, "I'd try to break up with her, and she'd trap me in the room and scream at me for hours. Then she'd force herself on me, and declare that she knew I wanted it because she knew I was so committed to healing from my childhood abuse that I would never have sex I didn't want. . . . This basically happened dozens of times."

Courtney's experience is quite recent. A white lesbian, last year, when she was twenty-three, she and her partner were engaging in consensual sex

until she pinned me in the sag in the mattress. She knew I don't like to be held down and I don't like being told to suck on anything due to what happened to me when I was four, but she did this anyway. She pinned me down and started riding me, would not let me up. Then she took her shirt off and told me to suck her breasts. When I refused she pushed her chest into my face so hard I couldn't breathe without opening my mouth. She forced me to suck her. She had told me at some point that she was sick of women who let past abuse affect them, and that's when I told her about my experiences to try to change her mind. She finished when she came and got off me.

Brandie, age thirty-four, and Roxanne, age fifty-five, both experienced severe sexual assault when they were leaving their abusers. While in the midst of a breakup with a partner of one year, Brandie, a white lesbian who today is an executive secretary, recounts her story:

She showed up at my home and broke through the glass of the back door to gain entry. Before I could finish a phone call for help, she ripped the phone from the wall and bound me with it. She repeated over and over that she loved me and that no one else could have me. She then removed my shorts and panties and forced herself on me. Even with all of my kicking she was able to "gain entry." After doing what she wanted (she did not orgasm) [she stated] that I was still "hers" and that no one else would want me. She was able to do this again a few weeks later but was waiting inside on the second occasion.

Brandie took out a restraining order after this second assault, though her assailant did show up at her house again, this time with a knife.

A few years ago, Roxanne, a white lesbian, told her partner of about four years that she wanted to break off, as I could not handle her temper. I gave her back her ring and house key. She became furious, started throwing me around, then said, "I'll show you what you can do with my ring and keys." She held me down and shoved them into my vagina, then laughed at me. I was crying and felt so ashamed and she just said I deserved it for trying to leave her.

Different types of coercion typify many of the sexual violence situations. Kathleen Basile identifies several modes of acquiescence that wives use when sex is not physically forced but is nonetheless unwanted. In her interviews with forty-one women, she found themes of initially unwanted sex that turned into wanted, sex agreed to because women felt it was their wifely duty, sex when giving in was easier to deal with than resisting it, sex because of fear of what might happen if she refused, and sex agreed to because of knowing what would happen if she didn't agree (e.g., she would be beaten or punished).[11] The following stories demonstrate situations of acquiescence.

Liz, a white lesbian, now a thirty-four-year-old graduate student, tells of a rape that occurred toward the end of a one-year relationship that began when she was eighteen. At the time she was on an antihistamine for allergies and was groggy and not feeling well.

After several refusals to have sex with her, [my partner] took matters into her own hands one night. I said I didn't feel good, and she became furious. She told me it was my "job" as her "wife" to "give it up." She pulled me by the arm into the bedroom and pushed me down on the bed. I tried to get up and yelled at her to stop it, but she got on top of me and held my arms down. I remember being confused and scared, and disgusted, but not angry (then). I started to cry as she undressed me. . . . I did leave her finally, when I came home from work and found her kissing a friend of ours. It was as if I needed a "valid" excuse, and the sexual stuff wasn't valid to me at the time. I think I believed her rhetoric about "wifely duties" even though I was a lesbian.

Sometimes the emotional coercion is so draining that it is easier to "give in." This was the case with Shelley, Ariel, Danielle, and Carlin. Shelley, a white lesbian who is now twenty-two and a residential counselor in a group home for abused children, began a relationship as a first-year college student. The abuse began quickly and lasted a year and a half.

I remember one instance where I was visiting her in her room. I was not in the mood for sex, but she just kept saying, "Yes, you are. Don't you want me anymore?" She took me by surprise and tied my arms over my head to the bedposts. I was protesting and becoming panicky. She said, "You'll like it. It's fun," or something to that effect. She took my clothes off and dripped hot candle wax on me. I was squirming and telling her to stop. When I finally screamed at her to stop she left the room, and left me tied up naked on her bed. She came back awhile later and untied me and I left.

In another instance she pulled my hair until I agreed to go down on her. Lots of times I'd be lying in bed and she'd crawl in, and despite my protests she'd force my legs apart and go down on me, or put her fingers inside me. It was an unspoken rule that after these incidents I was expected to reciprocate. If I did not, I'd be subject to mental and emotional abuse, being tied up or even choked.

I also remember an instance when she tied me up against my will and sat on my face so I couldn't breathe. The only way she let me breathe was if I performed oral sex on her. There were many times when I was very emotionally or mentally abused because of sex. Sometimes it was just easier to give in. . . . At the end of [the relationship] I ended up in the hospital. I was suicidal, anxiety ridden, and paranoid. This was not the person I was when I entered college. My self-esteem was nil because I was so dependent on this woman, I thought, and she made me believe that I could do NOTHING without her.

Ariel, a white Latina lesbian, is now thirty. The relationship with her wife lasted seven and a half years. An established pattern around sex was that her partner would ignore Ariel's "no" and continue on to her own orgasm, which Ariel hoped would happen quickly:

I was asleep and was awakened by my wife, who was rubbing my vaginal area with her hand in my underwear. I told her to stop. She was obviously turned on because I can tell by her breathing and shakiness. I grabbed her hand to stop her. She grabbed my hand back and pushed it away. She forced herself on top of me and proceeded to penetrate me with so much force that she caused bleeding and cuts with her wedding ring that she was wearing. I remember lying there, crying, and wishing she'd just hurry up and get it over with. A part of me was very scared and another part of me was very angry. I stayed with her for five more years before I was able to break the circle of violence. She was good at apologizing and buying gifts after she assaulted me *but*, she never "said" she was "sorry." Her apologies were things like gifts, trips, or taking me out.

Messing with a partner's mind is a common effect of emotional abuse. Danielle, now fifty, is a white lesbian, today happily coupled after an eight-year abusive relationship in which emotional abuse took a toll.

We were on vacation at a resort. She began demeaning me, saying that it was my fault we never had sex. This escalated and she kept pushing me, saying various things like "You never show me that you want me." "If you loved me . . . it would be important to you." She pulled out a dildo and began waving it at me and wouldn't let me get away from her, yelling all the while. When she got me to where I was sobbing and apologizing she began to ignore me. I had the dildo at that point and bit the top of it off and threw it at her. Then she came at me and shoved me. I crumpled and was sobbing, begging her to stop and begging her to have sex with me to prove that I cared. [It] felt very sick and twisted around. We were not high or drunk. More than abuse; it felt like my mind had been scrambled.

Carlin's lover of two years forced her to have sex against her will many times. A white lesbian, now fifty-five and on disability, a dozen years ago she was in the early stages of a disease that hadn't yet been diagnosed. Her partner "figured if I was in bed that meant that I wanted sex. And that's how it started." Another example of being forced to do things against her will was when she told her partner about a sexual nightmare. Her partner insisted this was a fantasy she wanted to act out. Carlin adds,

I was also told, and it was most amazing cause I had been a lesbian from a very young age, out and about—with her I chose not to, I did not want to have oral sex—so I was basically told that I was not a lesbian. Which was pretty devastating, I remember at the time. It really started with emotional abuse and mental abuse, and then went to the sexual part of it being forced to do things that I did not want to do.

Stacy, a white bisexual, now forty-three, has had to rebuild her life many times. From repeated childhood incest to several battering relationships she "learned at a young age that if I did what the person wanted me to do it would be over faster. In my opinion, it's a form of prostitution, you just don't get paid." Similarly, Rhonda says,

It seems that many times within my current relationship I have been coerced into sex to "keep the peace." Such times have included: unwanted kissing and rubbing while out at gay bars, and unwanted sexual contact when my girlfriend would come home drunk. The latter of the two would consist of penetration of my vagina with fingers or dildos or just grinding of our vaginal areas.

Sex after fighting was not uncommon. Here is a typical example, found in Nora's experience:

Several times after [my partner] was physically violent, she would initiate sex as a way of reestablishing the relationship. I don't remember her *ever* apologizing or acknowledging what happened. I was so confused and "numbed out," I never questioned the violence or the sex following violence. I felt incredible shame later.

Natalie, white and lesbian, now thirty-eight and disabled, describes that her current partner gets angry if she refuses her sexual advances. And Natalie knows she is capable of physical violence.

She tries to force me to have sex with her, I say, "Get off of me." An argument will ensue, every time. I'll have to push her away. "No, I told you, I'm not going to do this." And stuff like that. Then she gets very, very angry. . . . To me if they want it and you don't want to give it, and they keep pushing it, what are you gonna do?

As with wife rape, few of these women sought medical help for their injuries or reported their sexual assaults to the police. Most lesbians and bisexual women are unclear about their legal rights and are concerned about a homophobic response from authorities. The emotional impact of the battering and the sexual violence incapacitates many of them. Women in battering relationships, whether gay or straight, are at risk of repeated sexual violence. While it is true that women do leave their abusive partners, they may endure years of violation before they attempt to leave. Much damage is already done to their bodies and their spirits.

At this point researchers still do not have any prevalence studies for rape between women in same-sex relationships. Heterosexism in the legal system, the reluctance to report these rapes, along with the unique problems of identifying the lesbian and bisexual population, hinder attempts at random sampling. But I question whether it is so important to know the actual numbers when confronted with what researchers already *do* know. We need to keep pushing for the recognition of both wife rape and woman-to-woman partner rape as serious social problems. So defined, resources need to be mobilized toward prevention, treatment of perpetrators, and services for survivors.

Date and Acquaintance Rape

More than 80 percent of rapes are committed by someone the victim knows.[12] Over half of these occur during a date.[13] According to Robin Warshaw, a woman's risk of being sexually assaulted by an acquaintance is four times higher than the risk of an assault by a stranger.[14] Numerous studies have confirmed these facts; however, rape is one of the most underreported crimes. The Department of Justice estimates that only 36 percent of rapes are reported to authorities, while other studies give a figure of less than 20 percent.[15] Complicating these facts further is that lesbians and bisexual women are not reporting their rapes by female perpetrators. If we knew of these sexual assaults, what would the numbers look like? At this point, researchers don't know. We also don't have accurate numbers of rapes of males. The scant research that does exist suggests that males are also most often raped by male acquaintances, not by strangers. The impacts appear to be very similar, with the added stresses that men are not expected to be victims (making it hard for them to come forward or be believed) and that males are automatically assumed to be gay if another man assaults them. If a woman sexually assaults a man, there is complete disbelief that this could have occurred. Yet, it does occur, and males can have an erection from the stress or fear of the abuse.[16] Stories of male-to-male rape are now being reported in the gay press.[17] Similar to woman-to-woman sexual violence, this issue is just now coming to the fore.

Of ninety-five perpetrators in this study, twenty-six fit into the category of acquaintance or date sexual perpetrators. This included acquaintances (fourteen), friends (nine), or dates (three). While partners are acquaintances, and some studies do include them in this category, I am not counting them in this classification; they are in the previous section. A contrasting characteristic between acquaintance rape and marital rape is that acquaintance rape tends to occur one time as opposed to repeatedly. Those involved may have known each other for years, a short while, or may have just met. In most instances, the survivor never sees the perpetrator again. If they do, the exchange is brief or awkward (at least for the survivor).

Many instances of acquaintance rape occur when one or both persons involved have been drinking. Alcohol often acts as both a facilitator of rape and an excuse for it.[18] While I have not heard of any cases where "date rape drugs" such as Rohypnol (flunitrazepam) have been used with lesbians or bisexual women, it certainly is possible. It is not a secret in the lesbian, bisexual, and gay communities that we have a serious substance abuse problem. Two factors seem to be prominent in explaining our higher rates of serious drinking and drug abuse: that much of our socializing occurs in bars (including during the important coming out period), and that queer community members use substances to cope with the impact of isolation, alienation, and oppression from societal homophobia and biphobia. Schilit, Lie, and Montagne reviewed studies that examined alcohol abuse among gay and straight women and men. The studies indicate that lesbians had more alcohol problems than the other group members did. While the researchers admit that the studies are not comprehensive, the studies suggest that approximately one-third of lesbians abuse alcohol.[19]

Alcohol and drug abuse did not figure prominently in my study. As Renzetti comments in reviewing the role of alcohol and drug use in gay and lesbian battering, alcohol and drug use "is neither a necessary nor a sufficient cause for partner abuse."[20] Overall, in fifty-seven situations (out of ninety-one, or 63 percent), the survivor or perpetrator used no substances. Alcohol and drugs were a factor in more of the nonbattering situations (forty-nine) than in situations of sexual abuse within domestic violence (forty-two). So, looking at the forty-nine situations without domestic violence (of which twenty-six were acquaintance rapes), alcohol or drugs were involved in 43 percent of the cases.

Ariel experienced a not uncommon situation when she was nineteen, visiting a friend from high school at her college.

> We had gone to a party, drank and went back to her dorm room. She began with kissing and petting but when I said "no" she forced me down on her bed and proceeded to fondle and grab me. She tore my shirt and at that point I became disengaged. She penetrated me with her hand/fingers and performed oral sex on me. I was too intoxicated and confused to fight. The next morning I got up very early and left. We haven't spoken since.

Judy, a twenty-four-year-old white lesbian, also went to see a friend from high school. She was twenty-two at the time.

> I went to see her and meet her girlfriend. We went out and they bought lots of drinks for me. I found out later that they had planned to get me very drunk so that they could "convince" me to have sex with them. Most of this was initiated by my friend's girlfriend. They forced vaginal and anal penetration with fingers, touched and sucked my breasts, went down on me and the girlfriend kissed me on the lips (actually as I said before most of this was initiated and orchestrated by the girlfriend). There was a lot of emotional manipulation and coercion of me on their part. After they were done with me I was pressured/forced to perform similar acts on both of them.

During this incident, Judy felt torn loyalties to herself and her friend. Immediately afterward she continued to interact with them and try to "go back to the way things were." But after awhile, Judy cut communication and interaction.

Diana is a white lesbian, twenty-two years old. Two years ago she was out of town with a group of friends.

[My best friend's friend] had been flirting with me all night. We had been at a gay bar and I had been drinking excessively. She continued to buy beer after beer for me. I was with my partner at the time (for about five to six months). I vaguely remember kissing her in a bathroom; I'm still not for sure it was her. Then we went back to the hotel and my partner was upset with me and friends because we were being loud and she wanted to go to bed. There were so many of us, we were sleeping four to a double bed. I remember begging my best friend and her girlfriend to sleep with my partner and me, 'cause I sensed this girl wanted to sleep beside me. They told me they would, and so I lay down with my partner, her on the edge of the bed and myself toward the middle. I fell asleep (or passed out) and at the point when I fell asleep no one was beside me. I woke up early the next morning (everyone else was dead asleep) to heavy petting and prickly legs rubbing against my own. I was still somewhat drunk/hungover. She continued rubbing me, eventually reaching private areas (breasts and under my boxers) and eventually went inside me with her fingers. (I was lying in bed on my back, my partner to my right, dead asleep and five other sleeping people in the room). I was not at all wet and she didn't seem to care. It wasn't painful, but it was uncomfortable. I was scared because my partner was beside me. If she woke up it would look like I was wanting this. If I screamed and said stop, I would appear a fool in a room full of my and her friends. I just laid there. She was moaning a little and breathing heavy. I don't think she saw anything wrong with what she was doing. To this day, I'm sure she doesn't know she raped me. After she was inside me she pulled my hand over to her privates and wanted my fingers to be inside her. She was so wet it made me nauseous. She guided my hand where she wanted it to go. There was some movement by others in the bed and I jerked my hand away. She later leaned over and said thank you. Later everyone woke up and I saw her whispering to some girl, then looking my way. The two girls laughed and gave each other a high-five and then glanced at me.

Diana felt in a state of shock after this incident and said, "[I] kept replaying the incident in my head, trying to think if there was something I could have done differently."

When Aileen, a white lesbian, was nineteen (she's now twenty-two) a heterosexual friend of hers attempted a sexual assault. Her friend was drunk; Aileen was not.

She pinned me against a wall, kissed me, tried to grab my breasts and kissed my face/mouth while I tried to get away. I broke away after about three or five minutes of being very scared and kicked her out. When I confronted her the next day she denied it happened. All the people I told did not take it seriously.

Lucy recalls a harrowing experience:

I am now twelve years sober, but in my drinking days, somewhere between the ages of twenty-four and twenty-six, I was raped by my then girlfriend. We were both drunk and high. She tied me to a bed and used a broom handle. I was seriously hurt. We broke up soon after. Till this day, if I see her I get physically sick and emotionally tore up.

Bea's story is one that demonstrates acquiescence, or what she called a "mercy fuck." Over twenty years ago an acquaintance began kissing and fondling her without her consent and would not stop. Bea is a white lesbian, now forty-four. "I was shocked and tried to get her to quit verbally and by laughing when she didn't respect that I felt unable emotionally to set a rigid boundary and make her quit. So I gave in and had [oral] sex with her against my will to get it over and ensured we were never alone together again."

Marcia, a twenty-three-year-old, white lesbian graduate student, found herself in an uncomfortable situation at eighteen when she was at a bar with someone she had met three weeks previously. This woman was drinking and hit on Marcia through verbal comments and provocative dancing, which Marcia tried to deflect. Marcia was giving the woman a ride home when she was sexually assaulted:

She started by talking to me, telling me how hot she thought I was, how she was in an open relationship, how badly she wanted to kiss me, to taste my skin. I told her in every way I could think of that I was not interested, did not want to kiss her and could she please tell me where I needed to turn.

Then she put her hand on my leg, my right leg by my knee and I pushed her hand off. Turn right here, make a left there. And her hand was on my leg again, on my thigh this time. "Cut it out! I told you to stop!" "Okay, okay, I just can't help myself." Her hand back on my leg while I'm making a turn with both hands on the wheel. I guess my one-second delay led her to believe she could fumble to get under my shorts. "Hey! Will you fucking stop! Just tell me how to get home and keep your hands to yourself!" "You want me to stop?" All innocent like, as if she's got no idea why I'm getting angry. "Yeah, stop." "Stop what? Stop this?" Both hands, her full concentration, all over me. One up my right leg, so far up the inside of my leg she's almost touching my underwear. The other trying to untuck my shirt, pawing all over my stomach. Where are my hands? One on the wheel, the other putting her hand out of my pants and grabbing the other off my shirt. But they keep coming back and it's my hand to her two, and I'm trying to keep us on the road, to not get into an accident, and get her the hell off of me. "Stop it! Get the fuck off me!" "Okay,

okay," all calm with a big smile on her face. "I'll stop, but on one condition."
"What?" (I felt so defeated, anything just stop) "Kiss me. Just give me one kiss and
I'll stop." "No way!" "Look, just one kiss. I'll even close my eyes. Just a quick one.
Just one sweet kiss." Why didn't I just kick her out? Drop her off at a gas station?

"Okay, fine. One kiss. But you promised, you'll stop." "Yeah, I know, I know."
So she closes her eyes and I think, why can't this light turn green? Why is this the
longest light in fucking history? So I lean over, suppress my urge to vomit all over
her, and kiss her quickly high on her cheek. God I think I'm going to get sick. Light
turns green and I peal out with my foot heavy on the gas, as if it's her I'm leaving
behind. But I'm not and she's still sitting there next to me and I still don't know
where I am and she decides that that kiss was not good enough and so doesn't
count. I've got to kiss her on the lips for it to count. "That's not fair! You said all
I've got to do is kiss you and you'll leave me alone! You didn't say what kind of kiss
it had to be." So she didn't stop. She kept trying to touch me but I don't think it
was as bad as before. . . . When we got to her house, she got out of the car, she
put both her hands on the roof and leaned in towards the passenger side window
and told me to give her a call, that she really had a good time. I couldn't believe
what I was hearing. . . . I saw her two to three times afterward around town after
that, like the following week or so when she came up and accused me of telling lies
about her. That she had attacked me or something.

Marcia was shocked that another woman was behaving in this way, and she
felt betrayed that the woman took advantage of her and went back on her
word.

Many scenarios of acquaintance or date rape occur when the abuser
won't take no for an answer. They disregard the harm being done to the
other person. When Renee, a twenty-eight-year-old lesbian Creole, was dating at twenty-six, she agreed to have her date use a strap-on dildo.

She got it and put it on and bent my legs up above around my head area/ears and
had me penned. Then she started pushing it in and out and kept going faster until
my cervix started bleeding. I asked her to stop and struggled but was penned even
further. She was a lot bigger than me and I couldn't get up. So finally I got up and
she took me home. I lied and told her that I liked it just to get home to my daughter.

When Lauren, a thirty-seven-year-old white lesbian, was twenty-four, her
softball team was on a road trip to a national tourney. The team manager
roomed her with a woman she'd known for a year:

She started with telling me she had hit her long time partner just before leaving. She
did not want to be that way. She wanted to talk about why and learn to be better.

> She said she felt real badly about it. She wanted to snuggle to feel better. I was not interested. She was persistent. I gave in hoping she'd stop it. She kissed me. I stopped it and said no—I wasn't going there. She stopped. Later after I'd gone to sleep, she rolled over and started touching me. I said no (verbally) but my body reacted. I asked her to stop. She held me down with her body and made love to me digitally. I thought I owed her back but she said it did not work that way. Later that night/early the next morning, she digitally brought me to orgasm again (I disassociated). This pattern continued for the length of the trip (five nights). It occurred again about six weeks later on another trip, this time with others in the room. She held her lips over mine and my body still with hers and digitally fucked me. I hated every moment of it. I hated that my body responded. I now hate that I thought this was love.

At the time, Lauren felt it was her fault. She did not have the self-esteem and support to stop this woman from using her sexually. She had trouble believing a woman "would take that away from another woman," and she was confused by her body's sexual response.

Some situations, such as the next two, involve more terror and unpredictability. In a situation with a violent, wild younger woman, Margot, a white and American Indian lesbian, had been stalked for several years when her predicament came to a head. The acquaintance had been in reform school and in and out of jails. She was domineering and a stone butch. Margot writes, "I was terrified of her, especially when she was drinking, which was basically all of the time." One night Margot, who was forty-five, was visiting the acquaintance (who was nineteen) and her partner:

> After her partner went to bed, [she] began touching my breasts, put my hand on her breast, kissing me. I asked her not to, said I didn't like it and she got furious. No one is allowed to not like anything [she] does. She beat women up regularly. . . . She was verbally abusive. She had two vicious dogs, who would not let me out of the apartment. She dragged me to her bed. I was terrified of resisting much because I knew if I did she'd beat me. She licked and sucked my vulva and clitoris, rubbed herself (in her jeans) on me. She forced me to take all my clothes off, very embarrassing to me as I am quiet, gentle, inhibited. She kissed my mouth and face, fondled my breasts. Basically all I did was lie there. . . . She kept on drinking. Finally she got drunk enough to want to pass out. I rushed into my clothes and had her hold the dogs so I could get out.

Another terrifying occurrence happened to Leigh, a white heterosexual, now age forty-three and a CEO, who at age twenty-eight was kidnapped and forcibly held for three days in a hotel room by a woman who had been her best friend for five years and her boyfriend. The motive apparently was ransom, since the kidnappers did have Leigh call her parents to demand one hundred thousand dollars (her parents were not at home). The kidnap, however, included sexual threats and assaults. Leigh recalls:

> What I do remember overall is being terrified I would be killed or kept there forever. The woman periodically used the man as a tool to hurt me at her order, to punch me, etc. I was forced to smoke crack cocaine (I am not now nor was I ever a drug user). I was forced to kiss her on the lips, she fondled my breasts, I was forced to perform oral sex on her while she called me a bitch and a liar and told me I was no good because I couldn't make her orgasm. She threatened to burn me with the crack pipe; she threatened to shove wire coat hangers and bottles up in me (she held them in front of me while yelling at me). . . . She threatened to pick up men on the street, bring them back and have them rape me while she took photos. She had me perform oral sex on her boyfriend for four hours while she screamed at me that I was no good, called me derogatory names, etc. She often screamed at me that she wasn't a lesbian and that no man would want me after she was done with me. She once told me I could leave naked if I wanted, but then said if I told anyone she would kill me.

Leigh escaped and the perpetrators were arrested. However, it took her six years to reach out for help to deal with the trauma of those three days.

The previous stories of acquaintance and date rapes and sexual assaults are disturbing. People who have seemed safe turned out to not be trustworthy, and furthermore disregarded intimate boundaries, caused emotional and physical pain, and shattered once-held notions of the safety and security in being with other women. Following patterns of heterosexual acquaintance sexual assaults, alcohol is often involved, the assault generally occurs once, and the perpetrator is usually out of the survivor's life afterward. Power over other individuals to get them to do what the perpetrators want whether they want to or not seems to be the "reward" perpetrators receive. I now turn to other forms of sexual violence: sexual harassment, abuse of authority, and abuse of minors.

Sexual Harassment

The term *sexual harassment* came into use in 1980 when it was defined legally. The focus has been on workplace harassment, with well-publicized cases such as Clarence Thomas's Supreme Court confirmation hearings and Senator Bob Packwood's resignation. While there has been a surge of discussions and writings on the subject, studies reveal that only 5 percent of victims ever report their harassment to authorities.[21]

Most sexual harassment cases occur in the workplace or in settings such as schools. A study analyzing data from the National Violence Against Women Survey examined the prevalence and characteristics of coworker violence in the United States. The study only looked at coworker forcible rape, physical assault, stalking, and threats to physically harm or kill. Researchers found that 100,697 women and 92,748 men eighteen years or older are victimized by a current or former coworker each year—a rate of 1 adult per 1,000. This figure underrepresents the actual amount of coworker violence, since other types, such as sexual assaults other than forcible rape, were not included. However, it does indicate that this is serious abuse.[22]

Sexual harassment reports of lesbians, bisexuals, and gay men are nearly invisible. Perhaps a major reason for this silence relates to the discussion by Jeff Hearn and Wendy Parkin. They claim that much of sexuality is constructed in public places and a good deal of sexual interaction takes place in public. Given that public displays of sexuality between women are frowned upon, and in fact often draw hostility, public reporting of sexual harassment would be minimal. Lesbian and bisexual sexuality continues to be constructed and affirmed primarily in private or in traditional spots such as gay bars or gay-related events. Taken-for-granted displays of sexuality for heterosexuals (hand-holding, photos, sexual teasing, rings, hugging, kissing, etc.) are negotiated acts for lesbians. Therefore, healthy displays of sexuality as well as sexual harassment reports are muted.[23]

I have three cases of sexual harassment to relate, by three "typical" abusers: a stranger, coworkers, and a college classmate. Three other cases of sexual abuse by coworkers are included in the category of abuse of authority (see next section), since they were by supervisors or employers. It is crucial in thinking about the continuum of sexual violence to admit how "normal" sexual harassment is for women, including lesbians and bisexual women. Although lesbians and bisexual women have not been incorporated in the conceptualization as survivors or perpetrators of sexual abuse, sexual harassment is a fact of everyday life, and lesbians and bisexual women are not immune to it.

Alice, a white lesbian, now thirty-eight and a manager, was stopped in the bathroom of a gay bar when she was in her early twenties:

A woman repeatedly told me of her interest in me sexually as she blocked my exit from the bathroom and popped her knuckles. (She had previously described to me how she had beaten her ex-lover but it was her ex-lover's fault.) I began repeating to her, "If I wanted to be with a man, and experience what it is like to be with a man, I would do so." I then explained to her that I had been molested as a child and also experienced rape. I clarified to her that her behavior communicated a threat of sexual assault to me. She then stepped away and allowed me to leave the bathroom.

In this case, Alice was able to draw upon her past sexual abuses to give her the strength to defuse this situation. She also thought it likely that this stranger may have been abused and that "this woman's behavior was mostly due to her own confusion and possible identification with the abuser(s) of her past."

A first-year college student, Jude, eighteen, a white bisexual woman, was shocked and dismayed when another student started to hit on her during a class:

She began by whispering "Do you want to make out?" (loud enough for a few others in the class to hear). She's pretty funny so I laughed thinking that was a bit of a more absurd joke. It continued, along with her panting, touching my thigh, writing on her hand "I heart Jude," and asking me out for that Friday night. I considered leaving the class but realized how much I was paying to be there and would not let her win. When class was over I called my Mom and cried; I was so angry that this student could be disrespectful enough to waste my time and make a class I was paying to be in to learn an unsafe place. . . . This is obviously not a physical violence situation but it is a case of woman-to-woman disrespect. I have a list on my wall of what constitutes sexual harassment and this situation meets the qualifiers.

Jude also found that this brought up memories of past sexual harassment from jobs and teachers, which increased her anger. In the following days, Jude did not sit near this woman, but the verbal harassment continued. Jude confronted her outside of class (though not as directly as she would have liked), and the harassment stopped.

Lorraine, a forty-two-year-old white bisexual, experienced workplace sexual harassment on more than one occasion. This harassment made her nervous and anxious, particularly because the abusers thought their actions were a joke. She points out, though, "that I think there's an overlap between heterosexual and female-to-female harassment because I think there's also a lot of men who would say that they're just joking, that it's funny, afterwards." In one instance, a coworker of Lorraine's punched her in the breast. Lorraine turned around and pulled the woman's hair. Later she heard the coworker say she was trying to make Lorraine laugh, a claim Lorraine discounts because "it was a pretty hard blow." In the second instance, at another job, Lorraine was lying down in the rest room because of lower back pain. "[The coworker] laid down on top of me and started bouncing up and down." Lorraine regrets that she never reported either incident to work supervisors.

While harassment may not be accompanied by physical injury, there is psychological damage. As part of Sheffield's description of sexual terrorism, women do not know when it will happen—a factor that destabilizes us in our everyday lives. Harassment, then, becomes part of the arsenal of power and control, employed by males *and females* who seek to dominate others.

Abuse of Authority

Some professionals sexually exploit their clients, patients, students, and mentees. Because of their societal positions of authority and power, they are able to manipulate those vulnerable to them. Because of their relationships to those under them, they have opportunity and access unique to them. According to the Web site, Advocate Web:

> If a client's dependence on a professional is exploited, the client is almost always injured and the professional has betrayed the client's and society's trust. When a client is sexually exploited, the wounds can be particularly deep. It is a violation that goes beyond physical violation. It is an emotional, psychological, and sometimes spiritual violation.[24]

When the trust that is given to a professional and the respect that is granted the position are betrayed, it creates deep wounds.

Studies of therapist sexual relations with patients show that this is not a minor problem. Judith Herman cites surveys in which 5 to 10 percent of male psychologists have admitted to intercourse with their patients. Another survey showed that 20 percent of male therapists thought sexual relations with patients should not be prohibited, and 70 percent said they knew of male colleagues who engaged in sexual relations with patients.[25]

Seven women responded with stories of sexual violation by authorities. Three were abused by therapists (in one case, the therapist also employed her), two by teachers (and a third as a minor, which will be discussed in the next section), one by a doctor (who was also her employer), and one by a mentor/work supervisor. The confusion and conflicts engendered in the abuse survivor are exemplified in Rita's story. Rita is a white bisexual, now forty years old:

> When I was in college, at age nineteen, my school therapist pushed me up against a closed door in her office at the college where she had been counseling me for several months. I felt very uncomfortable about this. She invited me to a hotel on my birthday, promising me dinner. We ended up in a hotel room having sex. I was very confused. I wanted to be loved. I felt more trapped than anything. . . . This went on until I graduated and later, in counseling, I realized that none of this should have happened. It was inappropriate.

Giselle, thirty-nine, a white Latina lesbian, also felt vulnerable to her therapist, a well-known and respected, charismatic woman in the community.

> I was thirty-two, she was fifty-plus. She was my therapist and I had felt incredibly safe and vulnerable with her. She sexualized our friendship shortly after I knew her and I feel I was molested by her since I felt powerless to say no. We had sex numerous times and it was gross to me. I never had an orgasm or felt it was "consensual." It makes me sick to think of her now.

At first, Giselle felt flattered by her therapist's attention, as she put it, to "feel like the teacher's pet." But she says, "Looking back on it now, it feels like she was grooming me for abuse. And then I was hired to stay on and work for her in that group, where I became sort of her secretary, and did all the administrative work and picked people up from the airport, that kind of stuff. And at the same time she was my lover." Ultimately, Giselle "feel[s] she molested me and betrayed all kinds of ethical codes for a therapist and employer, abused power and control totally." Her biggest regret is that she didn't report her because she worries about this woman's ability to abuse other vulnerable young women.

Marielle, forty-one, white and bisexual, did report her therapist, who it turned out is not a credentialed therapist. She was immediately tied up in lawsuits, which continued at the time of our interview. She feels she was raped spiritually and reported the rape to the police, who took the report but told her the event did not constitute rape. The incident occurred recently, when she was forty years old. Several years earlier, Marielle had joined a church that turned out to be a cult connected to white supremacists. The therapist is connected to the same cult, and it took Marielle years to figure out she was being subjected to "thought reform."

Of the rape, Marielle writes,

It wasn't violent in the usual sense. It was carefully arranged in the context of a past event that I had described to her in therapy. Very confusing . . . only a therapist could devise a mental rape.

She took the elements of a disturbing sexual encounter (that was not rape) from my past and created a present situation that would call up that experience. I had told her the details of this and other confusing sexual encounters and she created a sexual scene in therapy, when I was vulnerable and crying and needed comforting.

Her reaction (orgasm) was totally inappropriate in the context of therapy, but was intentional to try to break me down emotionally; she was holding me as I was crying hysterically over my sister's death. She had an orgasm or pretended to as I was crying. Because she was my therapist this confused me.

Marielle continues to try to unravel her abuse and her connection with the cult. Not surprisingly, she doesn't trust anyone.

Aura's abuse by her acupuncturist/healer employer, who then became her doctor, has similarities to elements of the previous stories. Her abuser was a well-known healer in the community, a charismatic woman. She was held in such high regard that Aura describes this as "cult-like." This occurred when Aura, a white lesbian, now age thirty-seven, was in her early thirties. While they did not engage in sex, their relationship was sexualized:

From the beginning she crossed my boundaries in inappropriate ways while doing bodywork and acupuncture—caressing me in nonsexual but intimate/very close friend type of ways, telling me how much she loved me, telling me very personal information and stories about herself, eliciting such stories from me and reacting very emotionally (crying as she held me on at least one occasion), saying I should travel to Mexico with her, in every way acting as if I were a significant part of her life.

During our "nontreatment" encounters, I also felt there was a lot of intense energy between us. When we'd hug it felt a lot more than "friends." She would also make remarks with sexual connotations and talk about her sex life while in the office during my work shifts. I didn't know how to regard this. I didn't want a sexual relationship with her and couldn't even see how inappropriate she was being because I felt so much love for her, felt so fortunate to have this great "friend," and also deeply vulnerable to her as my doctor.

We had a disagreement when she tried to force me to work as an independent contractor. She took her anger out on me during my acupuncture treatments, with such sheer medical negligence that my immune system was nearly destroyed after nine months as her patient. She tried to blackmail me and forced me into filing a fraudulent tax return to protect her from having to pay higher taxes. One night this blew up in an intense emotional scene. She kissed me on the mouth, she called me "*mi amor*," and she said she loved me madly. She never touched me in a sexually explicit way, but the way she acted towards me emotionally, verbally and physically was as if I were a lover who had betrayed her.

Aura was fired from her job in a public and humiliating way and threatened with violence. She tried to speak out about her abuse but was silenced by the lesbian community, and she suffered for years from posttraumatic stress. In a telling statement confirming the depth of professional abuse, Aura admits, "I felt that my life was over when she fired me. I had not trusted anyone so deeply or let anyone so far inside my private self."

It took Erin's attending a group for survivors of professional abuse for her to realize that as a nineteen-year-old college student, she had been abused by a forty-eight-year-old female professor for three years. Erin is a white lesbian, now thirty-eight.

She was an alcoholic who cultivated me to meet her sexual needs. The harassment started with special attention I found flattering, compliments and invitations. She first asked me out on a date in the comments she wrote on my paper. She'd come to class drunk and touch my arm or shoulder. I remember her pinching my butt at a departmental reception when I was serving food. I spent more and more time at her house and she would be too drunk to take me home so I'd end up staying over. I remember her walking in on me once while I was in the bathtub. Once when she was very drunk she said we should have an affair and I said no and started making arrangements to take a semester off to steer clear of her. She begged me to stay, said she needed me, etc. And, by this time, I was very emotionally wrapped up in her and felt in love. All of it was complicated by her insisting she wasn't lesbian and we were just "kindred spirits." Eventually the contact turned sexual. I wouldn't describe it as violence but it sure was abusive. For example, she'd invite me into her bed, take off my pajama, touch my breasts, and then, when I responded and tried to kiss her. say that she didn't mean "sleeping together" to be sexual. I'd apologize, cry and feel terrible. I'd try to separate. Then she'd call and beg and we'd be back in sexual contact. She told me I was the sexual aggressor who initiated this relationship. Finally, after we'd had full out sexual contact she dropped me.

When Nina, a twenty-seven-year-old white lesbian, was an adolescent, she and her sister lived one summer with a modeling and talent agent for training. During this time she and her sister were sexually abused. She didn't hear from the woman until she went off to college, casting aside her dreams of modeling and turning to athletics. At that time the agent contacted her through her mother:

> My first thought was that she wanted to apologize, so I agreed to see her. I was not reluctant at all. In fact, I looked forward for a week to the visit.
>
> I was to meet her at her hotel, which I did on Saturday morning. She took me to a show, introduced me to a lot of important people in the industry, and led me to believe that I could in fact be a model, a thought that had not entered my mind since that summer. I was caught up in the moment as I was truly enjoying her company. By this time in my life I was having strong lesbian feelings, but had never acted on them. We had dinner that evening, and went back to her hotel room, where I had planned to spend the night.
>
> She DID apologize for the things that happened that summer, and she sounded very sincere. She asked me many questions about my sex life and I told her that I had never had a lover. She asked if I was still a virgin and I told her yes. She kissed me on the mouth, and I responded. Before I realized what was happening and could even think about resisting, she had me on the bed, ripped my bottoms off, and she got between my legs. She told me she had wanted my "cunt meat" since the summer she got my sister's.
>
> She used multiple fingers to then finger-rape me. I was in excruciating pain as it felt like she was trying to rip me open. Then she blindfolded me, and gagged me, and tied me to the bed. The last thing I remember before I passed out was her telling me that I needed a woman's dick, and I felt her insert the dildo in me.
>
> I woke up hours later to find myself a total mess but no longer tied up, and in massive pain. But, she was gone, with all her clothes. She left me new clothes to wear. I got some Tylenol and drove back to my college, and talked to no one until I went to class on Monday. At [sports] practice, I could hardly walk.

Many factors influenced Nina's decisions, not the least of which was this woman's summerlong abuse of her and her sister when they were young and her decision to keep this a secret. She also never expected an apology to turn into a rape.

Professionals who abuse are able to use their authority to catch their victims off guard, as well as silence them afterward because of their community positions. In Lila's case, her mentor/work supervisor got away with abuse of many clients, but not forever. Finally, Lila filed a lawsuit, which was settled out of court. As a client, then intern, then staff member of an agency that worked with women leaving prostitution, Lila, a white lesbian, then thirty-three, now thirty-seven, describes that her supervisor "methodically isolated me and blurred boundaries and combined seduction and terrorism to control me and abuse me. Once she kissed me and once she bit my breast. There were no circumstances to put these in context or label them. She just did them." In one specific incident,

> I had two beers at the bar and I expected [she] had a lot because she is a chronic alcoholic and drinks a lot of gin. We were at separate tables conversing with different people, so I don't know how much she drank right then. I drove her home four blocks away. An excellent old blues tune came on the radio and we high-fived our hands. She yanked me and kissed me. She broke open my jacket and flipped up her shirt and bra. She slapped me and pushed my face (pimpslap) and demanded, "Whose pussy is this?" She did not grab my genital area. She pimpslapped me a total of four times with the same demand until I said, "It's [your] pussy." I remembered she told me a story of some man in her life who made a claim of her that way and she told her men to "make it yours," so I said it and she stopped.

Lila's abuser is, once again, a charismatic woman, active in the movement against sexual violence. The lawsuit was Lila's attempt to protect other vulnerable women; it worked only partially, as this abuser continues in the movement work, and while some women won't work with her, others still do.

Abuse of Minors

Aside from studies on incest and some publicity of cases in which minors impregnate adults or the minors are impregnated, little is known about the extent and impact of sexual relations between adults and minors. Almost nothing is talked about in the lesbian, bisexual, and gay communities about these relationships, with perhaps the National Man/Boy Love Association (NAMBLA) the controversial exception. This silence makes it impossible for young women to speak openly about this abuse because their claims are given so little credibility.

Three women in the study discussed situations they now consider as abusive that occurred when they were fifteen, sixteen, or seventeen. The perpetrators were able to take advantage of very vulnerable young women, with lasting impact.

I begin with the situation of Claudia, a white lesbian, now forty-nine, whose abuser was a nun—one of her teachers in high school, and as such, this also fits under the category of professional abuse. The sexual abuse occurred during Claudia's junior year, while she was sixteen and seventeen. Previous to this, from infancy to about age eight, her parents had sexually molested Claudia. Claudia, a straight-A student, went for extra tutoring on the weekends for one of her classes. At first, there were passionate kisses and embracing. Then she began to meet the teacher every morning in the classroom before school:

> We would have ten or fifteen minutes of just standing in the room with passionate hugging and kissing, and it was wonderful, I mean it felt wonderful. I was totally in love with her, had always been teacher's pet and poured all my affection into the nuns; I was planning to be a nun.

Her teacher was helping her select a college to attend, and they went on a trip to look at one of the choices.

> That was the first time we had ever taken off any clothes. And at that point she actually touched my genitals once and asked me if I liked to be touched down there, or if I liked to be kissed and touched on the breast more. And, I just thought it was very odd to want to be touched down there, I mean I can't tell you how repressed I was. So I just said, "up here," and she respected that completely. So there was only that one time that there was anything genital at all and it was extremely limited. So primarily it was incredibly passionate kissing and sort of pressing our bodies together, that was the extent of it. And all of this ended after sometime over the summer between my junior and senior years, and she just told me that someone was suspicious and we had to stop this. It stopped to the degree that she acted like she barely knew me through all of senior year. And I cannot tell you how miserable that was. I went every morning still to the classroom, still hoping that she would come back, and then I would, before Mass, I would go to the bathroom. I had this acute diarrhea the whole year just from the stress. And I couldn't understand why she was doing this to me.

Claudia felt abandoned by the woman she felt she loved. They'd had constant contact not only physically but also through phone calls and passionate letters. Years later, after she graduated from college, she saw her teacher in Paris. They went for a walk:

> She sort of took my hand and said, "I guess you wonder why I never touch you anymore," and she said, "The doctor said it's like I have an allergy to you, it makes me sick to be around you." And now I see that as making me hate my body even more. And she said, I think she told me this before, that the doctor felt she had several broken ribs and it must have been because I hugged her too hard. And just this horrible stuff. Even then, even though I was still longing for her and everything, I knew this was not the truth. . . . I knew I was being lied to but I couldn't say anything, I didn't have the skills to say anything. I swallowed it all humbly.

Claudia feels her past incest "made me incredibly needy and probably an obvious target. And I was hyper religious and studious because that was the way I was coping with escaping from my home in ways that I could." After years of therapy, Claudia felt she needed to do something to protect other children this nun might be teaching. She wrote a letter saying she urgently wanted to speak to her. She heard back from another nun who told her this sister was ill and could not speak to her. The nun who called pressed Claudia for details, which Claudia would not give. In fact, she felt suspicious that perhaps they were protecting this sister's "secret"—perhaps even protecting the Catholic subset of the lesbian community.

It was decades before Claudia could put what happened into perspective. "It took my therapist quite a long time for me to accept that this was not the end of a beautiful love affair but that it had [always] been very inappropriate." The relationship had several uncomfortable facets, including the nun's hints that Claudia would find heterosexual sex distasteful and the stress that they were not lesbians. She was told, "Someday someone might try to tell you that this is homosexual, but it's not. It's different, so don't get confused. That's not what this is. This is very special."

Brooke was also sixteen and seventeen when she became involved with a married woman in her late twenties who was a coworker. Brooke, a white lesbian, now thirty-three years old, was a vulnerable teenager; her parents had separated when she was young, and her mother was depressed for as long as Brooke could remember. Brooke had been sexually abused as a child and had been diagnosed with ulcerative colitis at thirteen. She felt out of step with her classmates because of her illness. She also felt "in desperate need of an adult."

Their friendship included kissing, being held, and talking about all of the things Brooke felt she couldn't share with others:

I do not remember when things became more overtly sexual. When they did, we always kept our clothes on because we were in her car or on the couch in my apartment. She was always the one to push the sexual part further initially and then every time after that. She would touch my breasts with the bra on, and then I would do the same to her. I felt I had to equalize the exposure. Her hand would go under the bra, and I would do the same. I honestly can not remember if we ever touched each other's genitals. I remember, though, that we would rub up against each other, and use our hands. Now that I think of it, I may have a vague memory of touching her pubic hair, which means, of course, that she must have touched mine. . . . I remember feeling that I could not afford emotionally to lose her.

Because she was older, she did push me; she knew what sex was, I had very little idea. Although, given what a sexual relationship meant to her at twenty-seven, she did not push me as much as she might have, except once. We were at her apartment. I have to say, I have a hard time calling the general tenor of our relationship rape, but I will admit the level of sexual practice was not mutually consensual; however, this one time was rape. We had been kissing on her and her husband's bed; we did not usually do this. And all of a sudden she had my pants at my knees and she was going down on me. I had no idea that oral sex existed and asked her what she was doing and to stop. She said that she had wanted to do this for a long time, that I would enjoy it. I "checked out" and it was over. I realize now that part of what was so terrible about that moment was that I could not "level the playing field." Also, it was a vivid moment of the reality that nothing of the physical relationship had ever, really, been level, and that I was never, really, there in her relating, just as I wasn't in that moment.

For Brooke, this relationship was a mix of sweetness and secrets (from her parents and her friends, from the older woman's husband), of coercion and confusion. Today she is clearer that the situation was abusive, but it took years to sort out all the dynamics involved.

At age fifteen, Aura was part of a women's collective and participated primarily in an adult lesbian feminist community. One woman in particular sought her out and one day took her to a park:

[She barraged me] with reasons that I should have sex with her; saying that if I refused I wasn't a real lesbian; saying she needed me to take care of her; creating an atmosphere of fear and violence by telling me of a fourteen-year-old she'd slept with and how another woman had beaten her up for doing so, but it "was worth it"; telling me her current lover would beat both of us up if she knew about me, so we had to keep everything a secret; presenting this all as if it were some great exciting seductive "one night stand" and that it was up to me whether to proceed, while never letting up her verbal and emotional manipulations. At the same time much of what she said was designed to make me feel badly about myself, as a lesbian and a woman/girl and someone who could think for myself and make my own decisions. She never left me alone for a minute, never gave me a chance to clear my head and try and figure out what was really going on.

I finally acquiesced, never feeling that I'd been given a choice. We went to her place, where she performed a number of sexual acts on me (my participation was very minimal). It was physically painful and I had continued pain for a number of days after this happened. (She bit my breasts and was very rough in touching me. My clitoris hurt for days.) . . . I encountered her a couple more times after this. She acted as if we had some big romantic secret until one evening she was performing at the coffeehouse (she was a musician, though not a good one), when she put me down in front of a crowd of women for asking someone who came in late to buy a ticket. After the show, we had an emotional confrontation—not over the assault, but it shattered the veil of illusion and I began the process of naming what she'd really done to me.

Aura had a difficult time naming and understanding what had happened to her, in part because few around her took her seriously. She wanted to believe this was consensual, but her sense of violation was too deep. In her late thirties now, she feels the event has left her raw. She states,

There have been few instances where I have felt heard or supported, but the times I've written or/and published about it, reached out to other survivors—these have helped me in naming it as an instance of sexual violence, a misuse of power, a situation in which I didn't have the experience or understanding to possibly be able to consent to or desire or play an equal part or bear responsibility for what was done to me by this woman.

These last two sections, abuse of authority and abuse of minors, have clear overlap. In all the cases, the perpetrator is in a position of power over the woman she is abusing. And as in every section of this chapter, the sexual violence has left a very deep impact.

Sadomasochism and Abuse

The issue of the relationship between sadomasochism (S/M) and abuse is a sensitive one and is hotly debated. I bring it up here because 13 percent of the women in the study mention S/M. Joelle Taylor and Tracey Chandler remind us that "abuse occurs across all sexualities and across all sexual politics."[26] This includes lesbian and bisexual feminists as well as those engaged in S/M. It is erroneous and damaging to claim only one type of lesbian or bisexual woman or one type of same-sex sexual practice is abusive. In September 1983 the Lesbian Task Force of the NCADV published this statement:

We as leaders of the Battered Women's Movement are seriously concerned that we have received reports from lesbians involved in sado-masochistic relationships; that the relationships moved into battering, or in retrospect always were battering. We ask that lesbians engaging in sado-masochistic behavior carefully examine the nature of consent since it is our experience as advocates for battered women that in any relationship that involves violent activity, the lines between consent, compliance and coercion tend to blur.[27]

This statement, the first public statement of concern about abuse and S/M, wasn't made to single out S/M but to suggest a careful consideration of one's sexual practices.

S/M has been criticized by lesbian feminists as an "outlaw sexual practice" on the grounds that it introduces the power inequalities of heterosexual relations into same-sex sexual behavior and has no place in lesbian utopia. It was particularly contentious in the 1980s when S/M lesbians and bisexual women faced exclusion from many organizations and venues.[28]

While proponents of S/M say that sadomasochism is consensual and that they are free to choose to act on fantasies or desires, Nichols, Pagano, and Rossoff question why sadomasochism would be desirable and where the fantasies come from.[29] The issue is not sexual "freedom"; the issue is the context within which our freedom operates. They claim that sadomasochistic behavior reproduces the power imbalances and destructive aspects of our lives. The fantasy that women believe is freely chosen is one that comes to us through advertising, pornography, sexism, and power-over models. Others criticize eroticizing power-over as well. M. Kornak states, "The consequences of incorporating the power of the patriarchy in our lives, whitewashing it, and calling it our own are deep and far-reaching."[30] "There's something wrong," writes Marissa Jonel, "when a woman has an orgasm when beating or fist-fucking another woman, when pleasure is derived from degrading nicknames like 'stupid cunt' and 'fucking whore,' when we put energy into building torture chambers and buying wrist restraints."[31] To Jonel, a former masochist, S/M is a cover for violence.

But to adherents of sadomasochism, eroticism is found in the consensual exchange of power.[32] According to Jennifer Margulies, S/M takes place within a set time and place, or "scene," and the players have defined limits and roles. The partners agree on a safeword that either player can use at any time. The S/M community places emphasis on safewords and safety.[33] Writings such as "Playing and Staying Safe: Six Thinking Points Before Playing with Someone New" by Gloria Brame[34] and checklists about domestic violence and S/M are geared toward emphasizing safe, consensual sex.[35] Margulies states:

This is not to say that batterers can't use s/m to hurt their partners. Women can and sometimes do coerce and manipulate their partners into "agreements" to which they don't really agree. Women can and sometimes do ignore their partner's safewords, violate their boundaries and dishonor their limits. S/m can be a powerful weapon in the hands of a batterer, but so can the issue of when you have sex with each other, what you wear to a party or who you talk to when you're there. Battering consists of skillful manipulations that turn the air you breathe into an atmosphere of abuse. When a woman uses s/m to batter, the problem is battering, not s/m.[36]

Several women in the study agreed to S/M in a manner I referred to earlier as "acquiescence"—in other words, consent that was not freely given, though it was consent. For example, Marti, a white lesbian, now thirty-one, saw her S/M experiences at age twenty-two with her partner as sexual abuse:

> She was into this, what do you call it, the domination, S & M–type stuff, and when I would try to think that that's what she wanted, I would actually try to get into that. . . . I would try to please her and it didn't work, the more I tried to please her, the angrier she got. . . . It was some of the time. I knew that she was into it and I thought, well, maybe if I try to get into it, which I didn't, I didn't even want to deal with it, for the benefit of the relationship, and as mentally as she had me abused I thought, well, what the hell. I tried it, and it was not pleasant.

Christy, the twenty-seven-year-old lawyer mentioned earlier, experimented with S/M at age twenty-four with her partner and at first found it fun and exciting. Then it started to become more controlling. "At the time, our sex life was aggressive with S/M aspects. I think she thought I liked to be held down, tied up. At times, I did. But after a fight where she humiliated me and hurt me—I did not. I think the lines became blurred."

In one case, an abusive partner used the idea that the S/M they had toyed with "excused" the abuse. Gita, a South Asian lesbian, age thirty-two, claims,

> Part of what was used against me by her after the rape was the notion that we were in an S/M relationship. Although we had "fooled around" with certain aspects of S/M I certainly hadn't defined our relationship as S/M. Regardless, what she did was absolutely nonconsensual but she was able to gather sympathy or at least disbelief in my story by others by placing it in the S/M context.

Two study participants are active S/M players today and were at the time of their abuses. When Annie, a white lesbian, age thirty-two, was twenty-three, she and her lover were involved in S/M sex when her partner ignored her safeword and anally raped her with a dildo:

> The situation was a pre-agreed reenactment of a rape I'd experienced with a man. She disregarded my safeword. Remember the sex wars? This was then. We thought enacting the rape would give me power over it. She got "caught up" in her own trip. We were both experienced players. It is important to note this didn't happen because of S/M, but because of her power trip—like other rapes.
>
> The community I was part of was very unsupportive, partly because there was such a backlash at the time against S/M as rape. The feminist community I was a part of pretty much blamed my rape on my sexuality (S/M).

Another woman, Deirdre, a thirty-two-year-old teacher and white lesbian, recently ended her relationship. She felt S/M sex was the best part of her otherwise abusive relationship with her partner, who was a stone butch. Her rape, however, was all the more devastating because it involved rape by fisting, what Deirdre felt was the "most spiritual and emotional, intense way of making love that I know of. And we had practiced that as a form of making love together, and it's a huge deal to me. But it's also something that takes time and slowness, and there's nothing violent about it." After a particularly nasty verbal fight,

> [my partner] pinned me on the bed, and she had her boxer shorts on, and she held me pinned with her legs and her arms. And she yanked her boxers down and she took my hand and she physically forced it in her. And I was screaming and trying to pull back, and I was really freaking out and screaming "No." She forced it inside her and she's screaming at me "Is this what you want?" and this and that stuff. And I'm screaming, "Stop, no, don't do this." And she pulls it out of her and grabs me and rips down my pants, and I think I had on a long T-shirt, and I said, "Don't," and she said, "This is what you want." I said, "No, it's not, not this way, please don't do this." And she pried my legs apart and grabbed her hand and forced four fingers inside me and pulled out and forced her fist inside me. . . . In hindsight one of the reasons I guess she did it that way is because it would be the most emotional thing for me. And so she slam-fist raped me and I was screaming "No." I was screaming that she was hurting me, and screaming for her to stop. And she ended up putting her hand over my face and turning my head away, and continued. . . . Later that evening when she came back to say something to me, I looked at her and said, "You raped me." And she looked at me and said, "I gave you exactly what you wanted and exactly what you deserved."

A last story I want to share relates to a woman, Stacy, who was not into S/M herself but did hire a woman to take over gay/lesbian S/M chat rooms and message boards that she managed on the Internet. When this woman invited Stacy out to the coast for some rest, Stacy took her up on it. "When I got there, that's not what it was about. I was held hostage for two weeks. The telephone was taken out. I was locked into an apartment. I was beaten. I was raped repeatedly. . . ." When she convinced this woman she had to return home, they flew to another city where, instead of making a flight connection, "they took me to a house where they had a scene planned. And the exact words were, 'You think you're big enough to play with the big girls and hire us, you need to know what it's all about.' " Stacy escaped with a broken arm, broken shin, and other injuries. She managed to run out of the apartment and get the help of a cab driver. Back at the airport, the police were called, but Stacy refused to press charges out of fear.

My purpose is not to take a definitive stand on whether S/M is *always* abusive or not, but I am sure that S/M can be used as a tool of abuse. I find it difficult to believe it is as easily separated from abuse as proponents claim. To me, it is too pat to say that a player disregarding a safeword during a scene is no longer "really" doing S/M. I wonder what the internal meaning is for individuals who eroticize domination, especially those who are survivors of incest or rape (or both). In those cases, can participants truly give "consent" if their core boundaries have been violated?

It is easy to say as Arlene Lev and S. Sundance Lev do about clients they've worked with who were abused in an S/M context: "[They] needed to learn to set sexual boundaries and choose partners who treated them respectfully. They had to learn to distinguish abusive behavior from safe, sane, and consensual behavior."[37] That's fine *unless you are being abused.* We've certainly learned that abusers undermine our sense of self, destroy our sense of trust of our own judgment, and create conditions in which consent falls victim to power dynamics. This is what abusers do. Given this, I do question whether victims can be in complete control to set boundaries with the sexual dynamics occurring in partnering. Sexuality itself is confusing terrain, sexual behavior not so clear-cut. I've read the argument that being raped is not the same as fantasizing about rape (which seems obvious). But acting out a fantasy is not simply a fantasy either.

Concluding Comments

Where have all these stories taken us? While throughout society we may have thought sexual violence was the province of men, clearly women are capable of inflicting the same terror and harm as men are. The forms of sexual abuse are the same, and the outcomes to the survivors are the same. Female partnering is not automatically egalitarian or nonviolent. Sometimes it is abusive. Our first obligation is to admit that this is so. Those of us who care about these issues have an obligation to the survivors of this violence to end their isolation and to help them heal. We have an obligation to stop these perpetrators from moving on to the next victim.

It is a widely known fact that some men rape; in actuality we know that violence against women by men in our society is pervasive. This fact has been interpreted to mean that any man can be a potential rapist. Movements to stop male rape tend to exclude males except as they are targets of prevention programs or are under arrest facing legal charges. Acknowledging that some women are perpetrators· of sexual violence against other women implies that any woman can be a sexual perpetrator. This places antiviolence activists in a quandary. Who do we target and who do we include in our work?

Perhaps our analysis has been wrong all along. Instead of gender privilege being the source of power and control for males, perhaps power and control are equal opportunity variables available to both women and men, previously hidden in the privacy of interpersonal relationships and unspoken sexual violations, and under layers of homophobia and biphobia. If so, women and men must both be targets of prevention and accountability as well as both be activists addressing hierarchical structures of dominance. Women no longer "know when is the wrong time and where is the wrong place" when it comes to other women.[38]

5

Did She Call It "Rape"?

And when I said to her, "You raped me," she just laughed at me. She said, "That's impossible." (Roxanne)

I have a very difficult time saying, "rape." Mainly because I thought it wouldn't happen to me and if it did it would be a man. (Diana)

I would prefer to hear "sexual assault" and "nonconsensual sex." To me this really defines what is happening. Although it probably is still bottom line "rape." That, rape, has such a male-violence attached to its definition that lesbians would not respond to it. Women sexually assaulting other women really is different—at least in the mind's eye. (Blair)

I know [it was rape] in my mind, in my body, my heart, and my soul. Just, it's hard to talk about it in terms of rape. . . . I'm having some trouble with attorneys, and they're very, very, very uncomfortable with my using the term rape, and I'm not able to stand up for myself quite. It's their gestures, the fact that they're men, the fact that there's two of them in the room and then there's only me. It's the fact that I see disbelief on their faces that a woman could do this. It's all these things. And so, I'm like, well, I guess it wasn't really rape; I guess it's really more of a sexual abuse. (Marielle)

It is no accident that women struggle when we try to name what has happened to us. Within the context of lesbian and bisexual invisibility and societal sexism, females reside in alien territory. Language is a powerful mechanism of oppression. Language encodes our society's values and assumptions; it is the culture's way of classifying and ordering our experience, and it acknowledges what is possible. That women were excluded from the production of language means that our symbolic meanings, our experiences, and our understandings are omitted.[1] According to Dale Spender,

"If the rules which underlie our language system, our symbolic order, are invalid, then we are daily deceived."[2]

Sexism in Language

The sexism in our language, which frames the way we look at these acts, affects the study of sexual assault. Sexist language shapes our cultural understandings of sex acts, which limits us to possibilities ranging from "It isn't possible to rape your wife" to "Women aren't rapists." Muehlenhard, Powch, Phelps, and Giusti remind us:

> Rape, sexual assault, and related terms have the power to label some acts negatively, while ignoring and, by implication, condoning other acts. How these terms are defined affects how people label, experience, evaluate, and assimilate their own sexually coercive incidents. In addition, the definitions of these terms convey numerous assumptions about power and coercion, sexuality, and gender.[3]

There are an endless number of examples of the power of words and of who has the power to choose those words: referring to an African-American adult male as a "boy" or a "black man"[4]; using the term "people with AIDS" or "AIDS victim"[5]; calling a woman who has been raped a "victim" or a "survivor"[6]; or subsuming lesbians and bisexual women under the terms "homosexual" or "gay."[7] These examples point to controlling the dignity or the status of a person, or the invisibility of a person or group. Those in control might be the media, policy makers or legislators, or people outside of the targeted status group.

Other examples of the power of words include the terminology "battered woman," with the term "battered" implying ongoing physical assaults of the woman, while the usage by advocates includes nonphysical forms of abuse which may lead up to physical assault.[8] Many women may not define themselves as "battered" because they have not been physically beaten, yet they are abused verbally, psychologically, or sexually (or all three), and they are at risk. After striving to name the violence against us, advocates and researchers now realize that not all women identify with the established labels. And "domestic violence" sounds like it might not be so bad—*domestic* makes us think of the home and safety, and *domesticated* means "tamed." These terms are problematic when you are labeling potentially lethal situations.

According to Whorfian theory, language is not neutral but itself shapes the way we think.[9] A pertinent example here is the use of *he* and *man* to encompass both males and females. This is, according to Spender, a sexist linguistic structure. Neither women nor men see women in these instances.[10] Robert Baker tells us "humanity" is synonymous with "mankind" but not "womankind." Women cannot be substituted into any sentence. For example, "humanity's great achievements" can be substituted with "man's great achievements," but using "woman's great achievements" does not mean the same thing.[11] The invisibility of women is structured into our thought systems and into our reality, "so that it seems reasonable to assume the world is male until proven otherwise."[12]

Another example of sexism in language is the linking of male with godly and the female with evil, or of male spiritual activities as religion and female spiritual activities as cult. Patriarchal meanings favoring males over females are so common and have been used for so long they seem natural. A male "professional" might be a banker, while a female "professional" can mean a prostitute.[13] Many words for females have sexual overtones or are derogatory, while this is not the case for males. Examples include *master* and *mistress*, *king* and *queen*, *bachelor* and *spinster*. Yet another example is that there are 220 words for a sexually promiscuous woman and only 20 for a sexually promiscuous male.[14]

Invisibility and Silencing

Rich tells us, "In a world where language and naming are power, silence is oppression, is violence."[15] Women know we have been silenced when we cannot name what happens to us, thereby making our experience invisible. We need language to define ourselves, to see ourselves. Through language, we create ourselves.[16] Using language to "come out" as lesbians or bisexual women, as women with experiences not found in language, is a political act, acting against patriarchal control of language. Taking control of language becomes "a weapon in struggle" against a man-made language, which reflects the experiences of men.[17]

Frye points out a clear example of this regarding the impossibility of woman-to-woman sex. Dictionary definitions generally agree that "having sex" relates to intercourse. Intercourse involves vaginal penetration by a penis, with ejaculation. Given this defined usage, where does woman-to-woman sexuality fit in? The lack of acceptable language to express the sexuality of women in same-sex relationships renders this sexuality invisible. Given the heterosexist assumptions in our language, in the absence of men, women cannot be "having sex."[18]

Lesbians and bisexual women have been silenced because of compulsory heterosexuality. Women survivors of sexual violence in same-sex encounters have been silenced because of the perceived danger of admitting our vulnerabilities in a homo- and biphobic society. Women become complicit in a system that silences us or makes us lie, and we forget why we lie as we continue to do so. Rich points out that the danger powerless people run is that we carry the lying into our relationships with those who do not have power over us.[19] We have done this with battered lesbians and bisexual women and with woman-perpetrated sexual violence.

Woman-to-woman sexual violence has been unspeakable, and this unspeakable truth has blocked the dignity of the survivors of such abuse. Similar to the testimonies of women in truth commissions, which Margaret Walker has written about, these unspeakable truths are hindered by survivors' despair or intimidation, lack of vocabularies that are widely accepted and understood, lack of legitimate social and legal standing, and truths and tellers who are discredited by authorities. To challenge these blocks is to challenge an oppressive system.[20] Truths are not only "out there" to be known but rather involve a process of telling and being heard and believed; this telling is linked to the dignity of human beings being able to speak of their lives. As Walker writes, "To have voice is not only to be able to speak, and not only to be able to be heard, but to be able to speak and be heard as saying the kind of thing that you are intending to say."[21] Without this voice, we lose a basic state of "agency, choice and self-understanding."[22]

The Connection between Pain and Power

Inflicting pain is one aspect of wielding power. If pain cannot be expressed, power cannot be challenged. Expressing the experience of physical pain and emotional pain in language is difficult.[23] What is experienced as internal and unsharable is translated into "as if" statements: "It feels as if . . ."; "It is as though. . . ." Elaine Scarry tells us that "the problem of pain is bound up with the problem of power." One element, she says, is that a person can be in the room with another who is experiencing pain without having to know or share that experience in any way; in fact that person can be inflicting the pain and deny that the pain exists. Second, "there is no language for pain. . . . The relative ease or difficulty with which any given phenomenon can be *verbally represented* also influences the ease or difficulty with which that phenomenon comes to be *politically represented.*"[24] (italics in original) Even, for instance, an environment containing torture can be described as if the torture was absent, as when torture is described as "intelligence gathering."

To express the pain of sexual violence, as it is felt physically during the act, as it is felt emotionally during and afterward, words must exist to express our experience of the act. Words must be communicated—and understood—that express the pain and thus implicate the act. Politically oppressed group members will have difficulty stating their case, having their experience validated, if those in power—those in command of the language and of the meanings allowed in the culture—succeed in keeping oppressed members' experience inexpressible and their behaviors defined as impossible. They may be told their experience did not happen; it was not what they experienced. Furthermore, the lack of language makes it impossible to name the relationship of the actors—the powerful perpetrator and the powerless victim. Cultural and legal definitions established by those in power oppress and suppress people and their behaviors. Such is the case for lesbians and bisexual women and for the instance of woman-to-woman rape. Ending invisibility and silence, and hence challenging the political status quo, are the only means for proving we exist and for acknowledging the sexual violence perpetrated by woman-identified women. The expression of the sense of sexual violation women feel from other women must be allowed in order to acknowledge that some women are sexual perpetrators.

What this analysis shows is that language—how it is used and who controls it—is far from simplistic. If the experience of pain cannot be expressed, an aspect of power will not be acknowledged. The meaning of an act is found in the expression of the pain the act causes. The sexism and heterosexism in our language have rendered much of the sexual acts regarding women—lesbian sex, for example—invisible. This is especially the case with woman-to-woman sexual violence, where lesbians and bisexual women have not had the language to express their pain. Combined with the denial of females as perpetrators, this has denied the act of sexual violence. Women experiencing these violations are searching for ways to articulate their pain—in a culture that denies them the words to use for this expression. The following sections demonstrate this search.

Defining Terms of Sexual Violence

In the questionnaire the women answered, I defined sexual violence as

> any unwanted sexual activity. Contact sexual activities include: touching parts of the body, kissing, vaginal penetration by objects, vaginal penetration by fingers, oral sex, anal sex, rubbing, and being forced to do things to yourself. Noncontact sexual activities include forced viewing of pornography or other sexually explicit material and being forced to watch sexual activity of others.

I chose a broad definition of sexual violence because I did not want to exclude women who felt they had been violated sexually but might second-guess what I was looking for. I wanted to learn about the range of sexual violence women were experiencing.

Studies of rape and sexual assault suffer from the lack of universally agreed upon definition of terms, so comparing these studies is difficult. According to a study by Muehlenhard, Powch, Phelps, and Giusti, what some studies call "rape" another study might call "sexual assault" (e.g., comparing Russell with Kilpatrick et al.). Rape might mean penile-vaginal intercourse to one researcher (Russell) or any kind of unwanted sexual activity to others (Veronen and Kilpatrick). Other concepts used in these studies include sexual contact and sexual aggression. Similarly, criteria for establishing nonconsent differ. Some studies may use "when you didn't want to" (Koss et al.), while others use "victim fights, cries, screams, or pleads, etc." (Alder). Other consent factors such as intoxication, economic coercion, or compulsory heterosexuality are considerations for other researchers (Koss et al.; Muehlenhard and Schrag; Rich, respectively).[25]

There is precedent for asking women how they define sexual violence terms before applying labels to their experiences. Linda Bourque asked women in her study for their personal definitions of rape as well as what they thought the legal definition of rape was. She looked for specific concepts from the legal definition to see how closely aligned the definitions were.[26] And Kelly points out that very few studies ask women how they define the terms they are using, even though how acts are defined influences what women do about what happens to them.[27]

I asked my respondents to compare seven concepts: rape, sexual assault, sexual coercion, sexual abuse, rough foreplay, sexual miscommunication, and nonconsensual sexual activity. I was interested in how they defined these terms and how they distinguished one term from another. I also asked them if they used any of these terms to describe what had happened to them at the time. If not, I asked what other labels they did use.

One of my major concerns is how a woman defines sexual violence when the perpetrator is another woman. Are the prior concepts too male-identified as to be useless? Is the language of sexual violence too geared to mean male perpetrator and female survivor, in fact, to mean penile penetration in the case of rape? The answers to these questions are both yes and no. As discussed later, many women initially felt they had no words to describe what had happened to them, yet all of the women were able at some point to use one or more of these terms to label what had occurred.

The most common components mentioned by the study participants of the definition of *rape* were force, lack of consent, penetration, violations of boundaries or trust, and power and control. Typical definitions were: "forcibly penetrating another's body with a body part or object against their will" (Jannette), and "any sexual act that is forced against my will/choice. Also, I include any sexual act that I am forced to perform" (Evon). In more vivid descriptions, Samantha wrote, "I think of a man attacking a woman, like he wants to beat her to death from the inside. Implies struggle, force. It's a really small war." And Stacy defined rape as "when it strikes when I'm totally unaware that it's headed towards me. Like a body slam. I'm taken against all will, no me, nothing. I leave, I dissociate. I cease to be."

Of the women who separately defined the terms, more felt that *sexual assault* was the same or almost the same as *rape*. Many women felt assault implied greater violence and force. To Stacy, sexual assault was "more forceful. For me it's much more frightening. And for me, I have normally come away from it with physical injuries, which required medical treatment. The only time I ever had a broken bone, the only time I've ever been cut with a knife. The only time I've ever been beaten up senselessly . . ." Others mentioned elements of power and control, that it may or may not include penetration, that it was nonconsensual, and that *sexual assault* could be an umbrella term for many types of sexual violence.

The key aspects of *sexual coercion* were being manipulated, persuaded, or talked into sexual activity you did not want to engage in. Annie's definition echoed many others: "Being manipulated, forced through bullying or pressure to agree to a sexual act you didn't want to do." This pressure is primarily verbal and emotional; it "implies psychological/emotional force or pressure" (Monica). Imbalance of power was suggested by Liz, who wrote, "Someone persuading someone to do something they aren't sure they want to do, or should do, or someone being forced to comply by threat of punishment, as in a work situation where a boss threatens to fire an employee who refuses sex." Jannette added that sexual coercion was "being manipulated into performing a sexual act due to an imbalance of power."

Regarding *sexual abuse,* in addition to the nonconsensual element, many women referred to aspects of power and control, ongoing behaviors, and that this type of sexual violence more than any other implies that children are involved. To Christy, sexual abuse is "physical sexual contact other than penetration that is nonconsensual." Nora referred to "sexual contact between an adult and a child, or where there is a power imbalance, i.e., mentally incompetent adult or therapist-client relationship." And Cecile said it "usually applies to a relationship with a structural power imbalance and/or an ongoing dynamic." Others mentioned force, breach of trust, and abuse occurring within the context of domestic violence.

Rough foreplay was the only term on the list that many respondents defined as possibly or probably consensual and enjoyable. However, some felt that it could result in injury, could cause pain, could be used to gain control, or was as Lila said, "highly suspect." Ariel saw rough foreplay as "testing limits." Diana's comment sums up the ambivalence some women had: "It may be enjoyed by some, but may be physically harmful, and lead to a bad sexual experience." For others, rough foreplay heightened sexual arousal and was as Adele said, "fun."

The comments on *sexual miscommunication* fell into two categories: those with straightforward beliefs that one or both people misunderstood verbal or physical cues, and those who felt miscommunication was used as an excuse. In the first case, Leigh's definition is typical: "A lack of communicative clarity between people related to sex—one is unclear as to what the other wants or doesn't want." But Brooke points out that sexual miscommunication might be "the result of a conscious decision or internal resistance to listening to setting and respecting limits." And Allison feels, "If someone is pushing to have sex and the person they are with doesn't communicate well and the person who's pushing doesn't listen or read the person, then it's sexual miscommunication."

The last concept is *nonconsensual sexual activity.* This was regularly defined as a "blanket term which could include all the other terms" (Jill). Nonconsent was a factor in all of the other definitions (excepting miscommunication), so a range of behaviors (e.g., whether penetration occurs or not) is included: "Sex used to gain control over another person" (Courtney);

"Any kind of uncomfortable invasion of space with presence, or words, or actions. Anytime that someone puts her sexual wants before my right to respect" (Marcia); and "Covers any sexual activity that is not agreed to, and to me, is therefore always wrong and unacceptable. It may be different from rape, however, in that it may not be physically forced, or it may happen during otherwise consensual sex" (Liz). Rita felt the term was a "euphemism, neutralizing term for rape and assault," while Stacy said, "that's like waking up and having someone inside you. And yes, that's happened."

The study participants had commonly accepted definitions of what constituted sexual violence. Some specifically mentioned that the sexual violence was ordinarily expected to be male-to-female. As survivors of sexual violence by another woman, this certainly puts them in a dilemma. The predominance of linking penetration with rape has to do with the male-focused language in use. Intercourse has been defined as penis penetration by a male rather than engulfment by a female. The latter gives a distinctly different image of the act and might result in a different understanding of how society labels rape. The current language available to lesbians and bisexual women is limited, with the consequence that our experiences are not given voice. Only certain violations can be acknowledged, and only certain perpetrators can be blamed.

Did She Call It Rape?

We know from numerous studies that heterosexual women frequently do not define forced sex as rape or as a criminal act.[28] As Kelly tells us, "Women must define the incident first as lying outside normal, acceptable or inevitable behavior and, second, as abusive. Contacting support services or answering research questions involves a third step: naming the experience as a particular form of abuse."[29] In this regard, sexual violence against lesbians and bisexual women, as compared with heterosexual women, is similar.

It is significant that women have trouble "naming" these acts, an outcome of the historical exclusion of women from the process of naming and labeling. Additionally, women's gender roles include relationship maintenance. To name the abuse means they are departing from this conciliatory role. This leads to a "double difficulty" for lesbians and bisexual women.[30] Not only do they have to point to a breach of trust in a relationship because of violence, but in a same-sex relationship, they also have to acknowledge that it is other women who are causing the breach of trust to be named.

Lesbians and bisexual women have to overcome both language and gender role socialization.

Initial labels of the sexual violence that other women perpetrated against them varied widely among my participants, but one thing stands out: the label "rape" was rarely used *at first* to define forced sex. "Rape" alone or along with other terms (such as "sexual assault" or "sexual miscommunication") was used for fifteen situations (out of ninety-one) of sexual violence. Four other women used terms other than "rape" but added that privately to themselves they called it rape. For example, Diana said, " 'being taken advantage of' is what I called it to others, but I felt it was rape because I consider rape one of the biggest violations . . . and the feeling that first hits me when I recall the incident is being violated." And Renee used the terms "sexual abuse" and "unwanted penetration," "because sexual abuse is something I feel I'm able to repeat in conversation, with that lingo, without feeling dirty or in denial." Annie, whose situation was S/M sex gone awry, used the term "betrayal." "I felt like I'd been raped and coercion had occurred since I was very uncomfortable with the experiment, but I didn't use those words publicly."

In twenty other situations, participants labeled what occurred with multiple sexual violation terms but did not use "rape"; while in twenty-three situations, women used a single label to describe what happened. Cecile recounts using the terms "coercion," "pressure," "miscommunication"

> when I could bring myself to think about it at all. . . . "Miscommunication" in particular places blame equally on both partners while "rape" and "sexual assault" place blame pretty squarely on the perpetrator. This requires, in my case, admitting that someone I loved and trusted and needed had committed a crime against me. It also involved admitting that women rape, which my relatively unsophisticated feminist consciousness couldn't handle at the time. Also, no one in my immediate community was ready to deal with these things, either. Later, using "stronger" language about it helped me understand, stop blaming myself, and heal.

Aura, thinking back to her abuse as a minor, says, "I can't even recall now what other words I used or fumbled for at the time. That she'd 'seduced' me, that we'd 'slept together,' that she'd violated me, that she'd coerced me, that she'd hurt me."

Words that were used as single descriptors of situations were: "sexual coercion" (seven), "sexual abuse" (five), "nonconsensual sexual activity" (four), "rough foreplay" (two), "sexual miscommunication" (two), "sexual assault" (one), "domestic violence" (one), and "attack" (one).

But for over one-third of the situations (thirty-three) what really stands out is the lack of the use of sexual violence terminology. In half the cases, the women stated they used no label at all. They could not access words to describe their experience; hence no meaning could be established. The experience was there, waiting, in most cases, to be examined at a later date. But for now, it was a disembodied experience. Marianne "tried to pretend none of it happened or that it wasn't real or wasn't painful—I think if you asked me at the time I probably would have covered for her or said it was 'not too bad' or 'consensual.' At the time, however, I didn't have words to describe what was happening." Melanie was in denial: "At the time I forced myself to believe nothing happened. It took me eleven years to say anything to anyone." Polly felt "I had no words," echoed by Marielle: "I had no language to describe [it]."

Some women internalized the problems. Both Nora and Stacy felt there was "something wrong with me." Judy made "a mistake," while Erin was in "a bad relationship." Shelley and Claudia both called their situations "love," while Annie and Aura referred to "betrayal." For Jannette, it was "that stuff she does to me" or "the stuff she makes me do." Missy and Liz labeled their partners "assholes." For Lauren it was "lovemaking," Samantha "sex," and for Rhonda "sex play." Marti saw it as "mindplaying."

Missy's lack of labeling the situation was "mainly defensive. If she was a perpetrator, I was a victim. I don't want to be a victim." Liz tells us, "I didn't label those experiences in sexual terms at the time. The worst I probably did was tell her she was acting like an a——hole. The concepts of 'women together' and 'rape' or any form of sexual abuse just didn't go together in my mind at the time." Samantha

> called it sex. I mean, I was in my early twenties, I came out in the early eighties and I didn't realize at the time how out of control we were. I was scared of being beat by this womon [sic], afraid of pissing her off and getting my butt kicked, but I didn't question what was happening in bed. I did not question it because I was still obeying the message implanted by my grandfather to just "take it."

It is important to acknowledge that not all of the situations were, in fact, rapes as generally understood to encompass the primary elements of penetration, force, and nonconsent. However, the shift from the use of the word "rape" initially in fifteen cases *more than doubled* to thirty-nine uses of the label "rape" later, a significant shift. I use the word "shift" to mean a change in label (and understanding of the experience) regardless of how long it took for the shift to occur. For some women this took days, for others years. Where twenty women used multiple sexual terms to label their violence initially, later seventeen did (of course, some of these had been relabeled "rape," while others were shifts from the "no label" original category). Where originally twenty-three women used a single term to describe their situations, later thirty-one now used a single term. Regarding single terms, "sexual assault" alone accounted for twelve women, "sexual coercion" (six), "sexual abuse" (five), "nonconsensual sexual activity" (four), "sexual miscommunication" (two), and "sexual harassment" (two). Most significant, even if it was years later, *not one woman claimed to have no label to use*, though one woman calls it now "inappropriate behavior" and another "mindplaying," as contrasted with thirty-three not using a sexual violence label at the time of the event. In the vast majority of the cases, the label shifted to a more sexually violent term.

We see these shifts in what is now called "sexual assault," a range of sexual violence terms (but not including "rape"), and what is labeled "rape." For example, of the twelve who now use the label "sexual assault" alone, five had previously called their experiences "sexual coercion" (sometimes combined with "sexual miscommunication"); two had used no label; and others had used terms such as "attack," "rough foreplay," or "threat." Those who used a range of terms (but not "rape") most often went from labels of "nonconsensual sex," "sexual coercion," and "sexual miscommunication" to "sexual abuse," "sexual assault," "sexual harassment," and "sexual coercion." "Love" and "my partner needs help" both changed to the joint labeling of "sexual coercion" and "sexual assault."

Fourteen of the original fifteen "rape" labels stayed the same. Only Allison changed her "rape" label—to "sexual coercion." At the time, Allison named her violence "rape," "but with mild uncomfortability. [It] didn't feel quite right to say rape, since I didn't feel as forced as I could've been was I raped." Women changed their labels to "rape" in twenty-five (27 percent) of the incidents. Original labels that changed to "rape" included: "being taken advantage of" (Diana); "not too bad" (Marianne); "stuff she does to me" (Jannette); "I had no words" (Polly); "rough foreplay" (Rita); "a bad decision," "a mistake" (Judy); "lovemaking" (Lauren); "domestic violence" (Rhonda); no label (Nora, Meryl, Blair, Patti, Brandie, and Liz); "betrayal, nonconsensual sex" (Annie); "the closet" (Meryl); "sex" (Samantha); "coercion, pressure, miscommunication" (Cecile); "sexual miscommunication" (Brooke); "abuse" (Stacy); "something wrong with me" (Stacy); "rough foreplay, nonconsensual activity, sexual miscommunication" (Evon); "she seduced me, she hurt me" (Aura); "sexual coercion" (Jessica); and "sexual miscommunication, nonconsensual sex" (Carlin). What accounted for this renaming for these women?

Shifts in Terms over Time

Changes in a woman's labeling of her sexually violent incident over time are common. As Bergen points out, there is fluidity to the defining of an act as rape, leading to greater accuracy by naming the act.[31] Seventy percent of the sixty heterosexual women interviewed by Kelly changed their definitions over time generally in the direction of relabeling the incident as abusive. Kelly found that in relabeling, the "women were focusing on their own feelings and reactions rather than on stereotypes or limited definitions or the perceptions of others. They were no longer minimizing the severity of the assault(s) or the effects on them."[32] Bergen, studying thirty-five survivors of wife rape, found that most of them gradually came to define their experience as rape.[33] For many of them, the term "marital rape" was not popularly known when they were experiencing their rapes. It would be nearly impossible to name an experience as marital rape when rape was seen as something strangers did to you, not husbands—a parallel to the situation of naming sexual violence by a woman as rape when women are not seen as rapists. The women also looked at levels of physical violence, drawing upon the stereotype that rape is connected with brutal force. With increases in severity of violence, some women changed their definition of what was happening to them.

Often redefinition occurs after the women leave their partners. The process many women go through includes denial, forgetting and remembering, minimizing, and confronting in order to rename.[34] Some researchers find that the process of participating in an interview helps women redefine their experiences,[35] as do other interventions that involve discussing traumatic life events, such as therapy, alcohol recovery, and training to be an advocate for rape crisis or domestic violence.

By far, for those in this study who had a change over time in their label of the sexual violence, therapy was the predominant influence. Twenty-one women mentioned individual or group therapy as helping them to redefine what happened to them. This factor deserves greater examination. Therapists, as experts who listen to secrets others in society might try to silence and whose legitimate role is to examine, name, and give meaning to experience, are in a unique position to facilitate this shift. Jannette writes:

Years later when I was able to describe to a therapist what had happened, I learned that I had been raped and sexually assaulted by these women. My therapist listened to me and then described back to me what had happened as though it happened to someone else. Where I had little concern for myself I was deeply concerned for this fictional other. I am learning to apply the same concern to myself.

Lauren's journey involved dealing with previous abuse:

I ended up in therapy over what my brother did (which I also thought was ok) and described this event. It took the therapist (and group) about six months to convince me to relabel the rapes and the abuse. . . . To be honest with you, I was quite stunned at twenty-something years old to have the person I counseled with tell me that this was rape. It was; I mean, I had a masters, I had a bachelor's degree. I majored in journalism. I knew words, I understood. It just floored me, because everything I had been exposed to growing up was that rape was a man to a woman, and that there was no classification for this.

Marcia's therapist worked with her on a label:

I was almost nineteen when it happened and I used "attack" and just after I turned twenty-three I used the word "sexual assault." My label changed when I started to talk about it, for the first time in four years. I never labeled what happened in the car. I think my counselor had introduced the word sexual assault, along with a few others to get a sense of what I felt like had happened. Sexual assault was the term we came back to again and again, but it was awhile (maybe two or three months) before I'd accept that that's what happened. I didn't want it to be assault. That was something that guys did to women. Women aren't supposed to treat each other that way. We're supposed to know better and respect each other because we're women. But what she did was assault.

For Maureen, "realizing that this was sexual assault, not just pressure to perform sexually" had a big impact. "Influences were counseling by a lesbian counselor who knew about domestic violence and sexual assault in same-sex relationships, and learning about sexual assault. This has been a big influence in me becoming active in DV and sexual assault counseling for others." Leigh, who uses the term "sexual assault" for her experience, has had a similar story:

My label changed six years later when I went through training to become a counselor for survivors of sexual assault and domestic violence. As well, I changed my label for myself from "victim" to "survivor." As well, I got some counseling from a thera-pist specializing in sexual assault and was able to work out my feelings of guilt and shame, and finally feel my feelings and put them in their place instead of allowing this event to overshadow my life. I have "spoken" on TV, on radio, and to groups as a "rape survivor," but that is the only time I use the word "rape"—mostly because it is a word more accessible to the public and the message I want to get across is more important in those settings than the details of what happened to me personally.

Going through alcohol recovery was a major part of the process for Lucy ("My walk through recovery and intense therapy has helped me 'label' my abuse—it helped immensely because it gave validation to my intense feelings."); for Samantha ("Years later, after I got sober and began psychotherapy, that's when I reflected on that dark time of my life."); for Liz ("It changed after I spent some time in Alcoholics Anonymous, and then in therapy. . . . I was telling my sponsor about my relationship/sexual history, and told her about the incident in the car. She labeled it 'sexual abuse.' As I remembered more of that time, I told my therapist and she labeled all of it 'rape.' I began calling it 'rape' subsequently."); and for others.

Getting away from the situation also helped. Courtney found being alone to be a key:

> The influence I think changed it the most for me was my comfort level with being alone. Without her in my life I was without romantic company. The less I perceived I needed someone, anyone in my life, that's when I started calling it assault. Understanding that if I named it assault that I would not let myself go back to seeing her. I would be alone.

Getting away was a major factor for Cecile and for Evon. These were battering relationships in which abuse was hard to name while in the midst of the relationship. Nora tells us,

> I began to label the sexual violence in my [first relationship] as rape and sexual coercion [in the second] many years later. It changed because I realized it was part of the same pattern as the domestic violence—control and reestablishing of control—and that I did not choose to have sex with her in any of the incidents.

Erin fled for survival: "With lots of help I realized I'd been battered. My partner got unequivocally insane so other people started to believe me. The sexual abuse took longer to accept."

Time helped most women as they reflected on what had happened, "grew up" as several women mentioned, or began a slow healing process. "It took a few weeks for the entire event to sink in and what it meant to me.

. . . It was later, after the events that I realized that she had raped me" (Brandie). Time helped with Hannah's denial: "I've come to realize that it was really sexual assault, three to four years later."

Other influences included reading books, improved self-esteem, feeling emotions such as anger, pursuing legal avenues, dealing with previous abuse, education programs, and reaching out to others. In most cases, for the women in this study and in other studies, survivors of sexual violence need help "to revise and restructure their perceptions of what constitutes normal . . . behavior."[36] Therapists, rape crisis counselors, and domestic violence advocates often provide this feedback.[37] Plagued with self-doubt, and often guilt and shame, left with fractured boundaries, and feeling isolated, survivors of sexual violence need their experiences validated and a reality check on what has happened to them. Part of this process includes the redefinition of the events, which women achieve through the claiming of words that give meaning to their experiences.

Patriarchal Words or Just Words?

I argued at the beginning of this chapter that language shapes our approach to the world and that the language we have is patriarchal. Thirty-nine women were able to label the sexual violence against them—violence that was perpetrated by another woman—as rape. Yet, when asked if the term *rape* were male-identified or penetration-identified, most of the women who addressed this issue said it was. Several others felt the problem with the word *rape* was that it was too identified with force, brutality, or intensity. These associations, I would argue, are the result of rape's identification with brutal, particularly sadistic, stranger rape, and with masculinity. Most of the women used the term *rape* even though they felt it was male-identified in the society at large because the word *rape* carries the power to convey the violation of the acts they experienced. Only a handful of women claimed *rape* was a neutral word or a word easily applicable when the perpetrator was a female.

The problem with taking the male-identified word *rape* and applying it to woman-to-woman sexual violence is that society at large denies that women can be sexual perpetrators. Consequently, a disconnect occurs when a woman is called a rapist or a woman tells someone she has been raped by another female. A lack of fit remains between what the word means to the woman who experienced the act and the person trying to understand what happened to her. There is reluctance to view women as perpetrators of violence against children or even as aggressors in nonabusive situations such as women fighting in combat in the military. As Lauren says, "To be honest with you, I don't think straight society thinks about women being with women as rape. I'm not sure they're ready to hear that." Nora and others have been influenced by the notion that rape is male activity: "I have a hard time acknowledging that women can be violent and that a woman can rape another woman." Carole confirms, "The word rape, to me, is, probably because of how the word is used, it's always basically heterosexual." Marti states simply, "When you think of a woman being raped, you think of a man that attacked her." "You almost picture a man raping a woman when you hear the word 'rape,' " admits Giselle. Allison had trouble with other lesbians accepting the term *rape*

> 'cause those words just put women off. Like whenever I said I was raped or assaulted by a woman to a lot of different lesbians, they want me to explain. They can't believe it. It's not always that they don't believe me, it's they can't believe it can happen. And so that's a struggle because then you have the victim having to explain themselves away. If I said I was raped or assaulted by a man, every person I know would jump right on that bandwagon.

Ellen feels that rape has to be especially violent, "like with a broom handle or you have physical evidence of something" for lesbians and bisexual women to begin to admit this happens in our community. Similarly, Margot says, "I think that some women might feel only raped if the assaulting woman used her fist or used a dildo, with horrendous deep penetration . . . being terrified. I don't know, I just think women are so used to knowing that men can rape them that they change things in their minds so that you don't have to be afraid all the time."

But Nina tells us, "I could care less if some think 'rape' is male-oriented. Few women might be raped by another woman, but I was raped by a woman." Brandie came to the conclusion "that it was no different had it been a man or a woman. . . . A lot of women would not label rape between women as rape. Even though that is truly what it is. [It's rape because] of the violation. There could be a lack of penetration and still a sexual act towards another individual that is completely, totally unwanted." Liz found the term *rape* helpful: "It gave me a focus of feelings that I had," but she agrees that it is associated with males. She continues, "I think some feminists would go so far to say that a woman can't rape a woman because she doesn't have a penis. Which I disagree with. . . . I do associate it with penetration, but I would not go so far as to say it always has to be."

If society at large does not accept women as sexual perpetrators, the survivors of sexual violence in same-sex relationships will not find the acceptance of their experiences as valid or the resources they need to cope. Marcia calls for "creating more vocabulary because people aren't gonna initially accept that fact that a woman could rape another woman." Monica proposes another idea:

> I think that one of the most empowering things agencies (and anyone) can do is encourage individuals to define their own experiences. I don't think that there is *a* word that can resonate with "our" experiences because they are as varied as those of any other segment of the population. Yes, rape may be too harsh for some (myself included) but not for others, and it is particularly important to keep that word in the vocabulary of lesbian violence precisely because it holds so much power.

Feminists have fought to label women's experiences as rape, battering, and sexual harassment. We have brought new terms into public use through liberation movement work. For the most part, these were white, middle-class, and heterosexual feminists, who twenty to thirty years ago were not aware of early feminist heterosexism, racism, or classism. The heterosexist meanings embedded in our understanding of interpersonal violence turned out to disadvantage women whose violence is perpetrated by other women. Rather than create new words, perhaps it is more realistic to advocate for new meaning to existing words. There is precedent here in the legal arena, where words are defined in certain ways and their application to situations changes based on new legal meanings. This could be extended beyond the legal arena to the general public.

Whether new word or old word applied with new understandings, *rape* has a huge hurdle to clear in applying to women-perpetrated sexual violence. Throughout our culture, sexual violence is male-associated. It is a challenge to sexism and heterosexism to accept that women are sexual perpetrators. These are not "masculine" women acting out a male behavior; these are women acting out a behavior for power and control. Perhaps when society meets the challenge of accepting that women do in fact perpetrate sexual violence we will be clearer on what to label the acts they perpetrate. In the meantime, it appears sexual assault counselors, therapists, and domestic violence advocates will continue to apply the male-dominated language in use and continue to influence the many survivors that make their way to their offices. But advocates should be heartened by the voices that are now raised to break silence. As Mary Daly tells us, women create new meaning through listening to each other—listening to the reality of our lives,[38] that there are female perpetrators and female survivors of rape. What was previously hidden and unaccounted for now needs to be acknowledged. Most important, this acknowledgment allows us to challenge models of power and control more forthrightly.

6

The Emotional Impact
of Sexual Violence

I was terrified and mistrustful of everyone I met and knew. I had constant night-mares. I eventually began studying karate in a "dangerous" part of town with the purpose of learning to seriously injure or kill people. I trained three days a week, always living in fear that someone was "after me." It took me eight years before I stopped looking over my shoulder. For a week after my assault I slept at a friend's house with a loaded shotgun under the bed, refusing to leave the house, carrying the gun from room to room with me. (Leigh, fifteen years ago, kidnapped by her best woman friend and her boyfriend, held for three days, and forced to perform sexual acts)

I found all this brought up for me memories of past sexual harassment from jobs I've held and [from] teachers. The fact that it was from another woman also made me realize how much more I was willing to accept from her in the form of abuse and how that serves neither she nor I. I'm dealing with it by working on my 'zine. This issue is focusing on sexual harassment. (Jude, sexually harassed by a college classmate within the past year)

I have a lot of safety issues around touch/physical contact. High anxiety, mixed feelings [of] pleasure and fear. Many times I will numb out or dissociate. I carry a lot of emotional tension in my body. Part of me associates touch = sex = rape. I've avoided intimate relationships. I struggle with depression. (Nora, recurring sexual violence within a battering relationship, fifteen years ago)

Every woman who is included in this study has experienced sexual violence by a woman at least one time. That is difficult enough for her to admit and cope with. But an astounding 71 percent of the participants also have incest (which includes a few cases of statutory rape) in their background, and just over half (51 percent) have been raped at least once by a male. Forty percent have both incest and rape by a male in their life experience. These reflect much higher rates of victimization compared with most studies of sexual violence. For example, the currently accepted national rate for incest is that one in four females (25 percent) is sexually abused by the time she is eighteen years old.[1] A survey on lesbian health by Judith Bradford and Caitlin Ryan found that 21 percent of their sample had been sexually abused as children.[2] In Loulan's survey of 1,566 lesbians, 38 percent were sexually abused before age eighteen.[3] This matched Diana Russell's 1986 findings of 930 women in San Francisco (also 38 percent). In a study of battered women inmates in California, Elizabeth Leonard found rates of 55 percent of childhood sexual abuse and 48 percent of childhood sexual assault.[4] Sue Blume believes the number is more likely to be closer to more than 50 percent of all women because many women do not remember their childhood sexual trauma until late in life, if at all, because of repression.[5]

While I can't explain the much higher numbers in this study, I do not doubt them. I do not believe that women who are abused seek out or are attracted to abusers later in life. Rather, I think it is an unfortunate reality that there are many abusive people in society who seek to control others. While there may be a certain "familiarity" with abuse, making it more difficult for a victim to identify it when it is happening, I do not accept that anyone willingly wants to be abused or mistreated. Another consideration is that women who experience multiple traumas are more likely to identify the traumas they have gone through as abusive rather than minimize them. With each successive traumatic event, they may be more likely to see earlier experiences as abusive. They may have gone to therapy or read books on sexual trauma; they learn to identify and name the events. In what follows, I look at how trauma has affected these women. How does it affect their daily lives, and did the incest and previous male rapes affect how they dealt with their sexual assault by women?

Impact of Incest

According to Christine Dinsmore, "Incest survivors often feel different from the rest of the world. . . . In our heterosexist culture, lesbians, too, feel different."[6] Consequently, a lesbian or bisexual woman who is also an incest survivor may deny her lesbian or bisexual identity to feel "less different." She may feel the incest caused her lesbianism or bisexuality, an idea reinforced by living in a homophobic society. This, of course, is contrary to the knowledge that sexual identity is a natural part of the self and is not "caused" by external influences. Research does not show a connection between sexual victimization and sexual orientation.[7] Dinsmore points out, "The connection is based on the misconceptions of a culture in which heterosexuality is assumed to be the healthy norm, and in which lesbian existence is assumed to be an unhealthy deviance in need of explanation."[8] Still, internalized homophobia and biphobia compound the problems of misogyny for the incest survivor who is a lesbian or bisexual woman.

In my survey, fifty women (out of seventy) are survivors of incest (a betrayal of trust in overt or covert sexual acts over a child or adolescent, which I am defining as under the age of eighteen, including statutory rape). For only five women was the incest a one-time event. For thirty-one women, the incest took place over a period of years. Twenty women named one perpetrator. Thirty women had two or more perpetrators. I am looking at a group of women who have been repeatedly abused, usually as very young children, and by several different perpetrators. While the sex of the perpetrator was sometimes not specified, the majority is male. Perpetrators named include (in order of frequency mentioned): fathers, boyfriends, mothers, uncles, neighbors, cousins, male cousins, brothers, male and female baby-sitters, sisters, stepfathers, family friends, grandfathers, neighborhood boys, acquaintances, family members, and mother's boyfriend. Mentioned one time each were: priest, teacher, foster mother, minister's son, father's male friends, grandfather's girlfriend, mother's female lover, sister's boyfriend, set designer, female talent agent, day care workers, older kids, someone else, male friend of family, brother-in-law, half-brother, bus driver, and male buyer for alcohol.

Women with a history of sexual abuse as children tend to experience a range of problems in their adolescence and adult life. These may include adolescent "acting out" (delinquency involvement, school troubles, conflict with authorities, promiscuity, prostitution often connected with running away), sexual difficulty, depression, guilt, poor self-esteem, feelings of inferiority, promiscuity, alcohol and drug dependency, self-destructive behaviors, dissociation, isolation, anxiety, suicidal feelings or attempts, and relationship problems.[9]

David Finkelhor and Angela Browne apply a model in which four trauma-causing factors are used to analyze incest impacts. The four factors, which they call traumagenic dynamics, are traumatic sexualization, betrayal, powerlessness, and stigmatization. Finkelhor and Browne report that children who have been traumatically sexualized "emerge from their experiences with inappropriate repertoires of sexual behavior, with confusions and misconceptions about their sexual self-concepts, and with unusual emotional associations to sexual activities."[10] Betrayal refers to the feeling that results when someone you depended on (a family member or other trusted person) has caused you harm. Betrayal comes into play even with strangers if the child has felt taken in by that person. This sense is enhanced when children are not believed, are blamed, or are ostracized after disclosure. Incest is "a rape of trust," according to Blume.[11]

Powerlessness results when a child feels an inability to function when actions are done against her will or from an inability to stop the abuses. The child learns she must surrender in order to survive.[12] Fear adds to a sense of powerlessness, as does the response of disbelief if she discloses. Stigmatization, or the feelings of shame, guilt, and badness, may become incorporated into the child's sense of self in a number of ways. The abuser may blame the child for the behavior, she may be pressured to keep secrets, and she may hear about acts such as these in the community or family connected with negative associations. After disclosure, she may find herself negatively labeled and may internalize shame.[13]

Grief is another powerful emotion children deal with following incest. They grieve the loss of the safety of family, the loss of innocence and freedom of childhood. The world as a safe place is also lost.[14] Children rarely are able to get help for their abuse at the time it occurs. This is most likely because so many perpetrators are family members, the very people she needs to turn to for help. Yet, the impact is deep and can be lifelong if left unresolved. As Jannette said, "That's the first place, that's where you learn how much power you're going to have. And then you learn that you don't have any power, and that's going to have to be relearned someday."

Most of the women in the survey who spoke about this issue felt their incestuous abuse did affect how they dealt with their adult sexual violence because it had remained unresolved. On the other hand, Melanie, who was sexually abused at age nine and again at age thirteen, felt that her blocking out her adult sexual assault was unrelated to her incest. She said, "I never let anyone know in my family of either incident, but as I was a teenager dealing with other issues, I did discuss and resolve any unresolved issues I had regarding them." Russell points to some reasons why childhood incest might not be as traumatic for some children as others: the incident might have been relatively minor, such as kisses or touching, the perpetrator might have been a distant relative or unimportant person to the child, or the abuse might have occurred only once. Some children might have been able to stop the abuse from becoming more serious and felt competence rather than paralysis.[15]

For some women, the woman-perpetrated sexual violence they experienced as an adult pushed resolution of the past incest. Roxanne, a survivor of incest by her stepfather at age seven and then of sexual assault and rape by a woman when in her fifties, says,

I didn't realize I hadn't resolved it, I just kept pushing it back, I guess. And I didn't really start resolving it until I got counseling for all this other. So, it's taken a long time. I still go to counseling in group. I have days when it's just really hard. And, one thing that really, it's hard to really trust anyone anymore. And as I look back I realize I hadn't trusted anybody most of my life.

Claudia, age forty-nine, didn't have memories of her childhood abuse by her parents until she was in her late thirties, starting therapy. She feels her sexual abuse as a sixteen- and seventeen-year-old by a high school teacher was definitely connected to being "incredibly needy and probably an obvious target." When she confronted her family with the childhood abuse, they disowned her. Still, her actions helped in her resolution because she not only faced it but also had warned her sister to protect her children from their grandmother.

Other women also wanted to protect children from abuse. Samantha, whose abuser seduced a teenager in her presence, worried that one of her abuser's other girlfriends had a young daughter who might be at risk. Given Samantha's background of incest by her grandfather and his girlfriend, and by baby-sitters, she felt it "was too close for comfort [to] repeat in my young adult life." She was concerned about the "predatory-like nature" of her abuser and said that "out of the whole thing that's what still eats me up inside." Meredith reported her abusive partner to child protective services. Sensitized by her own incest when she felt vulnerable, she did not tolerate the sexualizing of her partner's daughter and took action. Meredith was abused by her father at a very young age, and raped three different times by different men in her early twenties. She felt these experiences delayed her realization of her adult abuse by two different women: "It took me longer to come to the opinion I have now because of what happened to me when I was young. Maybe I was surprised and thought that women were different than men, and then I thought well, maybe that's just the way life is. . . . It made it easier for me to discount the way I felt and how I thought."

Annie feels that her incest and date rapes affected her choice of adult partners on an unconscious level. While not a weak person, she always chose "extremely domineering people." Shelley, who never told anyone about her childhood abuse by her father, a baby-sitter, and a neighbor because she didn't feel she'd be believed, feels it affected her self-esteem. There would, therefore, be a connection between these events and her adult abuse. Brooke, a survivor of incest by her father, has begun to connect that abuse with her abuse at age sixteen by an older female coworker: "I am beginning to see that this is connected to a lot of things, including my childhood sexual abuse experiences. She would comfort me. She would make me laugh. I could call her when I was upset. She would hold me, pat [my] head, and we could sit like this talking. It was these kind of moments that I needed so much."

Several women have experienced statutory rape (which they called date rape), which they felt had had repercussions. Olivia felt she suffered from a lot of guilt out of her sense of responsibility from her incest at five years old and especially her date rape at fourteen years old. In the latter case, she felt she "got myself into that situation. [But] today I would say there was no way that that person should have done that. They were totally responsible because they were an adult and I was a child." Monica's boyfriend pressured her for sex when she was sixteen. She felt this was important because it was "my first sexual experience in which I learned to focus on my partner's needs and to be completely oblivious to my own. . . . I had also learned, as a woman, to be other-directed and caretaking all the time, and that extended through all aspects of my life including into sex. That left me ill-prepared to have any other sort of experience with women." Blair's date rape at sixteen left her very cautious with men: "I no longer trusted any and even very few people for a long time. I had to grow confident with my boundaries. I didn't tell anyone because I didn't know what it (assault) was or where to go or how to take care of myself in this dynamic. I lacked the confidence to say, 'Hey, this happened to me!' "

Impact of Rape by a Male

In the survey, males had raped thirty-six women at least once as an adult eighteen or over. Two of them had children as a result of their rapes. While most of the rapes were one-time events by a single man, it is hard to calculate the total number. Most of the women reported "several rapes" or "many times." "Thousands of times" was reported by one woman who formerly was involved in prostitution. It would be safe to say that there were over one hundred rapes in this survey count. Only sixteen of the women (out of thirty-six) had been raped only one time. Perpetrators (all males) included acquaintances, employers, boyfriends, strangers, friends, classmates, police officer, building superintendent, neighbors, deputy sheriff, husbands, boyfriend's uncle, salesman, doctor, coworkers, and prostitution tricks. The majority of the rapes occurred when the women were in their twenties.

The most commonly cited impacts of rape found in the literature include fear, vulnerability, depression, negative impact on sexual satisfaction, promiscuity, prostitution, suicide attempts, loss of trust, loss of self-esteem, loss of a sense of control over one's life, loss of confidence, drug abuse, and flashbacks. Many concrete losses may be experienced, such as loss of jobs, relationships, and the ability to drive or to leave the house.[16] The ongoing sense of fear, guilt, numbing out, nightmares, trouble concentrating, and reexperiencing the memories of violence are referred to as *posttraumatic stress disorder*, or PTSD.[17] PTSD is seen as resulting from a trauma outside the realm of normal human experience. In the American Psychiatric Association's *Diagnostic and Statistical Manual of Mental Disorders*, third edition, revised (*DSM-III-R*), rape is one of the many events that can lead to PTSD. Posttraumatic stress disorder is also quite common among battered women.[18]

Patricia Resick's 1993 overview of the psychological impact of rape pointed to fear and anxiety as the most frequently noted symptoms. She cites a study by Kilpatrick, Edmunds, and Seymour wherein they estimated that 3.8 million adult women have had rape-related PTSD and that 1.3 million women currently have rape-induced PTSD.[19] Many studies in Resick's review noted depression as likely, and suicidal thoughts and attempts were found to be much higher among rape victims than nonvictims. In looking at social adjustment, work adjustment suffered the most compared with marital, parental, and family adjustment.

Most studies found that sexual dysfunctions are among the longest lasting problems of rape victims. This includes avoidance of sex altogether, less sexual activity, and less sexual satisfaction. Kelly found that sexual violence affected women's attitudes toward sex in several ways. Because sex triggered memories of abuse, some women chose to be celibate. Some women expected all sex to be coercive and so avoided it. Many women viewed sex as dirty. For others, promiscuity became a way to seek a type of revenge and a way of expressing anger. The need for sexual control became dominant in their sexual relations.[20]

Warshaw, in discussing date and acquaintance rape, points to seven reactions survivors tend to experience: denial that a man they know harmed them, dissociation during the actual rape, self-blame that they must somehow be responsible, self-doubt and ignoring inner signals that something is wrong, not fighting back because of fear or socialization to think of others before themselves, not reporting the rape because of expected responses of disbelief or blaming, and, because of these prior reactions, putting themselves in a situation to be raped again by the same person.[21]

In Kelly's research on women who had experienced incest, rape by men, and domestic violence, the primary long-term consequences were negative impact on attitudes toward men, negative impact on attitudes to sex, flashbacks, nightmares, cues that reminded them of their abuse, and forgetting or cutting off to cope. Forgetting is often a coping strategy to deal with the violence, and while remembering through dreams and flashbacks is painful and draining, it is, to some extent, essential in the process of dealing with the past.[22]

Safety and security, which are basic needs in our daily lives, is threatened if the perpetrator is a family member or friend with whom survivors will repeatedly come into contact. The vulnerability that women feel if they have been assaulted in what they thought was a "safe place" may lead to coping strategies involving new behavior changes (keeping doors locked, adding new locks, carrying a weapon, not going certain places, not going places alone, and so forth). A sense of distrust of men is affected by who the abuser was, how survivors explained the man's behavior, and the reaction to the violence by others. This distrust may extend to women if mothers or other women did not believe or failed to support them.[23]

Ronnie Janoff-Bulman and Irene Frieze propose a framework that organizes the psychological responses of victimization into three areas: the belief in personal invulnerability, the perception of the world as meaningful where everyday life makes sense, and the view of the self as positive. Victimization shatters these assumptions, and coping means dealing with this fracture. Redefining the events, searching for new meaning, reestablishing control over the environment, and social support from friends and family and possibly through therapy all help in the healing process.[24]

Emotional Impact of Sexual Violence from a Woman

The consequences I now discuss cannot be separated out from previous sexual abuse experiences of incest or rape by men as adults. Rather, meaning and response are constructed based on those events as well as the contexts of homophobia, biphobia, transphobia, heterosexism, lesbian community myths, and societal ideas of women and violence.

Many women described a state of devastation after their sexual violence. Kara, whose partner hit her, restrained her with binds, and raped and sodomized her with a dildo, said, "I was totally and completely devastated, both physically and emotionally." Hannah said, "I was completely shattered. I had subjected myself to contact with another abuser and could not believe that a woman would do that to another woman," after her partner tried to force herself on her and became violent when she resisted. Hannah ended up in the hospital after the ensuing struggle. Bea, who had two different lovers abuse her sexually, felt "very vulnerable, insignificant, de-humanized, disrespected, confused, guilty, ashamed, dirty, weak, stupid, wary, untrusting, angry, betrayed."

Depression and suicidal feelings were common. Erin felt "devastating depression; lacking confidence; isolation and wariness; guilt and self-hatred" after sexual exploitation by a professor/advisor in college. Carlin "withdrew from life" after her battering relationship, which included forced sex when she was ill, ended. After Lucy's girlfriend tied her to a bed and raped her with a broom handle when they were both drunk and high, she was suicidal: "It nearly killed me," she said. "I had to choose to live. First I stopped drinking and drugging, and then, years later, the deepest depression set in. The total impact has made me also a recovering sexual addict. It is still a daily struggle."

Aura also struggled with devastating effects from an older woman who manipulated her into sexual activity when she was a minor: "I was already suicidal and self-destructive and deeply unhappy due to the amount of abuse and neglect I'd lived through in my family and earlier life. This experience destroyed the budding trust and hope I'd had in venturing into this world of women and damaged my sexuality and ability for intimacy in ways I still haven't healed." Sixteen years after her first experience with a female abuser, Aura was sexually abused by her doctor/employer, with deep consequences:

> I felt my life was over when she fired me. I had never trusted anyone so deeply or let anyone so far inside my private self. . . . I was in full-blown post-traumatic stress mode with constant flashbacks for at least three years and still am affected on a daily basis. I'm also confused about the sexual element. I haven't dated or been involved with anyone since then, and am certain that to do so would bring up a lot of unresolved feelings from this experience.

Several other women mentioned flashbacks and nightmares. Marianne, a survivor of incest and a four-year battering relationship with frequent sexual violence, said the impact of her abuse included "flashbacks, fear, pain, a sense of haunting, a sense of defeat that I hadn't managed to escape my childhood after all, incredibly low self-esteem, nightmares, a wish to die or hurt myself physically, hopelessness." Gita's losses were many after her abusive ex-lover returned for "one last time":

> I cried much more easily, I felt like my emotions controlled me completely—and throughout my life I have kept them well controlled. I was scared. I was numb, and I felt a complete inability to give love or care to somebody else. Nonemotional. I became dyslexic. I lost my sense of direction (literal). I could no longer multitask. I sold my vehicle because I couldn't deal with the stress.

Denial, numbing out, or blocking what had happened were not uncommon reactions. Melanie told me she "immediately had no emotional response. I simply blocked out what had occurred. Years later, the emotional impact was so great I quit a $50,000 a year job, was unemployed, went through two years of therapy, and had to learn a lot of new behaviors, patterns, and emotional responses." This was after two acquaintances she had known for only a few hours raped her while a third knew what was happening. Judy was "deadened to the experience." Lauren "buried the pain as I had done with the early childhood experiences." Stacy "dissociated," as did Nora and Lila. Courtney and Brooke "numbed out."

Most women did not mention anger, though Lila referred to her "consuming anger." Margot, who was raped by a much younger woman who stalked and harassed her, said, "I was terrified, angry, humiliated, disgusted with myself for being so wimpy and weak, and so scared. Then later, when I found out I was 'just a statistic' to her, I felt even more humiliated. She did it to 'put me in my place,' etc., so more anger and fear."

Several women discussed sexual problems, usually low interest or holding back. A few women said they experienced confusion about their sexuality. Monica has "ongoing discomfort with sex and I 'shut down' sometimes—but I'm not sure where that comes from. I'm working on it in therapy right now." Some women went into therapy because of sexual problems in their relationships, such as Patti, who felt "stressful, lonely, sad, angry, all internalized! I was numb. Now, I have PTSD and once after that with my partner couldn't have sex until we went to therapy." Polly is healing, "but it took me years to get here. The rape in itself was bad enough but it also caused confusion with my sexual identity." Brandie is "now more reserved sexually. Certain actions on the part of a lover trigger memories that put me right back in the experience." Brandie's girlfriend showed up at her house in the midst of their breakup and raped her—the first time by tying her up, the second time by brandishing a knife. Several women chose to be celibate for a period of time or permanently (Missy, Ellen, Olivia, and Nora, for example).

The symptoms of feeling fragile, hopeless, and worthless figured prominently into the emotional aftereffects of sexual violence for many women. To make sense of your world and to view yourself in a positive light is difficult when you feel as Ariel and Jannette did: "I felt hopeless and worthless and doomed to a life of being exploited to the benefit of others and used and abused" (Jannette); and "It has scarred me emotionally. I have had to overcome feelings of helplessness and unworthiness. I continue to battle with self-esteem and being a victim—which makes me feel less than I am" (Ariel). Meredith, after two violent relationships, said, "I felt shame because I thought (although I wished for different intimate relationships in my life) these relationships were what I *deserved*. I felt disappointed and depressed and doomed to sacrifice my self-respect for love, or else be single." Echoed by Jessica, "I felt like I somehow deserved it, though I couldn't see why." These feelings were certainly reinforced by comments from abusive partners, such as this one from Courtney's partner who, when Courtney tried to explain why certain behaviors were difficult for her, replied, "I don't want to hear about any of that incest crap."

Looking back at Warshaw's typical reactions to date and acquaintance rape, we see that all of them hold in the case of date and acquaintance rape by women.[25] In different combinations, it was common among the survivors to find the denial that a woman they knew could hurt them, dissociation during the assault, self-blame, self-doubt, putting others' needs ahead of their own, not reporting the violence, and repeated victimization by the same perpetrators.

Women's Response to Victimization

The majority of women did not respond immediately to their victimization. This is not a surprise given the consequences discussed earlier. Some women did tell friends, and in one case the woman told "anyone who would listen, in excruciating detail" (Aura). Some went to therapy. A few called police or a battered women's shelter agency. More women, though, waited months or years before talking about the sexual violence. Some in therapy at the time of the sexual assaults did not discuss them. Many waited until the relationship was over before talking about what had happened. In general, there is a delayed reaction to dealing with the sexual violence. The reasons for this are the interrelated impacts of previous violence, homophobia, biphobia, and fear of not being believed because the perpetrator was a woman.

I asked participants to look back on how they had responded and to think now about what they wish they had done differently. While a few women felt there was nothing they could have changed—"I was in no condition at the time to do anything differently" (Carlin); "Looking back, my actions were appropriate for my mental state. I was used to abusive behavior from a 'loved one.' I had learned to be submissive" (Lenore); "During the incident, I do not believe I *could* have done anything different. I believe I did only what I could do to survive" (Melanie)—most women identified something they wish they had done. These actions fall into the categories of telling others, seeking help (therapy or police or agency), leaving, and recognizing their needs and acting in their own best interests.

Lucy states, "I wish I would have had one single adult in my life who I could have bonded with—told the truth and who would have believed me. No one in my hometown would believe me, even to this day." And Nora also feels telling would have helped: "I wish I would have confided in my best friend about the sexual coercion and rape. She had been my 'reality check' in other aspects of the relationship. I might have felt less shame had I told her instead of keeping this *secret*." Christy had several opportunities to tell others, but did not. She was protecting her abuser—and also frightened of her:

> I wish I would have told my friends. I hid it from them, made excuses. I even denied it when they asked. My friends were finally the ones who got me out of it. I feel that the relationship could have ended earlier if I had told them sooner. I also wish that I would have been honest at the hospital regarding how I got the injury. The one incident when I went to the hospital, I told the nurse and doctor I hurt my knee moving furniture. I should have told them she hurt me and maybe they could have helped.

Seeking help from a therapist, an agency, or the police looked like a better option in retrospect years later than it did at the time when survivors felt shame, feared their abuser, or were uncertain of police response. Deirdre, for example, said, "I wish I had reported [the rape] to the police that day but it would have been traumatic and caused more problems." The threat of harm from the perpetrator held some women back: "I wish I would have gone to the police immediately—but I was afraid she would kill me,"

Roxanne recounts. Several women wished they had entered therapy or told their therapist at the time of the violence. And agency support might have been helpful, but many did not know if they'd be welcomed as lesbians or bisexual women: "I wish I had called our local womyn's shelter. I didn't know they were there. I now know it would have been safe. At the time I wouldn't have believed that" (Polly).

Leaving was a common wish for both long-term and short-term relationships. Kara relates that she wishes "I would have left her immediately instead of hanging around for another two years—waiting for her to kill me." From a different motivation, Carole recounts, "I should have pushed her off of me and left the room. I wasn't ready to deal with the consequences of leaving. After all, it was just an hour of my month to keep the peace between us." Most leaving comments were to have left after the very first incident, whether dating or in a relationship. Many wished they had never met or gotten involved with the women—a leaving before the fact.

The most common type of response related to wishing for courage or more self-awareness to act in self-interest. A good example of this is Jannette's comment: "In both relationships I wish I'd have had the courage and self-regard to set clear boundaries and not relinquish so much of my own power over my own life to another woman. A healthy person would have either ended or scaled back both relationships long before the sexual violence occurred." Monica feels she wasn't acting in her self-interest: "I wish I had said something to her when she started touching me. I wish I had realized what was going on and trusted myself enough to say it's not okay." Several women wished they had had the inner strength to resist physically: admits Judy, "I wish I had been 'stronger' during the incident—to have fought back or resisted more, but I wasn't in that place yet . . . also as I mentioned before there was a lot of emotional manipulation and confusion and I had torn loyalties to myself and my friend." Marcia wishes she had taken more direct action as well:

> I wish I had kicked her out of the car. I wish I hadn't ever given her a ride home. I wish I left her at the club. I wish I had elbowed her in the face. I wish I had punched her in the stomach or anywhere I could. I wish I had prevented the whole thing. I wish when I had seen her afterwards and she tried to talk to me, that I had punched her square in the face and knocked her out cold. I wish I had known what to do. I wish I had known that women could hurt you the same way that men could.

Several women wished they could have defended themselves; however, there were women who did fight back with mixed results—either the assault stopped or they were hurt worse.

Revictimization Issues

Evidence indicates that victims of childhood sexual abuse are more vulnerable to further sexual violence in childhood, adolescence, and later adulthood.[26] Some studies show a high rate of sexual revictimization as adults of those sexually abused in childhood—between two-thirds and more than three-fourths.[27] Mary Koss and Thomas Dinero found that sexual abuse during childhood was one of the best predictors of sexual victimization as an adult over other factors.[28] Gidycz, Coble, Latham, and Layman found that a history of childhood or adolescent sexual abuse led to increased risk of adult sexual victimization. They pointed to factors of poor adjustment and unresolved trauma.[29]

Several theories exist to account for these high rates of revictimization. Finkelhor and Browne, as discussed earlier, offered a model of trauma-genic dynamics.[30] Koss and Dinero proposed a vulnerability hypothesis that focused on previous child sexual abuse, liberal sexual attitudes, and above average rates of sexual activity as an adult as factors predictive of adult rape.[31] Jianfang Chu suggested that dissociation and posttraumatic stress symptoms made victims vulnerable to revictimization.[32] Liz Grauer-holz offers an ecological model to examine this link. This model considers personal, interpersonal (family and intimate relationships, and formal and informal social structures), and sociocultural factors (cultural values and belief systems) that combine to contribute to sexual revictimization. The ecological model differs from the others in expanding the examination from factors of the individual alone.[33] In other words, the individual is placed in a context.

Personal factors include aspects stemming from the initial victimization, such as traumatic sexualization, alcohol and drug abuse, dissociative disorders, powerlessness, stigmatization, learned expectation of victimization, and so forth. Early family experiences such as family dysfunction and breakdown are also part of personal history. Interpersonal factors include risks that increase exposure to abusers, such as alcohol and drug use, involvement in deviant activities, stigmatization, and others. Other interpersonal considerations relate to increased aggression by the perpetrator, such as seeing the victim as an easy target, feeling justified in acting aggressively, and the victim's decreased ability to respond defensively and effectively to stop the sexual aggression. Structural factors include lack of resources related to poor economic position, early childbearing, and unsafe living conditions, as well as lack of alternative sources of support because of weak family ties and social isolation. Sociocultural factors include the cultural tendency to blame the victim and viewing victims as "bad girls."[34]

These categories flow one into the other, with some predisposing the development of others. However, many questions remain about how these factors work together, whether they are all necessary (or only some), the relative importance of each, whether each additional victimization makes one increasingly vulnerable, and so forth. What the ecological approach does is to move beyond individual explanations of victimization into examining the complex interactions of the contexts in which individual lives are lived.[35] Furthermore, this analysis points to social change elements that could decrease sexual victimization.

Of the fifty women who had incest in their background, twenty-eight of them were raped by a male (56 percent). Of the twenty women who had not experienced incest, eight were raped by a man (40 percent). Since all of the women had been sexually violated by a woman, the majority had repeated sexual victimizations throughout their lives. While too many variables are involved to definitively state a connection, it is clear that the impacts of sexual abuse through incest and rape (by male or female) are severe and long lasting. It appears that women sexually violated by women experience the same impacts as when they are violated by men. Physical illness, food bingeing, intestinal distress, low self-esteem, sexual problems, depression, fear, and anger were problems most of the women were left with as a result of their sexual abuses. Healing from this kind of distress is challenging under the best circumstances (which most women did not have).

Women who endure multiple victimizations need personal and societal supports, therapeutic intervention, and legal assistance in many cases. The ability to get these supports runs contrary to the state that many survivors are in at the time of their abuses. Those who reached out were often rebuffed. Instead of reaching out, many turned inward. If a woman is terrified of everyone, mistrustful, doesn't tell anyone, and doesn't want to leave her house, she cannot receive support.

Many eventually took direct actions in which they used their experiences to help others. Almost one-third (31 percent) of the women have in the past worked or presently work as a volunteer or staff member at a rape crisis agency or domestic violence agency. Aura is involved in self-defense work and sees that as a positive step toward trauma resolution in her own life and that of other women around her. Lauren is involved with victim impact panels in her state. She and others talk to offenders, police officers, and others involved in restorative justice efforts to educate and raise sensitivity to the survivors' perspective. She generally talks about her incest by her brother and her rape by a male. She has yet to discuss her rape by a woman, but sees that as a real possibility. However it is done, it is necessary to turn the experience of victimization—being a victim of someone else—into the state of surviving—being a survivor who has healed and overcome.

7

Heterosexism in the Legal System

I never considered legal response because one, she had a law degree and loads of friends who were/are lawyers, and two, I didn't want this kind of exposure and discussion about the incident in front of straight policemen, judges, courts, [and] court recorders, who, I thought, would go home and have either sick fantasies or ideas of violence. (Gita)

My own homophobia combined with the typical victim approach of deserving what I got prevented me at the time [from seeking legal help]. Subsequent events, however, have led me to believe that other people were victimized, and if I had reported this occurrence, someone else might have been spared. (Oona)

And [the police officer] put his hand on me and he said, "Are you okay? You don't have to put up with that." And at the time I didn't, I couldn't access that at that moment. He didn't even use the word "rape." I think if he had used that word "rape," I would have said, "Well, no." But he did understand what I was saying. He used the word "that." He said, "You don't have to put up with 'that.' " (Marianne)

I think it would be safe to say that any woman in our society would have mixed feelings about turning to the legal system in the aftermath of sexual violence. Though states have passed rape shield laws, many lawyers, judges, or jury members often still expect something in the survivor's previous sexual behavior or background to be related to the present rape (though inadmissible in court). Rape law reform of the early 1980s also did away with the need for corroborating witnesses or evidence of physical resistance. But the rape survivor continues to be suspect for the crime against her. Rape remains a highly stigmatized event in the survivor's life.

The Presumption of Heterosexuality

When it comes to lesbians and bisexual women, there are further problems. For the lesbian or bisexual woman raped by a man, well, he had to set her straight. In his twisted mind, she needed this sexual experience because of her own perversity. Because of homophobia, some people think that perhaps she deserved what she got. But heterosexism in the legal system is the main block for women whose sexual violence is by another woman. The presumption of heterosexuality slants the way the laws are written and applied, and makes lesbians and bisexual women either invisible or people whose behavior is illegal.

As an element of patriarchy, heterosexism ensures the institutionalized importance of the female need of men by requiring male-female relationships. Lesbian baiting and lesbian invisibility are forces that push women toward men, with an elaborate system of rewards and punishments that seem to be "everyday life." Many women fail to see their own misogyny when they exclude lesbian or bisexual concerns from their feminist agenda. Since the law is built around the male prototype, women enter into the law as they relate to men.[1] This approach is very limiting theoretically when we look at sexual harassment, rape, and domestic violence. The feminist analysis focuses on males changing their behavior without considering the experiences of all women. Not all women are in heterosexual relationships. Feminism has fought the notion that biology is destiny, yet heterosexism has blinded many feminists to the range of female experience.[2]

This chapter will examine how heterosexist assumptions and problems with application of the law impact same-sex access to and protection by the law in both rape and domestic violence. More legal issues have been raised related to same-sex domestic violence than same-sex sexual violence, so my discussion will of necessity be slanted in that direction. Regarding domestic violence I will discuss the definition of who the law protects when it comes to filing battering charges and filing restraining orders; police, judge, and jury homophobia; and the use of the battered women's syndrome defense. Regarding rape law I will look at how "crimes against nature" result in the possibility of the victim being charged with a crime (a discussion that also relates to domestic violence); the definition of normal sexual acts lesbians and bisexual women engage in as "deviate sexual intercourse"; rape law reform and gender neutral language (language that, again, also relates to domestic violence); and severity of punishment of sexual crimes as it relates to how female perpetrators could be charged.

Defining Terms in Domestic Violence

Nine states specifically exclude lesbians, some bisexuals, and gay men from domestic violence statutes by either stating that coverage is only in male-female relationships or stating that partners need to be married or formerly married.[3] Montana's statute claims to protect "partners"; but partners is then defined as spouses or former spouses. Georgia's statute covers married couples or formerly married couples. Delaware refers to heterosexual couples. Only fifteen states and the District of Columbia offer specific statutory protection for same-sex domestic violence.[4] Only Vermont explicitly states that all laws related to spouses extend to same-sex partners due to the civil union legislation recently passed. Because of the denial of protections to lesbians and bisexual women that heterosexuals are afforded, they are denied equal protection under the law.[5]

Terms of eligibility for criminal charges of battering and civil restraining orders often differ within the same state. For example, in North Carolina the "personal relationship" between the parties must fit one of the following: are current or former spouses; are persons of opposite sex who live together or have lived together; are related as parents and children, including others acting in loco parentis to a minor child, or as grandparents and grandchildren; have a child in common; are current or former household members; are persons of the opposite sex who are in a dating relationship or have been in a dating relationship. Some of the states that use similar wording for personal relationships include Alabama, Connecticut, Illinois, Maine, Michigan, Minnesota, and Tennessee.

The phrase "are current or former household members" is the phrase that might allow a lesbian or bisexual woman access to legal protection. In North Carolina, this phrase was added to the civil code in 1997 and the criminal code in 1999. However, other parts of the statute refer to "persons of the opposite sex." And application of the law is another issue altogether. While some lesbians, bisexuals, and gay men are filing restraining orders, seldom do they get a domestic violence assault charge against their batterer. In practice, males battering females are charged with domestic violence "assault on a female," and all others are charged with "simple assault." This matters because the penalties differ.

Twenty-five states have the stipulation of living together as the only possible way lesbians and bisexual women could access these laws. In California cohabitation refers to an unmarried man and woman living together, while in Delaware, it can be an adult of the same or opposite sex. An Ohio statute states that couples must have lived or be living together as spouses. Courts have interpreted this to apply to same-sex couples, which is good unless, of course, the lesbians or bisexual women were not living together. If the cohabitation clause is the only access to protection and the women are living apart, they are out of luck. A problem with the application of the law is also well illustrated in Virginia. Virginia uses the same wording as Ohio, yet an opinion issued to judges by former attorney general James Gilmore in 1995 stated that "cohabitation" referred only to opposite-sex couples based on "customary legal usage." When the language changed to "household member" in 1997, queer activists were hopeful that lesbians, bisexuals, and gay men would now have access to the same domestic violence services as heterosexuals. Such was not the case, as the new attorney general agreed with the former interpretation.[6]

While ambiguous language might seem like an opening, in law it is highly problematic. The language needs to be court-tested to find out if it will be applied in the way we want—in this case, to same-sex victims of battering or sexual violence. Even when lesbians are eligible for restraining orders, that does not guarantee they will be granted. Because of the myth of "mutual combat," a judge may decide that the couple was fighting rather than that one was abusing the other. This myth is common with lesbians because the judge does not readily see a "dominant" partner and cannot stereotypically assign the role of abuser to one person. The sexist notion of women in a "catfight" also revictimizes the battered woman partner. Lesbians who fight back in self-defense might be charged by police with assault. This is very damaging to the victim of battering, since she is regarded as having equal responsibility for the abuse, and she will now likely have continued contact with the abuser through the courts. As Krisana Hodges points out, the courage it took to step forward to name the abuse and seek legal protection is undermined by her treatment.[7] Patti had this experience in court:

> When I ended the relationship in January I got a restraining order because she hit me. I never brought up the sexual incident. She countered my restraining order with one on me. The judge, a woman, criticized us both in the courtroom, saying, "This should be dealt with outside this arena," in a very patronizing tone!

Patti's situation did work out for her, as the judge took the restraining order off her and kept it on her ex-partner. Her ex-partner broke the restraining order several times, and Patti had to call the police to arrest her. She was put in jail overnight, and that was the last Patti heard from her.

Police, Judge, and Jury Homophobia

As Hodges remarks, "Inclusive statutes are the gatekeepers of legal protection for lesbian battered women."[8] But a major part of our protection is how members of the legal system—police, prosecutors, judges, and juries—behave. The legal system itself is abusive when "homophobia infects law enforcement and the courts."[9] When women in same-sex relationships seek legal avenues, they take a public risk of exposing themselves to homophobia, biphobia, and harassment not only in the courts but also with their jobs, families, and other relationships. As mentioned in chapter 2, the law has poorly enforced our rights. We have lost children in custody cases, we have no protection against employment discrimination, and police have historically raided gay bars and harassed gay men and lesbians in their custody.

Lenore, who works in a sheriff's department, had this to say:

They're very backwards here. . . . I can't see any woman reporting any type of abuse to the law enforcement people here. It's real macho. I see some gay guys that come into the jail that are charged with other things and, I mean, they're just made fun of, all that type of stuff. . . . They just have these really backward ideas on gay people.

In New York, lesbians and gay men cannot get protective orders in family court, though they can in criminal court if the police have intervened.[10] But in calling the police, lesbians, bisexuals, and gay men are taking a risk. Will the officers be homophobic or biphobic? Police often have legal "outs" regarding the handling of cases of domestic violence. Case law in North Carolina states that law enforcement can give assistance as "seems fit to give." It is not an affirmative duty on the part of law enforcement. Paula Martinac writes of a case in which officers laughed at the battering situations of gay men, put on gloves, and asked the abuser if he had AIDS.[11] Furthermore, police who are looking for a profile that fits the heterosexual male batterer may take both members of the gay couple to the station, even putting them in the same cell.[12]

Judges can hide behind ambiguous language to avoid appearing homophobic. This makes it harder for survivors not only to have their rights protected but also to call the judges on their homophobic attitudes. If a case is appealed, the appellate court might rule in favor of extending the rights, but not many lesbians and bisexual women appeal their decisions. Failure and exposure in the first trial can be personally devastating. As Hodges writes,

Without these explicit assurances from state appellate courts, the protections that these statutes afford the victims of same-sex abuse are delegated to the precarious discretion of the judges and prosecutors in each case. This creates a dangerous legal environment where lesbian battered women are unable to predict the responses they may receive if they seek out legal protection. While heterosexual women are not guaranteed a safe and receptive legal environment, lesbian battered women experience the courts as a legal crapshoot in a way that heterosexual battered women do not.[13]

Even if the legal definition opens protection to lesbians and bisexual women, if they live in a state with sodomy laws on the books, they will be criminals in the eyes of the law. This will be discussed more fully in a following section, but suffice it to say that these laws prevent many lesbians, bisexuals, and gay men from coming forward. Calling the police would involve admitting they are in an illegal relationship. Homophobic reactions and sodomy laws add to the other aspects of low reporting of these crimes: victim fear, feelings of helplessness, and threat of further victimization from the legal system.[14]

The courts have also proven discriminatory toward transsexuals. Witness the case of Christine Littleton, a postoperative transsexual woman whose husband died in Texas as a result of medical malpractice. When Mrs. Littleton tried to pursue the case and to collect benefits due her as a widow, the courts denied that she was in fact legally married. The courts ruled that she was legally a male and that her marriage was void. Both the Texas Supreme Court and the U.S. Supreme Court have refused to hear the case. Legal barriers facing transgender individuals are clearly linked to those suffering from homophobia and biphobia because of heterosexism in the law.

The Battered Woman's Syndrome Defense

Battered woman's syndrome expert testimony was introduced into the courts in the late 1970s. It alone is not a defense but is used along with a self-defense or temporary insanity plea. Often what this allows is a conviction to a lesser murder charge or a not guilty verdict. This testimony supports the argument that the woman on trial for murder was in a psychological state in which she felt her life was in imminent danger. To demonstrate this, evidence is presented about the impacts of abuse, such as low self-esteem and learned helplessness, the reasons why battered women cannot simply leave their relationships primarily because of fear for their lives and lack of resources, and the concept of the cycle of violence such that the abuser keeps the victim hoping for change (during the "honeymoon" stage) and in constant fear because of the unpredictability of the explosion of violence.

Of course, the syndrome is primarily used when a battered woman kills her male abuser. Can this testimony apply to a lesbian who has killed her lesbian abuser? Jeffrey Harkavy argues that lesbians are not any different than heterosexual women in personality, intellect, or any other attribute except for their sexual identity. He maintains there is no reason to expect a differing rate of abuse and possible self-defense murders occurring in lesbian couples than in heterosexual couples.[15] And lesbians stay with their abusers for the same reasons, with some additional pressures such as societal homophobia and fewer resources to get out. All the factors for the use of this defense are in place.[16]

However, Harkavy believes that judges will likely disallow this defense because of prejudice; and juries, if the testimony is allowed, may be similarly homophobic. In his view, until lesbians are accorded equal legitimacy of their relationships to heterosexual marriage, this defense is unlikely to be successful.[17] Similarly, Ruthann Robson believes that courts use a heterosexist standard of "couple" and are unlikely to view lesbian relationships in the same way. The situation of Annette Green is a case in point. The judge allowed the battered woman's defense, interpreting it as a "battered person's defense." The defense presented the compelling evidence of Green's abuse by her partner, including broken bones and being shot at, along with the testimony about the syndrome. The first degree murder conviction that resulted, the defense believed, was due to the homophobia of the jury and other court personnel.[18] Not surprisingly lesbians tend not to use the battered woman's syndrome precisely because they would have to admit they are in a lesbian relationship, which might "prejudice a jury."[19]

Crimes against Nature and Deviate Sexual Intercourse

One of the major legal problems lesbians, bisexuals, and gay men face is that many states define the sexual behaviors that are normal for us as illegal or deviant. These sodomy laws not only are damaging to our legal protection but also symbolically represent the widespread view that our sexual behaviors are sick, perverted, and abnormal. Clearly this is heterosexist, since what is deemed legal and normal is vaginal-penile intercourse. In fact, in some states—for example, New York—sexual intercourse is defined as having its "*ordinary* meaning" (emphasis added). Whether these laws are enforced or not, that they are on the books adds to the "hostile environment in the courts."[20]

While in the majority of states these statutes have been overturned, they stand in sixteen others.[21] Sodomy, usually defined as cunnilingus, fellatio, analingus, and anal intercourse, is a "crime against nature" usually whether it is consensual or not and whether the partners are heterosexual or homosexual. In Oklahoma it applies only to same-sex couples. What this means is that a lesbian or bisexual woman who wishes to press charges for a sexual assault involving one of the acts just listed could end up with a charge lodged against her for a crime against nature, even though the act was against her will. The act itself rather than the violence behind it is what zealous prosecutors focus on. In North Carolina, the charge would be for an "infamous offense." This would be up to the discretion of the district attorney, and few lesbians and bisexual women are willing to risk this possibility.

Many states view the sexual acts by lesbians, bisexuals, and gay men as unnatural in their legal definition of "deviate sexual intercourse." In New York, as stated earlier, sexual intercourse has the "ordinary meaning," while deviate sexual intercourse means "sexual contact between persons not married to each other consisting of contact between the penis and the anus, the mouth and the penis, or the mouth and the vulva."[22] Indiana law states that deviate sexual conduct is an act involving "a sex organ of one person and the mouth or anus of another person; or the penetration of the sex organ or anus of a person by an object."[23] Pennsylvania is unique in that deviate sexual intercourse also includes "digital penetration of a female by another female."[24]

Deviate sexual intercourse or conduct is criminal only when it is forced sexual activity. This might seem reasonable—that if it is *forced*, it is criminal. However, the separate "deviate" category is the result of using the vaginal intercourse standard. Why the distinctions between sexual penetration activities and the differing labels to the acts with different penalties attached if they are all forced? Why are some acts "deviate" and others "ordinary"? In North Carolina, the only person who can be raped is a woman, by a man. Other violations are called "sexual offenses," first to third degrees. Indiana law states that rape involves sexual intercourse with a member of the opposite sex. By using the heterosexual standard, lesbians and bisexual women sexually violated by other women will be treated less seriously.

The most common violations in this study were forced finger penetration (often with injuries) and vaginal and anal dildo penetrations. Since it is not possible for a penis to be involved, in some states why are these sexual violations not seen as serious as those involving a penis? In Georgia, rape is only "penetration of the female sex organ by the male sex organ." A case involving woman-to-woman digital penetration would most likely be defined as sexual battery, a misdemeanor.

That same-sex sexual behavior is seen as against "public decency and morality" is also shown in the use of the "homosexual panic" defense, such as was attempted in the defense of Steven Mullins and Charles Butler on trial for murdering Billy Jack Gaither in 1999. Homosexual panic refers to the violent emotional reaction a person might feel in a homosexual situation that triggers the person's own unconscious homosexual feelings. This is presumably an *understandable negative* reaction. Again, when Jonathan Schmitz shot and killed Scott Amedure after their appearance on the *Jenny Jones* show (where Scott's secret crush on Jonathan was revealed), jury members, family, and apparently the general public, understood why the public humiliation of just the suspicion of being gay was a *normal* reaction, even justifying murder as a response.

States should move toward the Washington State model. There, sexual intercourse has its "ordinary meaning" as well as

> any penetration of the vagina or anus however slight, by an object, when committed on one person by another, whether such persons are of the same or opposite sex, except when such penetration is accomplished for medically recognized treatment or diagnostic purposes, and also means any act of sexual contact between persons involving the sex organs of one person and the mouth or anus of another whether such persons are of the same or opposite sex. Sexual contact means any touching of the sexual or other intimate parts of a person done for the purposes of gratifying sexual desire of either party or a third party.[25]

Charges are of rape, in first to third degrees.

Gender Neutral Rape Language

In the late 1970s and early 1980s, reformers pushed for changes in the language of rape criminal statutes. The main challenges regarded who the laws covered, what counted as sexual conduct, and what made it criminal.[26] The most common reforms broadened the sex acts that were criminalized and used gender neutral language, changed the consent standard by altering if or how the victim resisted the attacker, eliminated requirements of corroboration, and introduced rape shield laws, which prohibited evidence of the victim's prior sexual history.[27] These changes were expected to have an impact on rape reporting, rape prosecutions, and convictions. However, a study by Ronet Bachman and Raymond Paternoster found that rape reform had little effect on victim reporting or changes in the actual practices in the legal system. There was a slight increase in reporting and a slight increase in rapists being sent to prison. The researchers suggest that much more work needs to be done to change societal attitudes before the criminal justice system will show significant change.[28]

Most reform statutes are now gender neutral. However, in some cases what "gender neutral" means is a woman can be charged with raping a man. It does *not* necessarily apply to same-sex rape. So, for example, in Massachusetts, where sexual intercourse is defined as penile-vaginal intercourse, a male or a female could be the perpetrator but only in a heterosexual situation. In Connecticut, the language is neutral because the statute specifies vaginal intercourse, oral sex, and anal sex between persons "regardless of sex." New York laws were gender neutralized in 1984, but when the definitions of terms used in the laws are examined, we find that they are heterosexist in discussing "any female person not married to the actor." Marital rape is discussed in separate statutes. Many states began to use the words "actor" or "person" or "victim," but we must dig deeper to find what type of actor or victim they are actually referring to. In states that do not have gender neutral laws, such as Georgia, rape can only be committed by a man against a woman.

The primary reason gender neutral language has not proven to be as beneficial as it seemed on the surface is because of the gender subtext of our understanding of relationships and of sexual behavior. "De-sexing" is not enough because our society associates perpetration of violence with males and victimization with females, making this a "gendered story."[29] The legal system uses this gendered view to understand domestic violence and rape, and police officers, judges, juries, and attorneys listen to these cases with this subtext in mind. Consequently, when lesbians and bisexual women tell of battering and rape, they tell a story with a different gender scheme, one that is at odds with the existing heterosexist subtext. This clash hurts their credibility and limits the logical extension of "person" to lesbian or bisexual women.[30]

Perpetrator Charges

One of the aspects of rape reform was a change in many states from using the term "rape" or using rape plus other offense labels. In Connecticut and Massachusetts, there are degrees of rape and degrees of sexual assault. Washington State uses degrees of rape, while Minnesota and Michigan use degrees of criminal sexual conduct. Florida uses sexual battery, while New York uses degrees of sexual abuse.

These changes matter to lesbians and bisexual women for two reasons. The first reason, related to what was discussed earlier, is that deviate sexual intercourse and situations in which female digital penetration is sexual battery (Georgia) might not carry the severity of rape or sexual assault charges. The charges may be misdemeanors instead of felonies, and the sentence imposed will be lighter because of the lesser charge. Therefore I question if a woman who is raped by another woman will feel that her assault is treated the same or taken as seriously as if she had been raped by a man. Interestingly, if a woman aids and abets a male assailant in the rape of another woman, the woman can be charged with and convicted of rape (or whatever the most serious terminology is in that state).

Second, the label "rape" has a societal meaning that conveys its "unique indignity."[31] Using these other terms obscures what rape is. As Susan Estrich states, "The fact remains, however, that a simple rape is a different and more serious affront than a simple assault."[32] I am particularly concerned that the sexual violence women experience at the hands of other women will never be validated as equally serious as rape by a man or even prosecutable under current laws in many states. What we call what happens to us makes a difference, particularly in legal language.

Legal Experiences among Study Participants

One night Hannah's lover tried to force herself on her. They struggled, and when Hannah tried to leave, her lover blocked the door. Hannah was hit and pushed but finally broke free. Because of a very bad bruise on the back of her leg, she—and her partner—went to the emergency room: "I panicked after I got there and everyone was talking about that [by law] they had to call the police, the police had to be there, had to be involved. [It] freaked me out and I ran." Hannah never spoke to the police, nor did she receive treatment for her injury.

Out of seventy study participants (and ninety-one incidents), only seventeen had police contact or used the courts. The majority related to domestic violence incidents. Restraining orders were sought and received by seven women. The police were called eight times when no charges were filed, once when charges were filed then dropped, and three times when arrests were made. Only once when an arrest was made did it specifically relate to sexual violence, and in the remaining three cases, one woman filed a lawsuit against her perpetrator and the organization at which they worked, and two women filed a rape report but no charges were pressed. Therefore, out of the entire sample, only four women followed up in any way on the sexual violence against them.

Lila's perpetrator was her work mentor and supervisor. A specific incident of sexual assault in a car took place, but numerous sexualized behaviors occurred in the office. Lila brought a lawsuit against her supervisor and the organization. Her lawyers labeled what happened to her "battery" for unwanted physical contact. After two years, the case was settled out of court and technically "resolved to the satisfaction of both parties." Lila agreed to the resolution because of her physical and emotional exhaustion. She originally pursued the lawsuit in order to protect other vulnerable women but was only partially successful. While this action confirmed the uneasy feelings some had about her perpetrator, the perpetrator is still active in the movement against sexual violence.

Leigh's case also headed for court. Leigh had been held against her will for three days and sexually assaulted by a woman and that woman's boyfriend. She was forced to perform numerous sexual acts on the woman (kissing, fondling, and oral sex, in addition to threats to prostitute her and to shove objects up her vagina) and oral sex on the man. The two were charged with multiple drug offenses, forced oral copulation, and false imprisonment. However, when they finally reached court, all the charges but the drug charges had been dropped. Leigh's perpetrators never spent time in jail but instead were court-ordered to drug rehabilitation. Leigh never testified in court. It was as if the acts against her were not important compared with the crack smoking of her assailants. As Leigh said, "What happened to me didn't count."

Both Marielle and Meredith filed rape reports with police but did not press charges. Marielle's perpetrator was her therapist, who had her create a sexual scene in therapy and then had an orgasm while Marielle was in trauma. In addition to trying to get the therapist's license revoked, Marielle wrote a fourteen-page detailed description of what happened and why she thought it was rape. The officer who read the complaint told her it was not rape, but Marielle needed to take this step for her own sense of self.

Meredith did not want to press charges against her partner, but she did file a report. This was after an incident of forced sex when she was physically restrained. She filed the report

> so that if something happened with somebody else and they went to the police, it would be on file. And along with making the report I put in there it would be fine to contact me, and I would say anything or testify to back up somebody if they wanted to do anything legally against [her]. So that's what all that was about. It was for the next person.

It is shocking to me that of ninety-one cases of varying degrees of sexual violence, many of them resulting in injuries, many of them involving forced restraint, so few women sought legal help. The two court cases were not resolved satisfactorily. Women who received restraining orders were helped (though often continued to have run-ins with their abusers), and only a few women felt that the police were helpful and encouraging to them.

However, what this review shows is that lesbians and bisexual women do not feel they can seek legal redress. This is based on heterosexism and societal homophobia, especially within the legal system, and their own feelings of lack of efficacy, common with sexual violence survivors. Yet, lesbians and bisexual women should be given equal protection based on the equal protection clause of the Fourteenth Amendment, which states in part: "No State shall make or enforce any law which shall . . . deny to any person within its jurisdiction the equal protection of the laws." Instead, laws are clearly written to omit lesbians and bi women, and laws are interpreted to exclude them. As Pamela Jablow suggests, it isn't the relationship between the parties that should matter, it is that the violence of battering and the violence of rape should be repugnant to us.[33] Woman-to-woman abuse should be equally an affront as heterosexual violence.

Overall, heterosexism in the legal system is found in how our sexual acts are defined and sometimes criminalized even when consensual, that gender neutral language is not necessarily sexual orientation neutral, that rape is not a charge that applies to us, and in fact, the charges that can be levied are most often misdemeanors. The treatment that abused women in same-sex relationships receive throughout the legal system is anything but protective. Their situations do not "fit" with gendered assumptions, a subtext that the legal system uses to understand the battering and sexual violence stories of women. Lesbians and bisexual women are so discouraged by their reception from the legal system that most do not even attempt to get protections they deserve. Those who go forward may be so dismayed that they are unwilling to appeal unfavorable decisions. These appeals are desperately needed to establish the statutory cases that will allow laws to be used in our favor. It is not enough that language may say "family-like" or "persons." We naively thought this gender neutral language let us in the door, but application has proven otherwise. Law must explicitly state "same-sex" or "lesbian" or "bisexual" for our protection to be guaranteed.

If you have any doubt that this should change, I suggest rereading the rape stories in chapter 4. As I made calls for information in this chapter, speaking to lawyers and advocates at rape and sexual assault agencies, I asked if they knew of any cases in their state in which a woman was charged with and convicted of sexual violence against another woman. Not one person knew of such a case, though a few said, "There must have been a case sometime."

8

Lesbian- and Bi-Friendly Services

The only way I felt I could leave the relationship was to die. It got to the point where my plans were set and I was driving within three feet of a semi driving 80 mph that I realized I needed to find someone safe to talk to. The hardest call to make was to Rape and Abuse Crisis Center. Would they accept me as a lesbian woman? Would they turn me away? Luckily, I wasn't [turned away]. (Ariel)

I went to a couple of groups for women with domestic violence, but had hetero-sexual partners, and I just wasn't comfortable. It was very hard to talk about things 'cause sometimes they look at you like, "how could this be?" (Roxanne)

[A shelter I worked at] was really invested in the whole analysis about the patriar-chy, and really into "We're all women here, therefore we're all safe" routine. Lesbians are going to start a utopia because we're all women. . . . So I remember sitting there through the training—'cause when I went to volunteer at the shelter I was already in this relationship—and I remember sitting through the training thinking, gosh, this sounds familiar, but thinking, but it's not a man. And it was laid out that simplistically. Obviously I was in some denial myself, but I think that their analysis of battering not only didn't include lesbian battering but made lesbian battering pretty much impossible. (Cecile)

How to best address woman-to-woman sexual violence? Homophobia, bi-phobia, sexism, and heterosexism condemn lesbians and bisexual women to inferior social status. Our society sexualizes violence in the media while denouncing sex education in the schools, thus encouraging sexual violence. As individuals, we balk at discussing sexual matters, abusive or otherwise. The idea of female perpetrators runs contrary to gender ideology and patri-archal analysis. Once survivors publicly give voice to their experiences of woman-to-woman sexual violence, how can we translate their needs and the needs of perpetrators into social services, laws, and public opinion that will work together to stop this violence?

Lack of Services

Sexual violence survivors are currently caught in a chicken-and-egg dilemma. Rape crisis and domestic violence agencies say they do not have lesbian-specific or bisexual-specific services because there are few or no requests for them. Are there no requests because lesbians and bisexuals do not feel welcome or that the services they seek are not available? In a survey about specifically lesbian services of 566 domestic violence service providers, Renzetti found that while the vast majority stated they welcomed lesbian clients, the majority did not act to ensure that lesbian clients were aware of their services. They did not promote services for lesbians, such as offering support groups for lesbians, brochures on lesbian battering, or ads in the gay/lesbian press. Similarly, while staff received training on homophobia, they rarely had training on lesbian battering.[1]

The result of these barriers and shortcomings is that services for lesbians and gay men are thirty years behind the battered women's movement, according to Diane Dolan-Soto, domestic violence program coordinator at the New York Gay and Lesbian Anti-Violence Project.[2] For many survivors, this lack of services is an old and familiar pattern. Their incest may not have been reported or dealt with appropriately by child protection agencies,[3] their rape by a male was not reported because of their fears of sexism in the legal system, and now their same-sex sexual violence or battering is not addressed by service providers either. Rape has the lowest report rate to police of all crimes,[4] and it will take extraordinary work to reach out to female survivors of sexual violence perpetrated by women.

In considering the context of agencies developing services, Juan Méndez reminds us of the obvious: "If one wants to serve a diverse population, then one's staff, or the people who are going to provide direct service, must reflect the characteristics of the population one aims to serve."[5] Agencies need to hire lesbians and bisexual women, lesbians and bisexual women of color, and perhaps bilingual staff as well. In addition, before any outreach can be done, we need to work on eliminating homophobia, biphobia, and heterosexism in the shelter and agency environments through staff and volunteer trainings.[6] Nomi Porat recommends concrete steps that help ensure the agency is a safe place for lesbians: the agency's mission statement should include that women are served regardless of sexual identity; antihomophobia training should be offered to staff, board, and volunteers; heterosexist language should be removed from agency forms and in crisis counseling, hot line counseling, and support groups; and opportunities should be available for battered lesbians to take leadership in developing their services.[7] Similar changes can be made for the safety of bisexual women.

Help-Seeking Behavior

We cannot definitively prove that if services were readily available, lesbians and bisexual women would go to agencies. The current climate of homophobia and biphobia stops many lesbians and bisexual women from going to service providers, where they will have to come out if they are honest about their abuse. Therefore, suggesting that only new services is the answer to connecting these women to the assistance they need is foolhardy. Social change advocates simultaneously need to address heterosexism, homophobia, and biphobia in the agencies as well as in the broader society.

Rarely will women victimized within same-sex relationships call the police or go to lawyers or doctors. For lesbians and bisexual women of color, justified fear of racism by professionals, especially in the criminal justice system, compounds their worries of homophobia and biphobia. The tarnished legacy of the racialized treatment of rape adds a unique dimension to same-sex sexual violence. Historically, and to the present, African-American men have been and are punished more harshly for raping white women than white men are. Racist attitudes permeate the criminal justice system, and women of color run a risk of negative stereotyping by police, judges, juries, and court personnel.[8]

We know that lesbians do not choose traditional sources of help when raped or battered. Few call hot lines or go to shelters. The most common sources of help are therapists and friends.[9] Lie and Gentlewarrier found that survivors and perpetrators of battering would also use support groups, but preferred that they be services specifically for lesbians.[10] A report on meeting the needs of queer women and girls who were survivors of violence in San Francisco indicated that these women and girls do not necessarily identify with violence-against-women services in general. They view these services as focused on females with male perpetrators. According to the report authors, even when lesbian or bi services are offered, clients still need to access services that are not queer-specific within those agencies. In addition, they often do not relate to the feminist model of domestic violence "with its emphasis on the 'cycle of violence' and a sharp dichotomy between the 'batterer' and the 'survivor.' " Lesbian and bisexual women may feel connected to the abuser because of societal reactions they defend against—

homophobia or biphobia. Women of color also may not want to leave their abusers but stand united against both the heterosexist and racist society.[11]

Renzetti examined not only what help battered lesbians sought but also whether the help was useful. Similar to other studies, Renzetti found that most women turned to friends, counselors, or relatives (in that order). Counselors were seen as the most helpful. For many women, it was the counselor who put the terms "battered" and "lesbian" together. Lesbians turn to family, but at a lower rate than heterosexual women do. Many women are not out to their families and so cannot readily turn to them as straight women can in an emergency. Out of one hundred women, nineteen of Renzetti's participants had turned to the police, but they did not find them very helpful. Only thirteen went to shelters. She discovered that some women did not turn to shelters either because they perceived the shelter was for heterosexual women battered by men or because their abusers worked at the shelter.[12] Again, this is very similar to my findings where the majority of the women did not respond immediately, but when they did, they tended to seek out therapists or they told friends.

Agency Outreach to Lesbians and Bisexual Women

The lack of services targeted to lesbians and bisexual women is often a result of societal homophobia and biphobia. Agencies are afraid of loss of public support or loss of agency funding if it is known that lesbians or bisexual women are served.[13] Yet, the women in my study urge specific programs and outreach measures that will assure lesbians and bisexual women that they are, indeed, welcome. As documented earlier, these women wished for specific lesbian services, preferably offered within the lesbian community. Many wished for support groups for lesbians, lesbian-specific hot lines, literature aimed at lesbians, and lesbian counselors. None of the bisexual women mentioned specifically bisexual services. I interpret this to mean that these women would be comfortable in lesbian services to address their violence at the hands of other women. Christy, who now works as an attorney helping clients get protection orders, finds that "people are more willing to call something offered within the community by the community than another domestic violence service trying to incorporate an additional element."

The reality is, however, that most services will have to be provided through existing mainstream agencies because of funding constraints in starting new and separate agencies. Study participants had many ideas how these agencies could reach out to them. For several women, the key factor was that agencies clearly state they are open to lesbians. Danielle said outreach literature needs to state

> something like, "sexual orientation safe," a "safe environment." . . . I guess I look at stuff that says lesbian. I have a tendency to certainly look more closely at it than if it just was written more generic. Because then it's like, wow, these people know we exist. And I think that's key, is that if you know that they can actually say the "L" word, you know, then somewhere in there there's got to be somebody that's dealing with this to make it come out enough that it's on a piece of paper.

Or as Marcia dryly stated, "Addressing lesbians in general would be a start." Related to the issue of specifically using the term "lesbian" and "bisexual" are the poster depictions used in outreach. Missy pointed out, "I think it's a lot of subtext problems. You get a brochure that, you know, it's nice to see 'partner' instead of husband or boyfriend, but the pictures are all of men holding women. It's the little things that people pick up on. We don't see a depiction of ourselves as lesbians in regular media." This is important because "if it's more inclusive that also helps because it lets us know that they're gay friendly" (Olivia). And Evon wants to see "posters that are for lesbians and gays and bisexuals and transgender, that when you see a poster that says here's a hot line if you've been sexually assaulted or you're in a domestic violence situation, and it could be totally geared for our population."

Rita suggests literature should be sent to queer businesses—bars, bed and breakfasts, and bookstores—and Evon wants to see more outreach to the queer press. Agencies that offer services to lesbians and bisexual women need to specifically advertise them rather than assume lesbian and bisexual clients will show up and inquire if the programs exist for them. "An agency would feel supportive if I KNEW they offered services to the gay and lesbian population," claims Melanie. Shelley refers to the invisibility of these problems in our community: "Well, I always see posters and whatnot for domestic violence around, but I never considered the relationship between two women could be, could have domestic violence in it. So, I think maybe that if there was, those hot lines and stuff were advertised for same-sex couples as well, that would have been a big help [to me]." And Deirdre would like to see signs that an organization is gay-friendly, such as "the [rainbow] flag on their symbol or advertisement."

Marti feels strongly that an agency that had lesbians serving lesbians would have "a lot more people turning to it." This is reinforced by Deirdre, who remembers how important it was to have staff at the agency she went to who had been abused by a woman "because getting the words 'I understand what you're going through,' from a woman who's been through it with another woman, to me that's almost the most important thing." Numerous women, looking for just that type of validation and support, mentioned a lesbian support group. But Annie reminds us that it isn't necessarily that simple:

> As far as what would I want from an agency, it would have to be a lesbian group because for me the dynamics between men and women and women and women are so different. And it would also have to probably be an S/M specific group because my experience has been that people who don't participate or haven't participated really don't have an understanding of what's going on. And they don't understand the dynamics and how things work. And they tend to say things that they think are comforting but really you end up explaining your sexual desire, which really doesn't help. It's kind of [like] if you're in a heterosexual group and you end up explaining your lesbianism, which isn't really the issue. . . . I think that was a really big factor for me, too, in my healing process, was feeling that there was something wrong with my basic sexual desire in addition to, which complicates how you can process the actual act of violence or abuse.

Deirdre left the support group for lesbians she was in primarily for reasons Annie mentions—she was inhibited by how she felt her S/M experience would shock the other group members. This contrasts with Aura's experience, where she was revictimized by her feeling unsafe at an agency where there were mixed services with women practicing S/M. This is yet another program issue to be taken into consideration.

Reaching out to lesbians and bisexual women of color requires additional strategies. Many women in these communities do not primarily identify as lesbian or bisexual; their identification is one of color. These women may not read the gay/lesbian press, so ads should also be placed in the paper(s) of the communities of color. Ads should explicitly say what sexual violence includes, as these women may not identify themselves as raped. Finally, lesbian and bisexual leaders in the diverse communities of color should be recruited by agencies as important resource persons, since people of color often turn to individuals before agencies.[14]

Outreach Words

Providing services to women who have experienced sexual violence in same-sex encounters is one part of necessary change. Another aspect is what

agencies should call this violence. In follow-up interviews I asked most of
the women what words they thought should be used that would reflect their
experiences. Interestingly, many women who labeled their violence rape
did not think the word "rape" should be used in outreach. Marianne felt
that "the word almost distances you from the problem. . . . [There are] so
many nuances to what that represents that I think it's easy for women to
say, well, that doesn't apply to me because there was something that was
'unrapelike' about it." Erin worries that survivors whose violation did not
result in injury or didn't involve a weapon would feel like they "don't qual-
ify." Monica points out that "in many states it is legally impossible for a
woman to rape another woman, and that definition of the word 'rape' automatically negates some women's experiences."

Many women felt that "assault" was the best word to use in outreach.
Aileen reasons

> I think that one of the reasons why rape is not a word that I would use very often,
> just because it's a much harsher word than assault is, and identifying as an assault
> survivor than a rape survivor, it's just an easier thing to do in life. It makes things
> less crisis oriented for the people involved.

Leigh based her use of the term "sexual assault" on her experience:

> I just think sexual assault is more encompassing, not only for non-gender bias but
> also because some women are raped by a foreign object, or that kind of thing, so
> that encompasses that as well. But, I don't know, I've had women that I've coun-
> seled say they really appreciated the fact that I used the term sexual assault instead
> of rape. That kind of made it inclusive for their experience.

In thinking back on her sexual violation, Roxanne says she preferred the
word "assault" because at the time she was "too frightened to admit" that
she had been raped.

Olivia suggests that

> sometimes the stronger words are the correct words, but they're not the words
> the victim identifies with. And maybe if you can get them into the door, then maybe
> you can get them to recognize the stronger words. Like they're at the clinic maybe
> they can recognize, oh, maybe that is rape and not only coercion or force.

Other words or phrases that were suggested to use in outreach included
"relationship conflict" (Adele); "sexual coercion" (Carole, Meryl); "sex you
don't want," "hurting you" (Marianne); "sexual abuse" (Deirdre, Renee,
Liz, Bea, Sonia); "partner abuse" (Giselle); "violence from another

woman" (Maureen); "nonconsensual sex" (Monica, Lenore); "a really broad range of definition" (Erin, Lorraine); and phrases such as, "Have you ever felt uncomfortable . . ." (Allison, Brooke).

For many women, rape *is* the right word to use. Polly suggests "maybe attack the myths around it but don't change the word." Melanie feels strongly that "in terms of outreach, rape is going to be key. People need to know rape happens in same-sex relations just as in male/female relations." Rhonda is concerned that "if a different term is used there would be different treatment. Yes, use the term rape." For Meredith,

> I think [calling it rape] is a good idea because from my perspective I felt a huge sense of relief to hear somebody name, use the word to name, some of the experiences that I'd had. Or to connect that word with women together as opposed to behavior between men and women. That kind of behavior is that kind of behavior whether you're a man or a woman and a lot of covering things up, or there has been a lot of covering things up in the women's community. And that's how I felt, that it was the same thing, even though it was something that happened with a woman rather than with a man. And I thought there was something wrong with me that I felt that way. So it was a huge relief. "Oh. Yeah, that's what I thought, that's how I felt." So, I think maybe it might frighten somebody, but just from my perspective it might be like, home base.

Would new vocabulary help if it both resonated with the experiences as lived and achieved societal acceptance? Marianne claims that we need to become like the Eskimos, who have multiple words for snow. Marcia suggests "creating more vocabulary because people aren't gonna initially accept that fact that a woman could rape another woman." Feminists fought long and hard for the legitimate use in public space of words such as "rape" and "battering." We fought for the right to name what was happening to us as women. Now there seems to be some doubt as to what these words mean in a somewhat different context. But when antiviolence advocates ask ourselves if these dynamics are the same or different, we must conclude they are the same. The behavior is the same. The impact is the same. It is the social meaning that is under dispute because our gender socialization does not accept women as sexual aggressors or sexual perpetrators. Our challenge is to demonstrate what some women are actually doing and have a cultural shift in response. This has happened before (think of the use of the birth control pill, men and women cohabiting before marriage, and the criminalizing of marital rape), and it will happen again.

The Lesbian Abuser

I did not interview any abusers in my study, though some of my study participants did comment on why they thought their perpetrators abused them. What I can say about abusers' motivations for perpetrating sexual violence or what kind of treatment is most effective is, for the most part, based on studies in which lesbian domestic violence survivors talk about their relationships or where respondents have admitted to having battered their partners. There are no studies focusing on female sexual violence perpetrators—clearly a research need. I am also unaware of research documenting bisexual abusers, though in this study Leigh's, Aileen's, and Brooke's abusers were heterosexuals who may have considered themselves bisexual.

The most common underlying causes of abusive behaviors by women to other women that are cited include power and control, dependency, jealousy, internalized homophobia, a history of childhood abuse, and alcohol and drug use. The dominant perspective in domestic violence is that batterers are hungry for control over some aspect of their lives and feel they can get away with abusing their partners.[15] Several of the study participants felt power and control were the main motivations for the sexual violence against them. Jannette felt, "It seems to me that there's a real need to feel control over somebody else." Bea took a macro view: "I think it's because we were all raised in the same patriarchal, abusive society, and there are people who are gonna identify with the perpetrator rather than deal with their victim issues. I think that's key." Courtney reflected, "Part of it [is] maybe the need to control their surroundings. I don't think they're immune from that, growing up and getting that message that somehow they're supposed to control their surroundings."

Ellen Meyers states, "If we see that domestic violence is about power, control, and change, we can apply these dynamics to any relationship because these behaviors are human and transcend the players in the relationship."[16] This is echoed by Adele, who told me,

I think what we forget often is that it really is about power and privilege and not about male and female, black and white. . . . Because I see it as a human struggle. . . . I think human beings are human beings. I remember in the early days [of feminism] when people, men were the mutants and women were the real human beings, and I really don't believe that. . . . I believe that we as a human race have some really sick patterns and power [dynamics].

Lauren was wistful: "We've spent our lives trying to end this power thing, so why would we do it to each other?" Meryl did not see power and control as male abusive behavior but as behavior of males or females:

> Maybe some lesbians are taking on male roles, but I don't really believe in that. Maybe some women need to be dominant, to be butch, more than their partners. According to society, taking on male conditioning is labeled "butch." Others might then label the women as butch, but maybe the women themselves didn't see themselves as butch. I didn't see my lovers as butch. They were older and needed to be in control in the relationship.

Abusers are not necessarily butch, nor are all self-identified butches abusive.

Ariel felt that "lesbians that are perpetrators are angry, and whether it's power and control issues with the person they're involved with or it's power and control issues with society as a whole, I think we're a minority in a majority world and a lot of anger can build up because of that." As sexism creates an environment for male abuse of females, homophobia creates the opportunity for lesbians to abuse other women.[17] Racism adds to the list of possible elements leading to battering, according to Waldron.[18] A white woman may assume that the cultural norms of behavior for a woman of color (louder voices, excited hand gestures) are signals of impending violence.

Lesbian batterers, as women and as lesbians, are "afforded substantially less power in the world than the heterosexual male batterer."[19] Internalized homophobia and a negative self-concept are common characteristics of lesbian (and gay male) perpetrators of abuse.[20] Ariel felt "the self-acceptance, the misogyny and hatred of women, the hatred of society and the condemnation that you live through" had a lot to do with abusers' behaviors. In her view, living closeted lives within a hierarchical context led to drinking problems, drug problems, and abuse. Roxanne worried that homophobia made it harder "in terms of getting help or admitting your behavior. That would be a very hard thing for a lesbian to do; there's one more layer of making it hard."

The balance of power in a relationship is not a clear-cut dynamic. Renzetti found in her study of lesbians in abusive relationships that respondents reported their abusers did tend to have more power, especially in decision making. But respondents also had personal power such as higher education levels, higher incomes, and greater occupational prestige. The unequal division of labor in the household was also mixed—sometimes it shifted over time, whether preceding abuse or in response to existing abuse was not possible to determine.[21] Merrill points out there is a difference between social power and personal power, and that personal power is a largely unexplored research area. He suggests that personal power can be undermined through psychological abuse where the efficacy to draw upon your personal resources is weakened.[22] This adds a further dimension to what Renzetti attempted to measure in her research.

Dependency was found to be the variable of greatest impact in the abusers' control over the respondents in Renzetti's study. Abusers were more dependent on their partners than vice versa, and as a partner desired greater independence in the relationship, this created conflict. The greater the struggle for independence, the more the abuser inflicted types of abuse with increased frequency.[23] Renzetti suggests that batterers feel ashamed of their overdependency on their partners, as this trait is associated with the traditional feminine role that lesbian feminists critique.[24] Liz Margolies and Elaine Leeder point out that dependency leads to violence, violence leads to isolation, and isolation increases dependency and violence.[25]

Childhood abuse, as witnesses to violence and/or as targets of physical or sexual abuse, has been connected to both abusers and victims. Margolies and Leeder, working with lesbian batterers in a clinical setting, found that all of them had a family history of violence, as did Ned Farley in his work.[26] Renzetti suggests that this is an intervening variable rather than a cause of abuse. While more perpetrators were abused when young than respondents in her study were, almost as many perpetrators were in nonviolent homes as violent ones.[27] Aileen recounts that in her case,

> the woman that I was with had been really severely abused, and that violence was kind of normalized for her. She was in foster homes growing up because her mother had abused her real badly; she had been sexually abused by her stepfather. It was a whole history of abusive relationships one after another and I've known that since she's broken up with me she's already been in three other relationships. I found out that two of those left her because she was beating them, too. . . . And it was also very difficult because she would use that a lot of times as an excuse. That would make me feel horrible and sorry for her, and make her not responsible for her actions. And helpless because all these horrible things had happened to her. She turned it around so I had to be comforting to her.

Aileen wonders about the abuse her perpetrator experienced: "She's got a million good reasons to turn out to be a perpetrator. Her parents were perpetrators and she was abused as a child, and she had all kinds of gnarly experiences. But then there are people who go through that and they don't become perpetrators, so, I don't know."

Jealousy was the most frequent source of conflict among the lesbians Renzetti studied.[28] Tied to a sexual component, abusers are often overly possessive of their partners. Other issues seen as related to abuser behavior are alcohol and drug use, low self-esteem, and fear of loss and abandonment.[29]

The complete lack of research on female sexual perpetrators hinders a thorough analysis of the sexual violations presented in this book. However, comparing the factors associated with lesbian batterers with male acquaintance rapists, we find some similar dynamics: power and control, sexual entitlement, hostility and anger, and acceptance of interpersonal violence.[30]

Healing from Abuse

Recovery from rape regardless of the sex of the perpetrator is not a return to where the survivor was before the trauma; rather it involves an integration of what occurred along with new insights about self and the world around her.[31] Stewart, Hughes, Frank, Anderson, Kendall, and West discovered a difference between those rape survivors who sought assistance immediately and those who delayed treatment. Those women who delayed treatment were more anxious, fearful, and depressed. They tended to know their assailants, and they were less likely to have physically defended themselves.[32] Most of the women in this study delayed treatment, if they received any at all. For some, their trauma remains untreated, and they are perhaps at increased risk of revictimization. Untreated trauma makes it difficult to build the psychological resources needed to fend off further abuse.[33]

We have seen the impacts of multiple victimization in the women in the study. The impacts of the sexual violence they experienced were severe and long lasting. I believe this is related to the fact that they had, for the most part, been victimized by people they knew—incest from family members, rape by male acquaintances, sexual assaults from women they, for the most part, knew well. When the survivor knows the perpetrator, she is more likely to blame herself for what happened and may not see the event at the time as rape.[34]

It is crucial for counselors to screen for sexual assault history when a client presents problems such as fear, anxiety, depression, sexual dysfunction, or social withdrawal.[35] Therapists especially need to ask about incest if a client has issues of battering, rape, drug or alcohol addiction, or has an adolescent history of running away.[36] The likelihood of posttraumatic stress symptoms is high. Treatment, according to Saunders, includes a gradual reexperiencing of the trauma, managing the accompanying stress, expressing emotions of shame, rage, and grief, and finding some meaning in the victimization. In addition to stress reactions, other issues from abuse within relationships that need to be addressed may include loyalty to the abuser, self-blame, and generalized mistrust.[37]

Whether working in individual therapy, therapy groups, self-help groups, or talking with supportive others, lesbians and bisexual women bring other issues in with them alongside the abuse trauma. Issues include living with the daily stress of homophobia and biphobia, and factors such as not being out to family, hiding a relationship, or being the only out lesbian or bisexual at work.[38] There are the issues related to the lack of legitimacy and social support for our relationships and the accompanying problems of overdependency, merger, coming out to family, and negotiating family life in a heterosexist society.[39] Counselors and group facilitators need to understand these issues and be comfortable dealing with them.

Arlene Istar discusses the dilemmas of homophobic counselors, agencies without services targeted for lesbians, and rural areas or small cities that don't have many lesbian, bisexual, or gay male friendly service providers. For a lesbian couple where domestic violence is the main issue, the optimum counseling situation would be for each woman to see her own counselor and ultimately see a third as a couple; in many situations, however, that is impossible. Lesbians are also searching for relationship validation, and refusal of couples counseling may alienate them.[40] Couples counseling, however, is viewed as dangerous for any battered woman. In the presence of her abuser, a victim is not free to speak the truth without possible consequences of beatings or worse. Abusers are known for manipulating police, judges, *and* therapists through their charm and deep-seated denial. Furthermore, the therapist would not be able to work on establishing a safety plan for the abused partner in the presence of the abuser.

In spite of this near-universal condemnation of couples counseling, there are times, in Istar's opinion, when the couple could benefit from therapy. They may go to a therapist who is ignorant about battering—a worse alternative. She also points out that a therapist assessing the couple together (who may have come in for "relationship problems") may discover power and control dynamics.[41] I feel that if these dynamics are, in fact, discovered, the couples therapy should be replaced by individual counseling as soon as possible before the victim is placed at further risk.

Healing from incest, rape, and battering requires greater sensitivity and understanding for lesbians and bisexual women. Female gender socialization plus societal homophobia, biphobia, and heterosexism alter dynamics sufficiently so that sexual abuse survivors need services concerned with additional issues. Furthermore, healing for the survivor is not separate from treatment for the abuser. The lesbian community's response to abusers has traditionally been either nonconfrontation or exclusion. Yet, Kaye/Kantrowitz asserts that if we are feminists, then women are our political community. Lesbians not directly harmed by a particular abuser could reach out to her. Kaye/Kantrowitz writes:

> The male batterer shores up collective male power. But the lesbian batterer, asserting her individual power, at the same time undermines collective female power. The problem is, if the community excludes her, we also undermine collective female power. If the concept of a people has meaning—and for a political movement dedicated to freedom, it better—we can't boot each other out. We have to rethink the meaning of solidarity, as well as the possibility that we—not they, we—must wrestle with using and misusing power, control, even violence, before we are free . . . and even then.[42]

But what does "reaching out" to the abuser, whether rapist or batterer, mean? Focus groups conducted by the Asian Women's Shelter staff in San Francisco found high levels of frustration by participants regarding *how* to deal with perpetrators. Overwhelmingly, survivors wanted services and treatment for their abusers so that the abuse will stop hurting others within the community. They did not want abusers marginalized; rather they felt "a community member, abuser or not, shares the same struggles against anti-immigrant sentiments, racism, and homophobia."[43] Consequently, they were wary of agencies that would ostracize abusers. Kaye/Kantrowitz and Cristy Chung and Summer Lee address unmet needs—to learn how to deal with abusers for the safety and well-being of community members, abusers included.

To prevent woman-to-woman rape and lesbian battering, to provide services for survivors, to treat abusers—none of this is possible in the present context of homophobia, biphobia, and heterosexism. Our challenge is to do more than raise awareness and piece together a program here and a study there. Now that we know, we can do no less than to have a bold campaign to dismantle the myths, form gay/lesbian/bisexual/trans and straight antiviolence coalitions, and push for our full civil and human rights.

9

The Vision and the Challenge

It's all about gender roles, it's all about sex roles, it's all about the way we've constructed violence. So then how do we break that down further and how do we get at that? (Aileen)

Society has to see two different items simultaneously: (1) since lesbian sex is "immoral and illegal," the victim isn't really a victim; (2) women are physically incapable of "rape," therefore, they cannot be perpetrators. Both thoughts and the lack of support of officials, agencies, and community need to be addressed. (Oona)

It all starts with understanding it. (Lila)

We have shared the "painfully resurrected" memories of seventy survivors of woman-perpetrated sexual violence.[1] Perhaps they have evoked fear or alarm, or triggered past hurts in you, the reader. They did in me. We now realize that the severity of sexual violence, as well as the forms and the impacts of this violence, are quite similar regardless of who your perpetrator is. It is not whether you are male or female, lesbian, gay, bisexual, or straight. Yes, individual factors will add to the complexity of the personal experience. But individual personality is linked to social status, socialization, and other macro factors. Theoretically our question is, if sex does not predict sexual perpetration and if sexual identity does not, then what is our framework to understand this interpersonal violence?

Theory Revisited

I return to hooks's challenge to the idea that "hierarchical structures should be the basis of human interaction."[2] I believe that the roots of oppression are in these hierarchical structures of society.[3] I believe we need to move forward beyond the patriarchal analysis to a broader framework that includes patriarchy as one component. The many forms of oppression work as an interlocking system of dominance, which requires an integrated analysis. The integrated analysis is necessary because oppressions are experienced simultaneously.[4] To answer questions I raised previously, the integrated analysis addresses all perpetrators, male or female, lesbian, bisexual, gay, or straight.

Second wave feminism elevated patriarchy in its theoretical analysis because sexism was the dominant form of oppression the early feminists identified. Sexism and male dominance neatly explained violence against women. Unfortunately, this ignored much of the experience of those who were not authoring the first theories—those women also oppressed by race, by class, by age, by ability, and by sexual identity. A broader framework is inclusive and also acknowledges internalization of different aspects of oppression, validates group culture, and recognizes the uniqueness of the individual human being.[5] This view does not downplay violence by men, but it does encourage us to examine how men and women both create and condone a culture of violence.[6] This broader framework is still feminist and reminds us that there are many feminisms. To claim that patriarchy is not *the* prominent oppression is not to say that it is irrelevant but to elevate the importance of other oppressions. Feminism as I understand it is multidimensional and necessitates examining the intersection of multiple status hierarchies.[7]

hooks calls the integrated analysis the white supremacist, capitalist, patriarchal class system.[8] Suzanne Pharr labels it the politics of domination.[9] Chesley, MacAulay, and Ristock refer to the structures of dominance.[10] My preference is to call it the hierarchical structures of dominance because I feel it is the aspect of hierarchy that allows the domination. The social controls of hierarchy are many. Whichever aspect of dominance you examine, the dynamics are similar. Whether sexism or racism, heterosexism or classism, the belief that one status group within that dimension is superior, natural, and right over and above the others keeps the others in their place. This similarity was noted in McIntosh's examination of invisible white privilege, which led her directly to parallels with male privilege and heterosexual privilege.[11]

It is essential to examine both macro social forces and individual personality, which are connected to each other. We all live out our daily lives in the framework of institutions, such as family, education, law, economy, and religion, that are hierarchically organized. Socialization teaches us to accept power and dominance, both through norms and values and through societal institutions. Traditional gender roles are reinforced in subtle and explicit ways—from children's toys to laws regulating sexual behaviors—again through cultural norms and institutions. But individual personality helps explain why not all members of a certain group abuse or are victims. Socialization may provide the teachings, but not all individuals learn the same lessons in the same way. This variation is significant.

We internalize oppression and domination, reinforcing the control of the system. Lesbian baiting is a constant reminder that to be who we are is not safe. Lesbians and bisexual women are not immune from the socialization of the culture, and we are products of a society that values power and control. Internalized biphobia and heterosexism destabilize bisexual women's sense of identity. Abusers can manipulate this doubting in their sexual violence against bi women, using their sexual attraction to men as excuses for abusive behaviors. As Chesley, MacAulay, and Ristock state, "Thus, reflective of existing social norms, hierarchies and abuses of power, entitlement, ownership and control can exist in lesbian relationships."[12]

We are surrounded by the messages that violence, power, and control get results, from a military budget that feeds the war machine to societal economic injustice where the poor get prison. No aspect of our lives is free of the dynamic of hierarchy, and the effects are played out in our interpersonal relationships. Unfortunately, at this point few studies have been done on lesbian rapists and abusers to understand the subtleties unique to them. There are no studies on bisexual rapists and abusers to my knowledge. The meager research on heterosexual women rapists are focused on the few documented cases of female rapists of males or females who were complicit in rapes of females by males.[13]

In understanding woman-to-woman sexual violence, the concepts of heterosexism, homophobia, biphobia, monosexism, and misogyny stand out because they are used against all lesbians and bisexual women regardless of class, race, or physical ability in specific ways. However, the various oppressions are factors of equal importance for those lesbians and bisexual women not in privileged positions on those hierarchical dimensions. It is crucial to use a broader framework to not silence lesbian and bisexual women survivors who are not dominant group members.

Furthermore, the broader framework allows us to examine oppression along the life course, so that the abuse of children—incest is particularly relevant here—is included in the analysis. The abuse of children occurs in a context in which children are powerless. Female children are particularly at risk because of misogyny and the sexualization of females that begins with little girls. Sexual revictimization is a major consequence of hierarchical control. What seems like an isolated personal experience is actually a widespread socially constructed phenomenon.

Certain factors have been critical throughout the stories in this book. Power and control exercised by perpetrators; cultural values and attitudes such as denial that women can be violent; denigration of lesbians and bisexuals; social isolation; internalized homophobia, biphobia, and misogyny; lesbian invisibility; revictimization; lack of legal protection; and dearth of services are all elements perpetuating sexual violence. To work on eliminating one aspect—for example, the myths about lesbian utopia—is powerful and important, but that alone would not stop interpersonal violence. In fact, I would argue that there is no possible way to work on any issue "alone," since we immediately are drawn into other realms—of cultural ideas, media, and institutions such as religion or law. To try to end homophobia and biphobia would mean working on several levels simultaneously—individual, cultural, institutional, and internalized. To begin the analysis of social change means understanding the big picture and challenging multiple levels concurrently. There is no challenging one form of violence without attacking the foundation: "the Western philosophical notion of hierarchical rule and coercive authority."[14] To take on these societal ideas and structures is a struggle for the long haul.[15]

Working toward Justice and Eliminating Sexual Violence

The alternative to a society organized on principles of hierarchical domination is a society organized around shared power based on human rights. To understand the depth and breadth of our oppression requires the development of a political or collective consciousness and a collective commitment to change.[16] We need enough progressive people to work toward this vision who will work on different aspects of the whole, reworking the existing social fabric. If people who believe in justice are honest, we will admit we need a system overhaul. It is the interconnection of the oppressions that makes this coalition work strong and brings us to a common agenda. Shared power is a key concept because this work requires working with people from different cultures by race, by class, by sexual identity, by age, and by ability, and with men as well as with women. "Diversity" is meaningless unless individuals from the different subcultures have input into coalition decision making at all levels.[17]

Homophobia, biphobia, transphobia, and heterosexism function to marginalize lesbians, gay men, bisexuals, and transgender people. In working to end interpersonal violence, it is imperative to ally with heterosexuals to bring us into the progressive agenda—not as a single-focus issue but as all the oppressions intersect in our lives as nonheterosexuals. We are not only lesbians and bisexual women. We are lesbians and bisexual women who have been sexually violated and battered, from all races and social classes.

My vision of a lesbian- and bisexual-safe society is one where we can come out without fear, ridicule, or question. Internalized homophobia and biphobia would not be a problem. We would honestly confront our abuse issues. There would be funding for lesbian- and bi-specific programs, crisis lines, and literature dealing with same-sex violence. There would be abuser treatment programs, and we would not fear calling the police or going through the court system. The end of the power-over model would mean that values of justice, respect, nonviolence, and cooperation would be part of our cultural socialization.

Summarizing some of the most important steps mentioned throughout the book, I suggest the following:

- We need education to challenge heterosexism starting in grade schools.
- We need to educate and train service providers about the issues of same-sex sexual violence (doctors, nurses, therapists, rape crisis advocates and staff, battered women's advocates and staff, shelter staff, lawyers, judges, police officers, security guards).
- Safety must be a priority in agencies by having lesbians and bisexual women on staff; lesbian- and bisexual-specific programming, literature, and outreach; and agency mission statements that include nondiscrimination based on sexual identity. Further, agencies must confront abusers who work or volunteer there by not allowing them to stay, but at the same time giving them referrals and resources for change.
- Rape crisis and sexual assault agencies need to take on this issue separately from domestic violence agencies where sexual abuse is a component of battering. Rape of women by women exists outside of relationships, and rape crisis agencies need to be the leaders in acknowledging this and in developing materials and programs.
- Domestic violence and rape crisis staff need to reexamine their use of

language. Further study is needed to determine the best outreach words to use for woman-to-woman sexual violence. Staff need to examine the impacts of heterosexism and monosexism on their use of language and how experience is framed.

- Agencies must be culturally competent and do appropriate outreach to women of color.
- We need support for queer agencies to provide shelter, crisis counseling, hot lines, and support groups.
- Therapists and health care providers need to screen for interpersonal violence—incest, rape, and domestic violence.
- Family violence must be challenged to end the role modeling of power and control within the family, and to stop incest and abuse that is the beginning of individual victimization.
- Media have a key role in increasing lesbian and bisexual visibility through roles on television and in movies, and through nonheterosexist language and story plots. Advertising needs to include lesbians and bisexual women. Ads for domestic violence and rape services must show same-sex relationships as well as heterosexual ones. Agencies can develop posters with visuals and wording depicting queer community members.
- Within the lesbian and bisexual communities we must acknowledge woman-to-woman sexual violence and lesbian battering. We must listen to survivors and question abusers. Education for community members about identifying types of violence, legal rights, reporting hate crimes, and where to seek help for all forms of violence should be a priority. We can form coalitions with other groups to work on these problems. Identified lesbians and bisexual women, especially community leaders, need to become resource people for lesbians and bisexual women in need.
- It is imperative for the legal system to acknowledge that rape or battering by a lesbian or bisexual woman is criminal behavior. Laws must be changed toward this end, and most important, laws need to be enforced. Heterosexism must be eliminated for the justice system to be just.
- We need to develop programs for abusive women in same-sex relationships. We need resources for them to encourage them to change. This is in the interest of all community members.
- Empowerment strategies such as self-defense, running for electoral office, and working on our own personal internalized oppression should be encouraged.

- The end to all interpersonal violence—including that against women by other women—must be seen as a human rights issue. *No one* deserves to be beaten, raped, or tortured.

The challenge is to see "our" issues as linked with "their" issues, that working toward the end of the hierarchy of dominance is in the interest of us all. The interconnection of oppressions leaves no one immune from some aspect of domination. I am challenging you to care that "injustice anywhere is a threat to justice everywhere," as Dr. Martin Luther King Jr. declared. Social change requires a commitment to the long-range vision.

Many of the stories in this book have been told for the first time, requiring courageous risk taking for the women involved. Now that you know, what small step can you take? Now that you know, can you extend yourself to work for equal rights, for nonexploitation, for safety? Perhaps you already knew of this violence; you yourself could have been in this book. Perhaps you have been nodding your head to every line, you've lost sleep, and you've had headaches. Tell someone! Be the first step in building your safety by breaking down the myths. We are not immune to the horror of rape. We must work to make it unthinkable. And the vision is nothing less than our liberation.

Appendix

Section I: Demographics

1. How old are you? _____ years

2. What is your race/ethnicity?
   - ☐ White, not Latina/Hispanic ☐ Latina/Hispanic ☐ Native American
   - ☐ African American ☐ Asian American ☐ Asian/Pacific Islander
   - ☐ Mixed (please specify)

   _____

   - ☐ Other (please specify)

   _____

3. Sexual identity? ☐ lesbian ☐ bisexual
   - ☐ transgendered/transsexual (living full-time)
   - ☐ pre-operative ☐ post-operative ☐ non-operative

4. Present partner status?

   _____

5. What is the highest educational level you have completed?
   - ☐ less than high school ☐ GED ☐ high school graduate
   - ☐ some college ☐ 4-year college graduate ☐ advanced degree after college
   - ☐ other certificate program (please specify)

   _____

6. What is your occupation?

   _____

7. What is your annual income?

   _____

8. How did you hear about this study?

   _____

Section 2: Sexual Violence Events/Experiences

I am defining sexual violence to mean any unwanted sexual activity. Contact sexual
activities include: touching parts of the body, kissing, vaginal penetration by objects,
vaginal penetration by fingers, oral sex, anal sex, rubbing, and being forced to do things
to yourself. Noncontact sexual activities include forced viewing of pornography or other
sexually explicit material and being forced to watch sexual activity of others.

1.   When you were a child or an adolescent (under 18), were you sexually abused/a
     victim of incest?   ☐ no   ☐ yes   how many times? _____

     who was/were the perpetrator(s)? _____

     how old were you at the time(s)? _____

2.   As an adult (18 and over) have you ever been sexually abused/assaulted by a male?
     ☐ no   ☐ yes   how many times? _____

     who was/were the perpetrator(s)? _____

     how old were you at the time(s)? _____

3.   Related specifically to sexual violence against you as an adult (18 and over) *by
     another woman* please describe what happened. If this has occurred more than once,
     please number and separate the events, and use additional paper if necessary. Please
     write legibly.

     In the description, include:
     • your age at the time
     • who this other woman was to you (date, partner, lover, acquaintance, etc.)
     • what she did to you
     • if either of you were drunk or high at the time of the incident(s)
     • any other significant aspects of the incident(s)

Section 3: Labeling the Event

Below is a list of words. The following questions address if, at the time, you felt any of these words "fit" what happened to you (that is, did you use any of them to describe what happened to you). If there was more than one event and the labels are different, please indicate if your labels of the events differ and why they differ. Otherwise, treat your multiple incidents as one time. Use additional paper if necessary.

- rape
- sexual assault
- sexual coercion
- sexual abuse
- rough foreplay
- sexual miscommunication
- nonconsensual sexual activity

1. What do you think is the difference between these terms?

2. Are any of these the label or labels you used at the time?

3. Why would you pick one over the other to describe your experience?

4. If none of the above words "fit" at the time, what word or words did you use to describe your experience?

5. Did your label of the event change from the time it happened to the next day, next week, next month, or years later? If so, how did it change, and what influenced it to change?

Section 4: Response to Sexual Violence

1. What was the emotional impact of the violence against you?

2. What were your immediate responses to what happened to you?
    ☐ I told someone (who?) _____
    When did you tell? _____
    ☐ I called the police   ☐ I called a hotline
    ☐ I called or went to rape crisis ☐ I called or went to a battered women's
                                          agency
    ☐ I went to the hospital   ☐ I went to a therapist
    ☐ I didn't respond immediately
    ☐ other (please specify) _____

3. Were you concerned about a homophobic/biphobic/transphobic reaction when
    you reached out as described in #2?
    ☐ yes.   Why?
    _____
    ☐ no.   Why?
    _____
    ☐ I didn't respond immediately

4. Were you concerned you wouldn't be believed?
    ☐ yes.   Why?
    _____
    ☐ no.   Why?
    _____
    ☐ I didn't respond immediately

5. Are there services that you wish had been available for you to use at the time? If
    so, please specify.

6. Looking back on it now, if there is something you wished you had done differently
    during and/or after the incident(s) please describe.

7. Is the perpetrator still in your life at this time? Describe your relationship.

Notes

Introduction

1. *Queer* refers generally to nonheterosexuals—lesbians, gay men, bisexuals, transgender individuals, intersex individuals, female-to-male transsexuals, and male-to-female transsexuals.
2. Lorde, 1984, 41.
3. McClellan, 1999, 249.
4. Ibid.
5. Brison, 1998, 578.

Chapter 1

1. Peplau et al., 1978.
2. Gusfield, 1981, 10.
3. Kanuha, 1996.
4. Rose, 1977.
5. Yllo, 1999.
6. Berrill, 1990.
7. Brand and Kidd, 1986.
8. Loulan, 1988.
9. Sloan and Edmond, 1996.
10. Waterman, Dawson, and Bologna, 1989.
11. Duncan, 1990.
12. Renzetti, 1992.
13. Waldner-Haugrud and Gratch, 1997.
14. Lie et al., 1991.
15. American Bar Association, n.d.
16. Brand and Kidd, 1986.
17. Coleman, 1990.
18. Lie and Gentlewarrier, 1991.
19. Baum, 2000. The reporting organizations are: Community United Against Violence (San Francisco); LA Gay and Lesbian Project and the STOP Partner Abuse Domestic Violence Program (Los Angeles); WOMAN, INC. (San Francisco); The Anti-Violence Program of Equality Colorado (Denver); Horizons Anti-Violence Project (Chicago); Fenway Community Health Center and Violence Recovery Program (Boston); New York City Gay and Lesbian Anti-Violence Project (New York City); Buckeye Region Anti-Violence Organization (Columbus, Ohio); Lesbian and Gay Community Service Center of Greater Cleveland (Cleveland); Network for Battered Lesbians and Bisexual Women (Boston); and Asian Women's Shelter (San Francisco).
20. McClennen, 1999a.
21. Eaton, 1994; Elliott, 1996; Faulkner, 1991.

22. Faulkner, 1991.

23. Bell, 1989, 29.

24. Thornhill and Palmer, 2000.

25. Ibid., 147.

26. *Heterosexist* refers to the assumption that only heterosexuality is normal, natural, and right, and therefore is the correct sexual standard.

27. Dr. Thornhill stated this at a meeting on 15 November 2000 when I asked him about women raping other women.

28. Waldner-Haugrud, 1999.

29. Eaton, 1994.

30. Bureau of Justice Statistics, 1994.

31. Eaton, 1994.

32. Island and Letellier, 1991.

33. McClennen, 1999a; Merrill, 1996.

34. Zemsky, 1990.

35. Merrill, 1996.

36. Zemsky, 1990.

37. Merrill, 1996.

38. McClennen, 1999a.

39. Hart, 1986, 174.

40. Appleby and Anastas, 1998.

41. Faulkner, 1991, 264.

42. Kaye/Kantrowitz, 1987, 12.

43. Eaton, 1994, 219.

44. hooks, 1984, 25–26.

45. Ibid., 31.

46. Ibid., 131.

47. Dobash and Dobash, 1988.

48. Hart, 1986, 173.

49. Stanko, 1997.

50. Ibid., 75.

51. Mattley, 1997.

52. Renzetti, 1997.

53. Mattley, 1997.

54. Riemer and Thomas, 1999.

Chapter 2

1. Adams, 1994.

2. Rich, 1980.

3. Neisen, 1990.

4. Appleby and Anastas, 1998.

5. Eliason, 1997; Ochs, 1996; Rust, 1999; Spalding and Peplau, 1997.

6. Ochs, 1996.

7. Hutchins, 1996, 251.

8. Ochs, 1996.

9. Rust, 1999.

10. See the "Remembering Our Dead" Web site at www.gender.org; Bolin, 1998; Lev and Lev, 1999.

11. Frye, 1983, 4.

12. Appleby and Anastas, 1998.

13. Combahee River Collective, 1995, 234.

14. Ibid., 236.

15. Lorde, 1983, 9.

16. hooks, 1989, 124–25.

17. hooks, 1989.

18. Collins, 1986, S19.

19. hooks, 1989; Kanuha, 1990.

20. McIntosh, 1988.

21. McCoy and Hicks, 1979, 66.

22. Goffman, 1963.

23. Appleby and Anastas, 1998.

24. Benecke and Dodge, 1992; Pellegrini, 1992; Pharr, 1988.

25. Radicalesbians, 1970.

26. Vaid, 1995, 18.

27. Ibid., 20.

28. Gamson, 1998.

29. Gentry, 1992; Herek, 1992; Markowitz, 1991.

30. Appleby and Anastas, 1998.

31. hooks, 1989.

32. Dalton, 1989, 217.

33. Blasingame, 1992.

34. hooks, 1989.

35. Vaid, 1995, 4.

36. Thirty-two states presently have such legislation, and nine states are considering laws banning recognition of same-sex marriages.

37. Klinger, 1996.

38. Herek, 1992.

39. Elliot, 1999; Hawaii, New York, Rhode Island, and Washington have bills pending in their state legislatures to recognize civil unions or marriages.

40. Obear, 1993; Price, 1994.

41. Colker, 1996; Faulkner, 1991.

42. Colker, 1996; Herek, 1992.

43. Benecke and Dodge, 1992; Colker, 1996.

44. Obear, 1993; Stelboum, 1994.

45. Gentry, 1992.

46. Klinger, 1996, 348.

47. Markowitz, 1991, 33.

48. Margolies, Becker, and Jackson-Brewer, 1987.

49. Ochs, 1996.

50. Hutchins, 1996.

51. Ochs, 1996.

52. Loulan, 1988, 223.

53. Moses, 1978, 87.
54. Bradford, Ryan, and Rothblum, 1994, 239–40.
55. Bay Area Reporter, n.d.
56. Garbo, 2000.
57. Gunther and Jennings, 1999; Hiratsuka, 1993.
58. Girshick, 1993, 1.
59. In Brownworth, 1992.
60. Levy and Lobel, 1991.
61. Sophie, 1987, 54.
62. hooks, 1995, 146.
63. hooks, 1994.
64. Ochs, 1996; Rust, 1999.
65. Szymanski and Chung, in press, 6.
66. "Assessment," n.d.
67. Bisexual Resource Center, 1996.
68. Szymanski and Chung, in press.
69. Bryson, 1991.
70. Bisexual Resource Center, 1996.
71. Pheterson, 1990, 45.
72. Appleby and Anastas, 1998.
73. Markowitz, 1991.
74. Forstein, 1988.
75. Hammond, 1988.
76. Banks and Gartrell, 1996; Gentry, 1992.
77. Benowitz, 1986, 200; Martinac, 1997.
78. Martinac, 1997, 17.
79. Hart, 1986; Renzetti, 1992.
80. Docis, 1991.
81. Hammond, 1988.
82. Schechter, 1982, 268.

Chapter 3

1. The concepts *lesbian utopia* and *lesbian invisibility* come from the 1970s when bisexual issues were not widely acknowledged. I use these original terms since those are the concepts of those times. Today we would include bisexuals and transgendered females.

2. Frye, 1983.
3. Rich, 1980.
4. Hoagland, 1989; Rich, 1980.
5. Hoagland, 1989.
6. Clarke, 1981; Rich, 1980.
7. Pearlman, 1987.
8. Appleby and Anastas, 1998, 81.
9. Krieger, 1982.
10. Appleby and Anastas, 1998; Krieger, 1982.
11. Miller, 1995.
12. Nichols, Pagano, and Rossoff, 1982; Kitzinger, 1987; Nestle, 1987, respectively.

13. Kitzinger, 1987; Nestle, 1987.

14. Davis and Kennedy, 1986.

15. Jeffreys, 1989/1996.

16. Jeffreys, 1989/1996; Nestle, 1987.

17. Phelan, 1989.

18. Ross, 1991.

19. Rosen, 2000.

20. Ross, 1991.

21. Davis and Kennedy, 1986.

22. Tanner, 1978.

23. Faderman, 1991.

24. Nichols, 1987, 116.

25. Miller, 1995; Pearlman, 1987.

26. Faderman, 1991.

27. Ross, 1991, 101.

28. Eaton, 1994; Faulkner, 1991; Morrow, 1994.

29. Burk, 1999, 9.

30. Elliott, 1996, 6.

31. Meyers, 1999, 241.

32. Bell, 1989, 26.

33. Sloan and Edmond, 1996.

34. Kaye/Kantrowitz, 1987, 12.

35. Meyers, 1999, 241.

36. McClellan, 1999.

37. Morrow and Hawxhurst, 1989.

38. Krieger, 1982.

39. Hammond, 1988; Ristock, 1991; Timoner, 1992.

40. Bernhart, 1975.

41. For example, see Eaton, 1994; Klinger, 1996; Krestan and Bepko, 1980; McClennen, 1999b; Renzetti, 1992; Toder, 1992.

42. Klinger, 1996.

43. National Coalition Against Domestic Violence, 1990.

44. McClennen, 1999c, 300.

45. Chung and Lee, 2000.

46. Rich, 1980, 649.

Chapter 4

1. Kelly, 1988b.

2. Sheffield, 1994, 111.

3. Randall and Haskell, 1995.

4. Finkelhor and Yllo, 1985; Resnick et al., 1991; Russell, 1990.

5. Finkelhor and Yllo, 1985; Pence and Paymar, 1993.

6. Campbell, 1989; Russell, 1982.

7. Mahoney and Williams, 1998.

8. Frieze, 1983; Russell, 1990.

9. Bergen, 1998.

10. Basile, 1999.
11. Ibid.
12. National Crime Center, 1992.
13. Rapaport and Posey, 1991.
14. Warshaw, 1988.
15. Fuentes, 1997.
16. Struckman-Johnson, 1991.
17. For example, see Goldman, n.d.; Lowers, 1995.
18. Richardson and Hammock, 1991.
19. Schilit, Lie, and Montagne, 1990.
20. Renzetti, 1997, 288.
21. Fitzgerald and Shulman, as quoted in O'Toole and Schiffman, 1997.
22. Tjaden and Thoennes, 2001.
23. Hearn and Parkin, 1987.
24. Advocate Web, n.d.
25. Herman, 1981, 187.
26. Taylor and Chandler, 1995, 43.
27. National Coalition Against Domestic Violence, 1990.
28. Taylor and Chandler, 1995.
29. Nichols, Pagano, and Rossoff, 1982.
30. Kornak, 1990, 5.
31. Jonel, 1982, 19.
32. Samois, 1982.
33. Margulies, 1996, 1.
34. Brame, n.d.(b).
35. Brame, n.d.(a).
36. Margulies, 1996, 6.
37. Lev and Lev, 1999, 53.
38. Sheffield, 1994, 111.

Chapter 5

1. Hoagland, 1989; Pellegrini, 1992; Spender, 1980.
2. Spender, 1980, 2–3.
3. Muehlenhard et al., 1992, 24.
4. Baker, 1998.
5. Callen, 1990.
6. Kelly, 1988a.
7. Pellegrini, 1992.
8. hooks, 1989.
9. Spender, 1980.
10. Ibid.
11. Baker, 1998.
12. Spender, 1980, 157.
13. Hoagland, 1989.
14. Spender, 1980.
15. Rich, 1979, 204.

16. Stanley, 1978.

17. Phelan, 1989. The postmodern theorists, especially the French feminists Cixous and Irigaray, lead in these discussions today. These theories are beyond the scope of this book, but interested readers may want to go to their works.

18. Frye, 1983.

19. Rich, 1979, 189.

20. Walker, 2001.

21. Ibid., 7.

22. Ibid., 13.

23. As discussed by Scarry, 1985.

24. Ibid., 12.

25. Muehlenhard et al., 1992.

26. Bourque, 1989.

27. Kelly, 1988b.

28. Estrich, 1987; Johnson and Sigler, 1997; Kelly, 1988a; Russell, 1982; Warshaw, 1988.

29. Kelly, 1988a, 140.

30. Thanks to Melissa Burchard for this concept and related points.

31. Bergen, 1995.

32. Kelly, 1988b, 129.

33. Bergen, 1995.

34. Kelly, 1988a.

35. This research and Kelly, 1988a.

36. Bourque, 1989, 291.

37. Loseke, 1987.

38. Daly, 1973.

Chapter 6

1. Finkelhor et al., 1990.

2. Bradford and Ryan, 1988.

3. Loulan, 1988.

4. Leonard, 2000.

5. Blume, 1990.

6. Dinsmore, 1991, 107–8.

7. See also Blume, 1990.

8. Dinsmore, 1991, 108.

9. Finkelhor and Browne, 1985; Herman, 1981; Kelly, 1988a; Runtz and Briere, 1986.

10. Finkelhor and Browne, 1985, 531.

11. Blume, 1990, 12.

12. Blume, 1990; Finkelhor and Browne, 1985.

13. Finkelhor and Browne, 1985.

14. Blume, 1990.

15. Russell, 1986.

16. Kelly, 1988.

17. Hammond, 1988; Janoff-Bulman and Frieze, 1983.

18. Saunders, 1994.

19. Kilpatrick, Edmunds, and Seymour, 1992.

20. Kelly, 1988a.

21. Warshaw, 1988.

22. Kelly, 1988a.

23. Ibid.

24. Janoff-Bulman and Frieze, 1983.

25. Warshaw, 1988.

26. Fromuth, 1986; Grauerholz, 2000; Kelly, 1988a; Lie et al., 1991; Lockhart et al., 1994; Loulan, 1988.

27. Grauerholz, 2000, 5.

28. Koss and Dinero, 1989.

29. Gidycz et al., 1993.

30. Finkelhor and Browne, 1985.

31. Koss and Dinero, 1989.

32. Chu, 1992.

33. Grauerholz, 2000.

34. Ibid.

35. Ibid.

Chapter 7

1. Leonard, 1990.

2. Ibid.

3. Arizona, Delaware, Georgia, Indiana, Louisiana, Michigan, Montana, North Carolina, and South Carolina.

4. Alaska, California, Colorado, Illinois, Massachusetts, Nevada, New Hampshire, New Jersey, New Mexico, North Dakota, Oklahoma, Pennsylvania, Rhode Island, Vermont, and West Virginia.

5. Jablow, 2000.

6. Jones, 1997.

7. Hodges, 2000.

8. Ibid., 319.

9. Ibid., 320.

10. Leland, 2000.

11. Martinac, 1997.

12. Baum, 2000; Leland, 2000; Martinac, 1997; Smith and Dale, 1999.

13. Hodges, 2000, 317–18.

14. Kidd and Chayet, 1984.

15. Harkavy, 1979/1980.

16. See also Dupps, 1990–1991.

17. Harkavy, 1979/1980.

18. Robson, 1990.

19. King, 1993, 75.

20. Hodges, 2000, 324.

21. Alabama, Arizona, Florida, Idaho, Kansas, Louisiana, Massachusetts, Minnesota, Mississippi, Missouri, North Carolina, Oklahoma, South Carolina, Texas, Utah, and Virginia.

22. New York State Penal Law, *Sex Offenses: Definition of Terms*, sec. 130.00.

23. Indiana Code 35-41-1-9, *Deviate Sexual Conduct*, sec. 9.
24. Pennsylvania Crimes Code, *Deviate Sexual Intercourse*, sec. 3126.
25. Washington State, *Definitions*, 9A.44.010.
26. Estrich, 1987.
27. Bachman and Paternoster, 1993.
28. Bachman and Paternoster, 1993; see also Estrich, 1987.
29. Hodges, 2000.
30. Ibid.
31. Estrich, 1987, 81.
32. Ibid., 81.
33. Jablow, 2000.

Chapter 8

1. Renzetti, 1996b.
2. In Dahir, 1999.
3. Herman, 1981.
4. Mahoney, 1999.
5. Méndez, 1996, 54.
6. Geraci, 1986.
7. Porat, 1986, 81.
8. Walker, Spohn, and DeLone, 1996.
9. Renzetti, 1988; Ristock, 1991.
10. Lie and Gentlewarrier, 1991.
11. Price, Lee, and Quiroga, 2001, 38.
12. Renzetti, 1992.
13. Eaton, 1994; Geraci, 1986; McClennen, 1999c; Renzetti, 1996b; Sloan and Edmond, 1996.
14. Waldron, 1996.
15. Elliott, 1996; Hart, 1986.
16. Meyers, 1999, 241.
17. Elliott, 1996.
18. Waldron, 1996.
19. Margolies and Leeder, 1995, 141.
20. Byrne, 1996; Leeder, 1988.
21. Renzetti, 1992.
22. Merrill, 1996.
23. Renzetti, 1992.
24. Renzetti, 1994.
25. Margolies and Leeder, 1995.
26. Margolies and Leeder, 1995; Farley, 1996.
27. Renzetti, 1992.
28. Ibid.
29. Margolies and Leeder, 1995; Renzetti, 1992; Waldner-Haugrud, Gratch, and Magruder, 1997.
30. Rozée, Bateman, and Gilmore, 1991.
31. Wiehe and Richards, 1995.

32. Stewart et al., 1987.
33. Wiehe and Richards, 1995.
34. Ibid.
35. Iasenza, 1999; Stewart et al., 1987.
36. Herman, 1981.
37. Saunders, 1994, 42.
38. Riddle and Sang, 1978.
39. Decker, 1985.
40. Istar, 1996.
41. Ibid.
42. Kaye/Kantrowitz, 1987, 12.
43. Chung and Lee, 2000, 11.

Chapter 9

1. Kane, 2000.
2. hooks, 1984, 131.
3. See also Ristock, 1991.
4. Combahee River Collective, 1995.
5. Butler, 1999; hooks, 1984.
6. hooks, 1984.
7. See also Renzetti, 1996a.
8. hooks, 1984.
9. Pharr, 1996.
10. Chesley, MacAulay, and Ristock, 1998.
11. McIntosh, 1988.
12. Chesley, MacAulay, and Ristock, 1998, 8.
13. Brown et al., 1984; Parrot, 1988; Russell, 1984; Sarrel and Masters, 1982.
14. hooks, 1984, 118.
15. Girshick, 1999.
16. hooks, 1984; Pharr, 1988.
17. Pharr, 1996.

References

Adams, M. L. 1994. Thoughts on heterosexism, queerness, and outlaws. In *Resist: Essays against a homophobic culture*. Edited by M. Oikawa, D. Falconer, and A. Decter. Toronto: Women's Press.

Advocate Web. n.d. "When professionals exploit their clients/patients/students." http://www.advocateweb.org/hope/whatissexualexploitation.asp. (25 August 2000).

American Bar Association. n.d. "The commission on domestic violence: Statistics." http://www.abanet.org/domviol/stats.html. (14 June 2000).

American Psychiatric Association. 1987. *Diagnostic and statistical manual of mental disorders*. 3d ed. Washington, D.C.: American Psychiatric Association.

Appleby, G. A., and J. W. Anastas. 1998. *Not just a passing phase*. New York: Columbia University Press.

"Assessment of internalized homophobia." n.d. http://psychology.ucdavis.edu/rainbow/html. (7 December 1999).

Bachman, R., and R. Paternoster. 1993. A contemporary look at the effects of rape law reform: How far have we really come? *Journal of Criminal Law and Criminology* 84 (3): 554–74.

Baker, R. B. 1998. "Pricks" and "chicks": A plea for "persons." In *Philosophy and sex*. 3d ed. Edited by R. B. Baker, K. J. Wininger, and F. A. Elliston. New York: Prometheus Books.

Banks, A., and N. K. Gartrell. 1996. Lesbians in the medical setting. In *Textbook of homosexuality and mental health*. Edited by R. P. Cabaj and T. S. Stein. Washington, D.C.: American Psychiatric Press.

Basile, K. C. September 1999. Rape by acquiescence: The ways in which women "give in" to unwanted sex with their husbands. *Violence Against Women* 5 (9): 1,036–58.

Baum, R. 2000. *Lesbian, gay, transgender, and bisexual (lgtb) domestic violence in 1999: A report of the national coalition of anti-violence programs*. New York: National Coalition of Anti-Violence Programs.

Bay Area Reporter. n.d. "Mental health: Depression." http://www.gay.net/community. (7 December 1999).

Bell, E. Summer 1989. With our own hands. *Trouble and Strife* 16: 26–29.

Benecke, M. M., and K. Dodge. 1992. Lesbian baiting as sexual harassment: Women in the military. In *Homophobia: How we all pay the price*. Edited by W. J. Blumenfeld. Boston: Beacon Press.

Benowitz, M. 1986. How homophobia affects lesbians' response to violence in lesbian relationships. In *Naming the violence: Speaking out about lesbian battering*. Edited by K. Lobel. Seattle: Seal Press.

Bergen, R. K. June 1995. Surviving wife rape: How women define and cope with the violence. *Violence Against Women* 1 (2): 117–38.

———. 1998. The reality of wife rape: Women's experiences of sexual violence in marriage. In *Issues in Intimate Violence*. Edited by R. K. Bergen. Thousand Oaks, Calif: Sage.

Bernhart, E. 1975. Friends and lovers in a lesbian counterculture community. In *Old family/New family*. Edited by N. Malbin. New York: Van Nostrand.

Berrill, K. T. September 1990. Anti-gay violence and victimization in the United States. *Journal of Interpersonal Violence* 5 (3): 274–94.

Bisexual Resource Center. 1996. "Bisexual internalized oppression." http://www.bire-source.org/internalized.html. (8 December 1999).

Blasingame, B. M. 1992. The roots of biphobia: Racism and internalized heterosexism. In *Closer to home: Bisexuality and feminism*. Edited by E. R. Weise. Seattle: Seal Press.

Blume, E. S. 1990. *Secret survivors: Uncovering incest and its aftereffects in women*. New York: Wiley.

Bolin, A. 1998. Transcending and transgendering: Male-to-female transsexuals, dichotomy, and diversity. In *Current concepts in transgender identity*. Edited by D. Denny. New York: Garland.

Bourque, L. B. 1989. *Defining rape*. Durham: Duke University Press.

Bradford, J., and C. Ryan. 1988. *The national lesbian health care survey*. Washington, D.C.: National Lesbian and Gay Health Foundation.

Bradford, J., C. Ryan, and E. D. Rothblum. 1994. National lesbian health care survey: Implications for mental health care. *Journal of Consulting and Clinical Psychology* 62 (2): 228–42.

Brame, G. n.d. (a). "Are you being abused? A notice about domestic violence in the sm/fetish scene." http://www.gloria-brame.com/domidea/abused.htm. (6 July 2000).

———. n.d. (b). "Playing and staying safe: Six thinking points before playing with someone new." http://www.gloria-brame.com/domidea/playsafe.htm. (6 July 2000).

Brand, P. A., and A. H. Kidd. 1986. Frequency of physical aggression in heterosexual and female homosexual dyads. *Psychological Reports* 59: 1307–13.

Brison, S. J. 1998. Surviving sexual violence: A philosophical perspective. In *Philosophy and sex*. 3d ed. Edited by R. B. Baker, K. J. Wininger, and F. A. Elliston. New York: Prometheus Books.

Brown, M. E., L. A. Drucker, L. A. Hull, and S. K. Panesis. October 1984. *Women who rape*. Boston: Office of Commissioner of Probation.

Brownworth, V. 2 June 1992. Abused and isolated: Gay and lesbian teens. *Advocate*, 63.

Bryson, B. J. Spring 1991. Choosing oppressions. *NCADV Voice*, 11, 17.

Bureau of Justice Statistics. November 1994. *Violence between intimates*. Washington, D.C.: U.S. Department of Justice.

Burk, C. Spring 1999. Rethinking femme and butch. *Network News* 8 (1): 1, 8–10.

Butler, L. 1999. African American lesbian women experiencing partner abuse. In *A professional's guide to understanding gay and lesbian domestic violence: Understanding practice interventions*. Edited by J. C. McClennen and J. Gunther. Lewiston, N.Y.: Edwin Mellen.

Byrne, D. 1996. Clinical models for the treatment of gay male perpetrators of domestic violence. *Journal of Gay and Lesbian Social Services* 4 (1): 107–16.

Callen, M. 1990. *Surviving AIDS*. New York: HarperCollins.

Campbell, J. C. 1989. Women's responses to sexual abuse in intimate relationships. *Health Care for Women International* 10: 335–46.

Chesley, L., D. MacAulay, and J. Ristock. 1998. *Abuse in lesbian relationships: Information and resources*. Ontario, Canada: Health Canada.

Chu, J. A. 1992. The revictimization of adult women with histories of childhood abuse. *Journal of Psychotherapy Practice and Research* 1: 259–69.

Chung, C., and S. Lee. 2000. *(Re)action: Queer Asian women's response to relationship violence*. San Francisco: Family Violence Prevention Fund.

Clarke, C. 1981. Lesbianism: An act of resistance. In *This bridge called my back: Writings by radical women of color*. Edited by C. Moraga and G. Anzaldua. New York: Kitchen Table Press.

Coleman, V. E. 1990. Violence between lesbian couples: A between groups comparison. Ph.D. diss., California School of Professional Psychology. *Dissertation Abstracts International* 51: AAG9109022.

Colker, R. 1996. *Hybrid: Bisexuals, multiracials, and other misfits under American law*. New York: New York University Press.

Collins, P. H. 1986. Learning from the outsider within: The sociological significance of black feminist thought. *Social Problems* 33 (6): S14–S32.

Combahee River Collective. 1995. A black feminist statement. In *Words of fire: An anthology of African-American feminist thought*. Edited by B. Guy-Sheftall. New York: New Press.

Dahir, M. 23 November 1999. Hidden bruises. *Advocate*, 25–29.

Dalton, H. L. 1989. AIDS in blackface. *Daedalus* 118 (3): 205–27.

Daly, M. 1973. *Beyond god the father*. Boston: Beacon Press.

Davis, M., and E. L. Kennedy. Spring 1986. Oral history and the study of sexuality in the lesbian community: Buffalo, New York, 1940–1960. *Feminist Studies* 12 (1): 7–26.

Decker, B. 1985. Counseling gay and lesbian couples. In *With compassion toward some: Homosexuality and social work in America*. Edited by R. Schoenberg and R. Goldberg with D. A. Shore. Binghamton, N.Y.: Harrington Park Press.

Dinsmore, C. 1991. *From surviving to thriving: Incest, feminism, and recovery*. New York: SUNY Press.

Dobash, R. E., and R. P. Dobash. 1988. Research as social action: The struggle for battered women. In *Feminist perspectives on wife abuse*. Edited by K. Yllo and M. Bograd. Newbury Park, Calif.: Sage.

Docis, D. Spring 1991. Homophobia in battered women's programs. *NCADV Voice*: 1–2.

Duncan, D. F. 1990. Prevalence of sexual assault victimization among heterosexual and gay/lesbian university students. *Psychological Reports* 66: 65–66.

Dupps, D. S. August 1990–1991. Battered lesbians: Are they entitled to a battered woman defense? *Journal of Family Law* 29 (4): 879–99.

Eaton, M. 1994. Abuse by any other name: Feminism, difference, and intralesbian violence. In *The public nature of private violence: The discovery of domestic abuse*. Edited by M. A. Fineman and R. Mykitiuk. New York: Routledge.

Eliason, M. J. 1997. The prevalence and nature of biphobia in heterosexual undergraduate students. *Archives of Sexual Behavior* 26 (3): 317–26.

Elliot, D. 20 December 1999. "Vermont begins to pave the way for fairness for same-sex couples." http://www.ngltf.org/press/122099.html. (14 February 2000).

Elliott, P. 1996. Shattering illusions: Same-sex domestic violence. *Journal of Gay and Lesbian Social Services* 4 (1): 1–8.

Estrich, S. 1987. *Real rape*. Cambridge: Harvard University Press.

Faderman, L. 1991. *Odd girls and twilight lovers: A history of lesbian life in twentieth-century America*. New York: Penguin.

Farley, N. 1996. A survey of factors contributing to gay and lesbian domestic violence. *Journal of Gay and Lesbian Social Services* 4 (1): 35–42.

Faulkner, E. Summer 1991. Lesbian abuse: The social and legal realities. *Queen's Law Journal* 16: 261–86.

Finkelhor, D., and A. Browne. October 1985. The traumatic impact of child sexual abuse: A conceptualization. *American Journal of Orthopsychiatry Quarterly* 55 (4), 530–41.

Finkelhor, D., G. Hotaling, I. A. Lewis, and C. Smith. 1990. Sexual abuse in a national survey on adult men and women. *Child Abuse and Neglect* 14: 19–28.

Finkelhor, D., and K. Yllo. 1985. *License to rape: Sexual abuse of wives*. New York: Free Press.

Forstein, M. January 1988. Homophobia: An overview. *Psychiatric Annals* 18 (1): 33–36.

Frieze, I. 1983. Investigating the causes and consequences of marital rape. *Signs* 8: 532–53.

Fromuth, M. E. 1986. The relationship of childhood sexual abuse with later psychological and sexual adjustment in a sample of college women. *Child Abuse and Neglect* 10: 5–15.

Frye, M. 1983. *The politics of reality: Essays in feminist theory*. Freedom, Calif.: Crossing Press.

Fuentes, A. November/December 1997. Crime rates are down . . . but what about rape? *Ms.*, 19–22.

Gamson, J. 1998. *Freaks talk back*. Chicago: University of Chicago Press.

Garbo, J. 25 July 2000. "Homophobia blamed for higher rates of mental disorders among gays and lesbians." http://www.gayhealth.com/templates/0/news?record = 147. (27 July 2000).

Gentry, S. E. 1992. Caring for lesbians in a homophobic society. *Health Care for Women International* 13: 173–80.

Geraci, L. 1986. Making shelters safe for lesbians. In *Naming the violence: Speaking out about lesbian battering.* Edited by K. Lobel. Seattle: Seal Press.

Gidycz, C. A., C. N. Coble, L. Latham, and M. J. Layman. 1993. Sexual assault experience in adulthood and prior victimization experiences. *Psychology of Women Quarterly* 17: 151–68.

Girshick, L. B. August 1993. Teen dating violence. *Violence Update* 3 (12): 1–2, 4–5.

———. 1999. Organizing in the lesbian community to confront lesbian battering. *Journal of Gay and Lesbian Social Services* 9 (1): 83–92.

Goffman, E. 1963. *Stigma: Notes on the management of spoiled identity.* Englewood Cliffs, N.J.: Prentice-Hall.

Goldman, D. n.d. "Same-sex rape is more common than many may realize." http://content.gay.com/health_gayrape_000107.html. (21 January 2000).

Grauerholz, L. February 2000. An ecological approach to understanding sexual revictimization: Linking personal, interpersonal, and sociocultural factors and processes. *Child Maltreatment* 5 (1): 5–17.

Gunther, J., and M. Jennings. 1999. Cultural and institutional violence and their impact on same-gender partner abuse. In *A professional's guide to understanding gay and lesbian domestic violence: Understanding practice interventions.* Edited by J. C. McClennen and J. Gunther. Lewiston, N.Y.: Edwin Mellen.

Gusfield, J. R. 1981. *The culture of public problems: Drinking-driving and the symbolic order.* Chicago: University of Chicago Press.

Hammond, N. 1988. Lesbian victims of relationship violence. *Women and Therapy* 8 (1–2): 89–105.

Harkavy, J. 1979/1980. The defending of accused homosexuals: Will society accept their use of the battered wife defense? *Glendale Law Review* 4: 208–32.

Hart, B. 1986. Lesbian battering: An examination. In *Naming the violence: Speaking out about lesbian battering.* Edited by K. Lobel. Seattle: Seal Press.

Hearn, J. and W. Parkin. 1987. *"Sex" at "work": The power and paradox of organization sexuality.* New York: St. Martin's Press.

Herek, G. M. 1992. The social context of hate crimes: Notes on cultural heterosexism. In *Hate crimes: Confronting violence against lesbians and gay men.* Edited by G. M. Herek and K. T. Berrill. Newbury Park, Calif.: Sage.

Herman, J. L. 1981. *Father-daughter incest.* Cambridge: Harvard University Press.

Hiratsuka, J. April 1993. Outsiders: Gay teens, straight world. *NASW News,* 3.

Hoagland, S. L. 1989. *Lesbian ethics: Toward new value.* Palo Alto, Calif.: Institute of Lesbian Studies.

Hodges, K. M. 2000. Trouble in paradise: Barriers to addressing domestic violence in lesbian relationships. *Law and Sexuality* 9: 311–31.

hooks, b. 1984. *Feminist theory: From margin to center.* Boston: South End Press.

———. 1989. *Talking back: Thinking feminist, thinking black.* Boston: South End Press.

———. 1994. *Outlaw culture: Resisting representations*. New York: Routledge.

———. 1995. *Killing rage: Ending racism*. New York: Henry Holt.

Hutchins, L. 1996. Bisexuality: Politics and community. In *Bisexuality: The psychology and politics of an invisible minority*. Edited by B. A. Firestein. Thousand Oaks, Calif.: Sage.

Iasenza, S. April 1999. The big lie: Debunking lesbian bed death. *In the Family* 4 (4): 8–11, 20, 25.

Island, D. and P. Letellier. 1991. *Men who beat the men who love them*. Binghamton, N.Y.: Harrington Park Press.

Istar, A. 1996. Couple assessment: Identifying and intervening in domestic violence in lesbian relationships. *Journal of Gay and Lesbian Social Services* 4 (1): 93–106.

Jablow, P. M. Summer 2000. Victims of abuse and discrimination: Protecting battered homosexuals under domestic violence legislation. *Hofstra Law Review* 28: 1095–145.

Janoff-Bulman, R., and I. H. Frieze. 1983. A theoretical perspective for understanding reactions to victimization. *Journal of Social Issues* 39 (2): 1–17.

Jeffreys, S. 1989/1996. Butch and femme: Now and then. In *Not a passing phase: Reclaiming lesbians in history, 1840–1985*. Edited by Lesbian History Group. London: Cox and Wyman, Reading, Berks.

Johnson, I. M., and R. T. Sigler. 1997. *Forced sexual intercourse in intimate relationships*. Aldershot, England: Ashegate.

Jonel, M. 1982. Letter from a former masochist. In *Against sadomasochism: A radical feminist analysis*. Edited by R. R. Linden, D. R. Pagano, D. E. H. Russell, and S. L. Star. East Palo Alto, Calif.: Frog in the Well.

Jones, C. 4 July 1997. New domestic violence law may not cover gay couples. *Washington Blade*, sec. A.

Kane, S. November 2000. Biography as counter-memory: The hustling wars and other events in the exemplary life of M. Paper presented at the annual meeting of the American Society of Criminology, San Francisco, California.

Kanuha, V. 1990. Compounding the triple jeopardy: Battering in lesbian of color relationships. *Women and Therapy* 9 (1–2): 169–84.

———. 1996. Domestic violence, racism, and the battered women's movement in the United States. In *Future interventions with battered women and their families*. Edited by J. L. Edleson and Z. C. Eisikovits. Thousand Oaks, Calif.: Sage.

Kaye/Kantrowitz, M. February 1987. Paradoxes of violence [Review of the book *Naming the violence: Speaking out about lesbian battering*]. *Women's Review of Books* 4 (5): 11–12.

Kelly, L. 1988a. *Surviving sexual violence*. Minneapolis: University of Minnesota Press.

———. 1988b. How women define their experiences of violence. In *Feminist perspectives on wife abuse*. Edited by K. Yllo and M. Bograd. Newbury Park, Calif.: Sage.

Kidd, R. F., and E. F. Chayet. 1984. Why do victims fail to report? The psychology of criminal victimization. *Journal of Social Issues* 40 (1): 39–50.

Kilpatrick, D. G., C. N. Edmunds, and A. K. Seymour. 1992. *Rape in America: A report to the nation.* Arlington, Va.: National Victim Center.

King, P. 4 October 1993. Not so different, after all. *Newsweek,* 75.

Kitzinger, C. 1987. *The social construction of lesbianism.* London: Sage.

Klinger, R. L. 1996. Lesbian couples. In *Textbook of homosexuality and mental health.* Edited by R. P. Cabaj and T. S. Stein. Washington, D.C.: American Psychiatric Press.

Klinger, R. L., and T. S. Stein. 1996. Impact of violence, childhood sexual abuse, and domestic violence and abuse on lesbians, bisexuals, and gay men. In *Textbook of homosexuality and mental health.* Edited by R. P. Cabaj and T. S. Stein. Washington, D.C.: American Psychiatric Press.

Kornak, M. 30 January 1990. Lesbian sado-masochism is violence toward women. *Minnesota Daily,* 5.

Koss, M. P., and T. E. Dinero. 1989. Discriminant analysis of risk factors for sexual victimization among a national sample of college women. *Journal of Consulting and Clinical Psychology* 57: 242–50.

Krestan, J., and C. S. Bepko. 1980. The problem of fusion in the lesbian relationship. *Family Process* 19 (2): 277–89.

Krieger, S. 1982. Lesbian identity and community: Recent social science literature. *Signs: Journal of Women in Culture and Society* 8 (1): 91–108.

Landes, A., S. Squyres, and J. Quiram, eds. 1997. *Violent relationships: Battering and abuse among adults.* Wylie, Tex.: Information Plus.

Leeder, E. 1988. Enmeshed in pain: Counseling the lesbian battering couple. *Women and Therapy* 7 (1): 81–99.

Leland, J. 8 November 2000. "Silence ending about abuse in gay relationships." www.nytimes.com/2000/11/06/national/06ABUS.html. (6 November 2000).

Leonard, E. D. November 2000. Convicted survivors: Comparing and describing California's battered women inmates. Paper presented at the annual meeting of the American Society of Criminology, San Francisco, California.

Leonard, L. M. Spring 1990. A missing voice in feminist legal theory: The heterosexual presumption. *Women's Rights Law Reporter* 12 (1): 39–49.

Lev, A. I., and S. Lev. 1999. Sexual assault in the lesbian, gay, bisexual, and transgendered communities. In *A professional's guide to understanding gay and lesbian domestic violence: Understanding practice interventions.* Edited by J. C. McClennen and J. Gunther. Lewiston, N.Y.: Edwin Mellen.

Levy, B., and K. Lobel. 1991. Lesbian teens in abusive relationships. In *Dating violence: Young women in danger.* Edited by B. Levy. Seattle: Seal Press.

Lie, G., and S. Gentlewarrier. 1991. Intimate violence in lesbian relationships: Discussion of survey findings and practice implications. *Journal of Social Service Research* 15 (1/2): 41–59.

Lie, G., R. Schilit, J. Bush, M. Montagne, and L. Reyes. 1991. Lesbians in currently aggressive relationships: How frequently do they report aggressive past relationships? *Violence and Victims* 6 (2): 121–35.

Lockhart, L. L., B. A. White, V. Causby, and A. Issac. 1994. Letting out the secret: Violence in lesbian relationships. *Journal of Interpersonal Violence* 9: 469–92.

Lorde, A. 1983. There is no hierarchy of oppressions. *Interracial Books for Children Bulletin* 14 (1 and 2): 9.

———. 1984. *Sister outsider*. Trumansburg, N.Y.: Crossing Press.

Loseke, D. R. 1987. Lived realities and the construction of social problems: The case of wife abuse. *Symbolic Interaction* 10 (2): 229–43.

Loulan, J. 1988. Research on the sex practices of 1,566 lesbians and the clinical applications. *Women and Therapy* 7 (23): 221–34.

Lowers, J. January 1995. Battered dreams: Gay and lesbian domestic violence and rape victims face a terrifying closet. *Outlines*, 20–21.

Mahoney, P. September 1999. High rape chronicity and low rates of help-seeking among wife rape survivors in a nonclinical sample. *Violence Against Women* 5 (9): 993–1,016.

Mahoney, P., and L. M. Williams. 1998. Sexual assault in marriage: Prevalence, consequences, and treatment of wife rape. In *Partner violence: A comprehensive review of twenty years of research*. Edited by J. L. Jasinski & L. M. Williams. Thousand Oaks, Calif.: Sage.

Margolies, L., M. Becker, and K. Jackson-Brewer. 1987. Internalized homophobia: Identifying and treating the oppressor within. In *Lesbian psychologies: Explorations and challenges*. Edited by Boston Lesbian Psychologies Collective. Urbana: University of Illinois Press.

Margolies, L., and E. Leeder. June 1995. Violence at the door: Treatment of lesbian batterers. *Violence Against Women* 1 (2): 139–57.

Margulies, J. Winter 1996. S/m and battering. *Network News* 5 (1): 1, 6–7.

Markowitz, L. January/February 1991. Homosexuality: Are we still in the dark? *Networker* 15 (1): 26–35.

Martinac, P. December 1997. Confronting violence in our relationships. *Baltimore Alternative*, 17.

Mattley, C. 1997. Field research with phone sex workers. In *Researching sexual violence against women: Methodological and personal perspectives*. Edited by M. Schwartz. Thousand Oaks, Calif.: Sage.

McClellan, D. 1999. Advocating on behalf of same-gender couples experiencing partner abuse. In *A professional's guide to understanding gay and lesbian domestic violence: Understanding practice interventions*. Edited by J. C. McClennen and J. Gunther. Lewiston, N.Y.: Edwin Mellen.

McClennen, J. C. 1999a. Prevailing theories regarding same-gender partner abuse: Proposing the feminist social-psychological model. In *A professional's guide to understanding gay and lesbian domestic violence: Understanding practice interventions*. Edited by J. C. McClennen and J. Gunther. Lewiston, N.Y.: Edwin Mellen.

———. 1999b. Partner abuse between lesbian couples: Toward a better understanding. In *A professional's guide to understanding gay and lesbian domestic violence: Un-*

derstanding practice interventions. Edited by J. C. McClennen and J. Gunther. Lewiston, N.Y.: Edwin Mellen.

———. 1999c. Future directions for practice interventions regarding same-gender partner abuse. In *A professional's guide to understanding gay and lesbian domestic violence: Understanding practice interventions.* Edited by J. C. McClennen and J. Gunther. Lewiston, N.Y.: Edwin Mellen.

McCoy, S., and M. Hicks. 1979. A psychological retrospective on power in the contemporary lesbian-feminist community. *Frontiers* 4 (3): 65–69.

McIntosh, P. 1988. *White privilege and male privilege: A personal account of coming to see correspondences through work in women's studies.* Wellesley, Mass.: Center for Research on Women, Wellesley College.

Méndez., J. M. 1996. Serving gays and lesbians of color who are survivors of domestic violence. *Journal of Gay and Lesbian Social Services* 4 (1): 53–59.

Merrill, G. 1996. Ruling the exceptions: Same-sex battering and domestic violence theory. *Journal of Gay and Lesbian Social Services* 4 (1): 9–21.

Meyers, E. A. 1999. Developing a successful community outreach program: A look at criminal justice and the lesbian and gay community. In *A professional's guide to understanding gay and lesbian domestic violence: Understanding practice interventions.* Edited by J. C. McClennen and J. Gunther. Lewiston, N.Y.: Edwin Mellen.

Miller, N. 1995. *Out of the past: Gay and lesbian history from 1869 to the present.* New York: Vintage Books.

Morrow, J. April 1994. Identifying and treating battered lesbians. *San Francisco Medicine* 17: 20–21.

Morrow, S. L., and D. M. Hawxhurst. September/October 1989. Lesbian partner abuse: Implications for therapists. *Journal of Counseling and Development* 68: 58–62.

Moses, A. 1978. *Identity management in lesbian women.* New York: Praeger.

Muehlenhard, C. L., I. G. Powch, J. L. Phelps, and L. M. Giusti. 1992. Definitions of rape: Scientific and political implications. *Journal of Social Issues* 48 (1): 23–44.

National Coalition Against Domestic Violence. 1990. To the lesbian nation. In *Confronting lesbian battering: A manual for the battered women's movement.* Edited by P. Elliott. St. Paul: Minnesota Coalition for Battered Women, Lesbian Battering Intervention Project.

National Crime Center and Crime Victims Research and Treatment Center. 1992. *Rape in America: A report to the nation.* Arlington, Va.: National Crime Center.

Neisen, J. H. 1990. Heterosexism: Redefining homophobia for the 1990s. *Journal of Gay and Lesbian Psychotherapy* 1 (3): 21–35.

Nestle, J. 1987. *A restricted country.* Ithaca, N.Y.: Firebrand Books.

Nichols, J., D. Pagano, and M. Rossoff. 1982. Is sadomasochism feminist? A critique of the Samois position. In *Against sadomasochism: A radical feminist analysis.* Edited by R. R. Linden, D. R. Pagano, D. E. H. Russell, and S. L. Star. East Palo Alto, Calif.: Frog in the Well.

Nichols, M. 1987. Lesbian sexuality: Issues and developing theory. In *Lesbian psycholo-*

gies: Explorations and challenges. Edited by Boston Lesbian Psychologies Collective. Urbana: University of Illinois Press.

Obear, K. 1993. Homophobia. In Beyond Tolerance. Edited by N. J. Evans and V. A. Wall. Alexandria, Va.: American Counseling Association.

Ochs, R. 1996. Biphobia: It goes more than two ways. In Bisexuality: The psychology and politics of an invisible minority. Edited by B. A. Firestein. Thousand Oaks, Calif.: Sage.

O'Toole, L. L., and J. R. Schiffman, eds. 1997. Gender violence: Interdisciplinary perspectives. New York: New York University Press.

Parrot, A. 1988. Coping with date rape and acquaintance rape. New York: Rosen Publishing Group, Inc.

Pearlman, S. 1987. The saga of continuing clash in lesbian community, or will an army of ex-lovers fail? In Lesbian psychologies: Explorations and challenges. Edited by Boston Lesbian Psychologies Collective. Urbana: University of Illinois Press.

Pellegrini, A. 1992. S(h)ifting the terms of hetero/sexism: Gender, power, homophobia. In Homophobia: How we all pay the price. Edited by W. J. Blumenfeld. Boston: Beacon Press.

Pence, E., and M. Paymar. 1993. Education groups for men who batter: The Duluth model. New York: Springer.

Peplau, L. A., S. Cochran, K. Rook, and C. Padesky. 1978. Loving women: Attachment and autonomy in lesbian relationships. Journal of Social Issues 34 (3): 7–27.

Pharr, S. 1988. Homophobia: A weapon of sexism. Little Rock, Ark.: Chardon Press.

———. 1996. In the time of the right: Reflections on liberation. Berkeley, Calif.: Chardon Press.

Phelan, S. 1989. Identity politics: Lesbian feminism and the limits of community. Philadelphia: Temple University Press.

Pheterson, G. 1990. Alliances between women: Overcoming internalized oppression and internalized domination. In Bridges of power: Women's multicultural alliances. Edited by L. Albrecht and R. Brewer. Philadelphia: New Society Publishers.

Porat, N. 1986. Support groups for battered lesbians. In Naming the violence: Speaking out about lesbian battering. Edited by K. Lobel. Seattle: Seal Press.

Price, D. 31 March 1994. "I lost my children because I'm a lesbian." San Jose Mercury News, 2C.

Price, J. L., S. S. Lee, and S. S. Quiroga. 2001. Violence against women and girls in San Francisco: Meeting the needs of survivors. San Francisco: City and County of San Francisco.

Radicalesbians. 1970. The woman-identified woman. In Come out! Selections from the radical gay liberation newspaper. New York: Times Change Press.

Randall, M. and L. Haskell. 1995. Sexual violence in women's lives. Violence Against Women 1 (1): 6–31.

Rapaport, K. R., and C. D. Posey. 1991. Sexually coercive college males. In Acquaintance rape: The hidden crime. Edited by A. Parrot and L. Bechhofer. New York: Wiley.

Renzetti, C. M. December 1988. Violence in lesbian relationships: A preliminary analysis of causal factors. *Journal of Interpersonal Violence* 3 (4): 381–99.

———. 1992. *Violent betrayal: Partner abuse in lesbian relationships.* Newbury Park, Calif.: Sage.

———. January/February 1994. Understanding and responding to violence in lesbian relationships: Part 3. *Treating Abuse Today* 4 (1): 20–24.

———. 1996a. On dancing with a bear: Reflections on some of the current debates among domestic violence theorists. In *Domestic partner abuse.* Edited by L. K. Hamberger and C. M. Renzetti. New York: Springer.

———. 1996b. The poverty of services for battered lesbians. *Journal of Gay and Lesbian Social Services* 4 (1): 61–68.

———. 1997. Violence in lesbian and gay relationships. In *Gender violence: Interdisciplinary perspectives.* Edited by L. L. O'Toole and J. R. Schiffman. New York: New York University Press.

Resick, P. A. June 1993. The psychological impact of rape. *Journal of Interpersonal Violence* 8 (2): 223–55.

Resnick, H., D. Kilpatrick, C. Walsh, and L. Vernonen. 1991. Marital rape. In *Case studies in family violence.* Edited by R. Ammerman and M. Herson. New York: Plenum.

Rich, A. 1979. *On lies, secrets, and silence: Selected prose, 1966–1978.* New York: Norton.

———. 1980. Compulsory heterosexuality and lesbian existence. *Signs: Journal of Women in Culture and Society* 5: 631–60.

Richardson, D. R., and G. S. Hammock. 1991. Alcohol and acquaintance rape. In *Acquaintance rape: The hidden crime.* Edited by A. Parrot and L. Bechhofer. New York: Wiley.

Riddle, D. I., and B. Sang. 1978. Psychotherapy with lesbians. *Journal of Social Issues* 34 (3): 84–100.

Riemer, B. A., and J. L. Thomas. 1999. Methodological issues in researching same-gender domestic violence. In *A professional's guide to understanding gay and lesbian domestic violence: Understanding practice interventions.* Edited by J. C. McClennen and J. Gunther. Lewiston, N.Y.: Edwin Mellen.

Ristock, J. L. 1991. Understanding violence in lesbian relationships: An examination of misogyny and homophobia. In *Women changing academe: The proceedings of the 1990 Canadian women's studies association conference.* Edited by S. Kirby, D. Daniels, K. McKenna, M. Pujol, and M. Valiquette. Winnipeg: Sororal Publishing.

Robson, R. Fall 1990. Lavender bruises: Intralesbian violence, law, and lesbian legal theory. *Golden Gate University Law Review* 20: 567–91.

Rose, V. M. 1977. Rape as a social problem: A byproduct of the feminist movement. *Social Problems* 25: 75–87.

Rosen, R. 2000. *The world split open.* New York: Viking.

Ross, B. 1991. Sex, lives, and archives: Pleasure/danger debates in the 1970s lesbian feminism. In *Women changing academe: The proceedings of the 1990 Canadian women's studies association conference.* Edited by S. Kirby, D. Daniels, K. Mc-Kenna, M. Pujol, and M. Valiquette. Winnipeg: Sororal Publishing.

Rozée, P. D., P. Bateman, and T. Gilmore. 1991. The personal perspective of acquaintance rape prevention: A three-tier approach. In *Acquaintance rape: The hidden crime.* Edited by A. Parrot and L. Bechhofer. New York: Wiley.

Runtz, M., and J. Briere. September 1986. Adolescent "acting-out" and childhood history of sexual abuse. *Journal of Interpersonal Violence* 1 (3): 326–34.

Russell, D. E. H. 1982/1990. *Rape in marriage.* Bloomington: Indiana University Press.

———. 1984. *Sexual exploitation: Rape, child sexual abuse, and workplace harassment.* Newbury Park, Calif.: Sage.

———. 1986. *The secret trauma: Incest in the lives of girls and women.* New York: Basic Books.

———. 1991. Wife rape. In *Acquaintance rape: The hidden crime.* Edited by A. Parrot and L. Bechhofer. New York: Wiley.

Rust, P. C. R. 1999. The biology, psychology, sociology, and sexuality of bisexuality. In *Bisexuality in the United States: A social science reader.* Edited by P. C. R. Rust. New York: Columbia University Press.

Samois. 1982. *Coming to power.* Boston: Alyson Press.

Sarrel, P. M., and W. H. Masters. 1982. Sexual molestation of men by women. *Archives of Sexual Behavior* 11 (2): 117–31.

Saunders, D. G. 1994. Posttraumatic stress symptom profiles of battered women: A comparison of survivors in two settings. *Violence and Victims* 9 (1): 31–44.

Scarry, E. 1985. *The body in pain: The making and unmaking of the world.* New York: Oxford University Press.

Schechter, S. 1982. *Women and male violence: The visions and struggles of the battered women's movement.* Boston: South End Press.

Schilit, R., G. Lie, and M. Montagne. 1990. Substance use as a correlate of violence in intimate lesbian relationships. *Journal of Homosexuality* 19 (3): 51–65.

Sheffield, C. 1994. Sexual terrorism. In *Women: A feminist perspective.* 5th ed. Edited by J. Freeman. Mountain View, Calif.: Mayfield Press.

Sloan, L., and T. Edmond. 1996. Shifting the focus: Recognizing the needs of lesbian and gay survivors of sexual violence. *Journal of Gay and Lesbian Social Services* 5 (4): 33–52.

Smith, R., and O. Dale. 1999. The evolution of social policy in gay/lesbian/bisexual domestic violence. In *A professional's guide to understanding gay and lesbian domestic violence: Understanding practice interventions.* Edited by J. C. McClennen and J. Gunther. Lewiston, N.Y.: Edwin Mellen.

Sophie, J. 1987. Internalized homophobia and lesbian identity. *Journal of Homosexuality* 14 (1–2): 53–65.

Spalding, L. R., and L. A. Peplau. 1997. The unfaithful lover: Heterosexuals' perceptions of bisexuals and their relationships. *Psychology of Women Quarterly* 21: 611–25.

Spender, D. 1980. *Man made language.* London: Routledge and Kegan Paul.

Stanko, E. 1997. "I second that emotion." In *Researching sexual violence against women: Methodological and personal perspectives.* Edited by M. Schwartz. Thousand Oaks, Calif.: Sage.

Stanley, J. Summer 1978. The transformation of silence into language and action. *Sinister Wisdom* 6: 5–11.

Stelboum, J. P. 1994. Sliding into home: Identifying lesbian sex. In *Resist: Essays against a homophobic culture.* Edited by M. Oikawa, D. Falconer, and A. Decter. Toronto: Women's Press.

Stewart, B. D., C. Hughes, E. Frank, B. Anderson, K. Kendall, and D. West. 1987. The aftermath of rape: Profiles of immediate and delayed treatment seekers. *Journal of Nervous and Mental Disease* 175 (2): 90–94.

Struckman-Johnson, C. 1991. Male victims of acquaintance rape. In *Acquaintance rape: The hidden crime.* Edited by A. Parrot and L. Bechhofer. New York: Wiley.

Szymanski, D. M., and Y. B. Chung. In press. The lesbian internalized homophobia scale: A rational/theoretical approach. *Journal of Homosexuality.*

Tanner, D. 1978. *The lesbian couple.* Lexington, Mass.: Lexington Books.

Taylor, J., and T. Chandler. 1995. *Lesbians talk violent relationships.* London: Scarlet Press.

Thornhill, R., and C. Palmer. 2000. *A natural history of rape.* Cambridge: MIT Press.

Timoner, R. 9 July 1992. Domestic violence silently threatens lesbian community. *Bay Area Reporter,* NG.

Tjaden, P. G., and N. Thoennes. 2001. Coworker violence and gender: Findings from the national violence against women survey. *American Journal of Preventative Medicine* 20 (2): 85–89.

Toder, N. 1992. Lesbian couples in particular. In *Positively gay.* Edited by B. Berzon. Berkeley, Calif.: Celestial Arts.

Vaid, U. 1995. *Virtual equality.* New York: Anchor Books.

Waldner-Haugrud, L. K. 1999. Sexual coercion in lesbian and gay relationships: A review and critique. *Aggression and Violent Behavior* 4 (2): 139–49.

Waldner-Haugrud, L. K., and L. V. Gratch. 1997. Sexual coercion in gay/lesbian relationships: Descriptives and gender differences. *Violence and Victims* 12 (1): 87–98.

Waldner-Haugrud, L. K., L. V. Gratch, and B. Magruder. 1997. Victimization and perpetration rates of violence in gay and lesbian relationships: Gender issues explored. *Violence and Victims* 12 (2): 173–84.

Waldner-Haugrud, L. K., and B. Magruder. 1995. Male and female sexual victimization in dating relationships: Gender differences in coercion techniques and outcomes. *Violence and Victims* 10 (3): 203–15.

Waldron, C. M. 1996. Lesbians of color and the domestic violence movement. *Journal of Gay and Lesbian Social Services* 4 (1): 43–51.

Walker, M. U. March 2001. Women's rights, rights to truth. Paper presented at the annual meeting of the Southeastern Women's Studies Association, Boca Raton, Florida.

Walker, S., C. Spohn, and M. DeLone. 1996. *The color of justice: Race, ethnicity, and crime in America.* Belmont, Calif.: Wadsworth.

Warshaw, R. 1988. *I never called it rape: The Ms. report on recognizing, fighting, and surviving date and acquaintance rape.* New York: Harper and Row.

Waterman, C. K., L. J. Dawson, and M. J. Bologna. 1989. Sexual coercion in gay male and lesbian relationships: Predictors and implications for support services. *Journal of Sex Research* 26 (1): 118–24.

Wiehe, V. R., and A. L. Richards. 1995. *Intimate betrayal: Understanding and responding to the trauma of acquaintance rape.* Thousand Oaks, Calif.: Sage.

Yllo, K. September 1999. Wife rape: A social problem for the twenty-first century. *Violence Against Women* 5 (9): 1,059–63.

Zemsky, B. 1990. Lesbian battering: Considerations for intervention. In *Confronting lesbian battering: A manual for the battered women's movement.* Edited by P. Elliot. St. Paul: Minnesota Coalition for Battered Women.

Index

CPSIA information can be obtained at www.ICGtesting.com
Printed in the USA
LVOW081238261112

308820LV00003B/367/P